To Sylvia and Karen Erikson
        and
        Sue, Amy, and Owen Hall III

# Computer Models for Management Science

# Computer Models for Management Science

## THIRD EDITION

*Warren J. Erikson, Ph.D.*
University of Southern California

*Owen P. Hall, Jr., Ph.D.*
Pepperdine University

*ADDISON-WESLEY PUBLISHING COMPANY*
Reading, Massachusetts • Menlo Park, California • New York
Don Mills, Ontario • Wokingham, England • Amsterdam • Bonn
Sydney • Singapore • Tokyo • Madrid • San Juan

**Library of Congress Cataloging-in-Publication Data**

Erikson, Warren J.
  Computer models for management science / Warren J. Erikson, Owen
  P. Hall, Jr.—3rd ed.
    p. cm.
    Includes index.
    ISBN 0-201-50046-9
    1. Operations research—Computer simulation. 2. Management
  science—Computer simulation. I. Hall, Owen P. II. Title.
    T57.6.E74 1989
    658.4'03'52—dc19                                    88-7889
                                                        CIP

3 4 5 6 7 8 9 10 - CRS - 98 97 96 95 94

# Contents

# 3 Linear Programming 19

# 4 Integer Programming 45

# 5 Transportation Model 55

# 6 Assignment Model 71

# 7 Project Scheduling 89

# 8 Network Models 107

# 13   Queuing Models  211

## Appendix:  Problem Solutions  235

## Index  261

# *Preface*

The computer programs described in this book can be used to solve problems on 11 of the more frequently covered topics in management science, decision science, and operations research courses. These topics include Linear Programming, Integer Programming, the Transportation Model, the Assignment Model, Project Scheduling (PERT/CPM), Network Models (Minimum Spanning Tree, Maximum Network Flow, and Shortest Route), Decision Analysis Models, the Decision Tree Model, Markov Models, Inventory Models, and Queuing Models. These programs can be (and have been) used by students in advanced courses, but they have been designed with features to help the beginning student learn quickly and easily.

We believe that the major value of this package of programs is its ease of use. The algorithms that solve the problems are all standard and commonly encountered versions that are probably similar to programs that are now running on your computer. Our major effort focuses on designing input and output that is easy to learn by the first-time user, but still is useful to the more experienced student.

This book provides all the information needed to run every program correctly the first time you try. We have tried to avoid the "computer programmer" style of writing that many people find both confusing and intimidating. If we have done the job right, everyone (including those who have no previous exposure to computers) will find the use of these programs to be a painless experience.

The programs have been designed for use with any textbook. We believe that the programs in this package can be used to solve almost all problems and cases (on the topic covered) that are contained in any textbook now being used. Naturally, some books cover a few topics that cannot be solved by our programs (e.g., game theory and dynamic programming), and our programs cover some topics that are not contained in all books (e.g., Markov Models and Network Models).

Each program's input and output have been designed to use the terminology and model structure that are most frequently encountered for that topic. There should be a minimum of differences between our version and the version that appears in most textbooks.

## Organization of the Book

Chapters 1 and 2 are different from the other chapters in the book. Chapter 1 contains a brief description of each program. (Most of these descriptions are also contained at the beginning of each corresponding chapter.) The purpose of Chapter 1 is to provide a quick overview of all the programs in the book.

Chapter 2 explains how to run these programs on an IBM PC or compatible computer. The material is written for the individual who has no previous experience with computers. Those who are experienced with computers can quickly skim this chapter to learn the relevant details regarding the use of the package and then go directly to the chapter describing the program they want to use.

Chapters 3 through 13 are organized in the same general way; each describes one program. The chapters begin with a brief description of the management science model that is solved by the program. This description is intended to provide a bridge between the programs and the textbook you are using.

The *Program Description* contains a brief description of the size and type of problem that is solved by the program.

The *Problem Preparation* section describes the steps that are necessary to prepare a problem for data input. This preparation is often the same as the steps you would take prior to solving a problem by hand. In almost all cases, you will find that a formulated problem taken from any textbook will need minimal changes to prepare it for computer solution.

The *Data Input Overview* section provides a general description of the data that must be entered to solve a problem. All data values are either typed one number at a time in response to prompts from the computer or are entered into an easy-to-use table (or spreadsheet) displayed on the screen.

The *Data Input Details* section contains a detailed description of the data entry sequence. The information in this section is generally the same as in the previous section, but here the intent is to provide detailed guidance to assist in data entry.

The *Program Output* section provides a general description of the output provided by the program.

Every chapter includes at least one example problem. Some of the chapters contain up to seven example problems. In each case, the problem is given and the complete set of input data is shown the way it would look on the screen. This is followed by a copy of the output that would be printed by the program when it was run. If the output is complex, there may be an additional explanation of how to read it.

Every chapter contains a set of problems that vary in difficulty. The easier ones are included to give you practice in using each program if you feel that the example problems are not sufficient. The more difficult ones are included to show you how to solve problems that include the complexities that are frequently a part of real business decision making. All problems are answered at the back of the book. Every chapter also contains one case study that is more complex than the typical problem. Answers are not provided for case studies.

## Changes from the Second Edition

In response to user feedback, we have corrected errors and modified some of the programs (both to make them easier to use and to extend their capabilities). The major modifications are described below. All of these changes (and this book) apply only to the IBM version of the package; the Apple II version is available, but remains as described in the second edition of this book.

Some of you may have already seen some of the new features, because they were included as upgrades in some of the later versions of the second edition. Now, however, every program matches its description in the book, and every problem has been run on the new edition and its answers checked.

### Data Entry Modifications

The primary change is the replacement of prompted input with a spreadsheet-type input procedure that each program explains at the bottom of the screen. Users appear to be unanimous in the opinion that this procedure is both easy to learn and easy to use. The data for a problem are entered into the cells of an on-screen table (where each cell is defined by the intersection of a row and column), and the arrow keys are used to move from cell to cell to edit previously entered data. This data entry procedure is used in linear programming, integer programming, transportation, assignment, decision analysis, decision trees (for Bayesian analysis only), inventory models, and queuing models. Network analysis uses a similar tabular data entry procedure, but the arrow keys cannot be used to edit previously entered data. The Markov model also uses a tabular response to prompts at the bottom of the screen. Only the PERT program does not yet have any spreadsheet-type data entry and editing features.

### Extensions

New features have been added to the transportation, assignment, project scheduling, decision analysis, and Markov programs.

Both the transportation and assignment programs now allow users to input their own row and column names. Each program asks if the user wants computer (C) or user (U) generated names.

Users of the project scheduling program now have the option of including PERT/cost in their analysis of a project (this option is only available for projects in which single time estimates are made for each activity). If this option is selected, the user must input the cost of each activity in the project (this will be prompted by the computer). Output will include total project cost and a cost profile (the minimum and maximum total cost that will be incurred by the end of each time period as the project progresses).

Sensitivity analysis has been added to the decision analysis program output. This new output section presents the upper and lower limits for every payoff value. The optimal alternative will not change unless one of the payoff values is changed to a new value that goes beyond its upper or lower limit.

The market share analysis in the Markov program now outputs the market share for all time periods. Earlier editions output only the last time period.

## Acknowledgments

We appreciate the help of others who have used previous versions of this book in their classes, assisted in programming, provided vital technical information, and generally provided us with the help, criticism, and support without which a book like this could never be written. They are in alphabetical order: Dean Baroni, Israel Borovits, Karl Dickel, Lance Eliot, Paul Grundeman, Steven Jew, Vikky Lawrence, David Mathews, Richard McBride, Don Murray, David O'Donnell, Jack Pounders, George Schick, Sam Stainbrook, Ephriam Turban, Charles Werneke, Terris Wolff, Jon Yormark, and Jacob Zahavi.

There is an even larger group that has provided invaluable assistance by contacting us regarding both errors and suggestions for improvements. We have resolved the impossible dilemma of deciding which ones to name and which ones to leave out by not naming any. This is not meant to lessen either their contribution or our appreciation. The changes, additions, and improvements in the third edition would have been of much lower quality without their input.

There are also others who did not contribute directly to the technical content of the book, but were still an important part of its creation:

Our families, who have contributed both by general encouragement and by direct help in cut and paste, program checkout, and word processing.

Marj Tamaki, who typed and prepared most of the manuscript for publication.

Diane Yeager, who assisted in debugging and testing the software.

Our past editors, Cindy Johnson, Chris Williams, and Herb Smith, who have encouraged us to create something better and helped us to do it.

Thanks to all; we appreciate it.

## Equipment Needs

These programs are designed to run on any IBM PC series computer or any IBM PC compatible computer with at least 256K memory.

Similar comments can be made regarding operating systems and printers. We have tested the package with IBM's DOS 2.0 and 2.1. Informal tests with later releases of DOS indicate that everything works, but we have not formally tested the package with other operating systems. All printed-output testing used Epson and NEC 8023 printers. Informal tests with other printers indicated no problems.

We cannot guarantee that every detail of every program will work on every system because there are more than 1000 different combinations of computers, disk drives, operating systems, and printers that can run this package. Testing all possible equipment combinations is just not feasible. We have had success in using this package on a wide variety of systems, and purchasers of the previous editions have informed us of success in using these programs on an even wider variety of systems.

If something does not work as described, however, we would appreciate being informed. If you do find a problem, please send a detailed description of both your computer configuration and the problem. In almost all cases it would be best if you also send a printout that shows a complete run of the problem situation.

*Los Angeles, California*                                             W.J.E.
*Palos Verdes, California*                                           O.H., Jr.

## Equipment Needs

These programs run on an IBM* personal computer. The minimum required equipment includes:

IBM PC
256K memory
One double-sided disk drive
PC DOS version 2.1 or above

Although a printer and a second disk drive are both optional, they are recommended. Detailed instructions regarding the use of this program are included in this manual.

*IBM is a registered trademark of International Business Machines Corporation.

# Computer Models for Management Science

# 1

## Overview of the Programs

This chapter contains a brief description of each program in this package. Each description covers the types of problems that can be solved, the types of answers that are output by the program, and the largest problem that can be solved. More details about each program can be found in its chapter.

### 1.1 Linear Programming

This program will solve a single objective function, continuous variable, linear programming problem with up to 50 variables and 50 constraints. The program solves for variable values, the objective function value, and slack and surplus variable values, shadow prices, right-hand-side ranging, and objective function coefficient ranging.

### 1.2 Integer Programming

This program will solve a single objective function, zero-one integer programming problem with up to 50 variables and 50 constraints. The program solves for variable values, the objective function value, and slack and surplus variable values. Unlike the linear programming model, this integer programming model does not output shadow prices, right-hand-side ranging, or objective function coefficient ranging.

Integer programming models tend to require more compute time than linear programming models, so be prepared for some time delays. The program runs quickly on most computers if the problem contains seven or fewer variables. If there are more than seven variables, the program uses a heuristic to solve the problem. The exact solution is not guaranteed for these larger problems, but all test problem runs have resulted in either the exact solution or one close to it.

## 1.3 Transportation Model

This program solves the classic transportation model by finding either the maximum or minimum total payoff that results when items are shipped from a set of sources to a set of destinations. The number of items to be shipped between each source and each destination is also output by the program. Problems with up to 20 sources and 20 destinations can be solved.

## 1.4 Assignment Model

This program finds the minimum or maximum payoff that can be obtained by assigning people to machines (or any one set of items to another set). Problems with up to 25 rows and 25 columns can be solved.

## 1.5 Project Scheduling

Project scheduling is discussed in most books as either PERT (Program Evaluation and Review Technique) or CPM (Critical Path Method). In most cases, you will be correct if you consider PERT and CPM as two different names for the same thing. Therefore, even if your book uses only CPM, most problems can be solved with this program.

The program computes the earliest and latest start and finish times for each activity (job) in a project that contains up to 99 activities. Slack for each activity, the critical path, and the expected project completion time are also output.

Time estimates can be entered as either a single estimate or as three estimates (optimistic, modal, and pessimistic). The program output will also include the variance of the expected project completion time if three time estimates were input. The program can also calculate total project costs when activity costs are known for single-time-estimate projects.

## 1.6 Network Models

All network problems are described by a set of nodes connected by links. The various types of network problems are distinguished by different interpretations of the nodes and links. Three types of network models are covered: minimum spanning tree, maximum flow, and shortest route. The program solves each model for networks with up to 25 nodes and 25 links.

In *minimum spanning tree* problems, the link lengths represent distances between nodes. The distance between any two nodes must be the same in each direction (symmetric). The program outputs the total length of the minimum spanning tree, and identifies all links that are included.

In *maximum flow* problems, each link length is used to  represent the maximum flow rate between two nodes.  All flow rates must be one-way flows (asymmetric), so if two-way flow is possible between two nodes, this link must be entered as  two one-way flows. The program determines the maximum flow  rate between any two specified nodes (called the *source* node and the *sink* node). The flow through each link in the network is also part of the program output.

In *shortest route* problems, each link length is used to represent either the distance or the travel time between two nodes. Problems with either symmetric or asymmetric links can be solved with this model. The program finds the shortest route between any two specified nodes (called the *starting* node and the *destination* node). Output includes the total length of the shortest route and a description of the complete route from the starting node to the destination node.

Some problems may have multiple optimal solutions, but none of these three programs indicates if multiple optimal solutions exist.

## 1.7  Decision Analysis Models

This program determines the optimal decision for problems involving either decision making under uncertainty or decision making under risk. For decision making under uncertainty, it determines the optimal decision using the five most commonly used decision criteria (maximin, minimax, equal likelihood, minimax regret, and Hurwicz). For decision making under risk, the program determines the optimal decision from a set of alternatives based on the maximization of the expected value of the resultant payoff. Both the expected payoff and the expected value of perfect information are also output. If additional information is available to the decision maker, the program also determines the marginal probabilities, the posterior probabilities, the expected payoff with sample information, and the expected value of sample information.

The program will handle up to 15 states of nature, 15 alternatives, and sample information with up to 15 different predictions.

## 1.8  Decision Tree Model

This program is in two parts. The first part (called Bayesian analysis) uses the prior probabilities and the conditional probabilities to compute the marginal probabilities and posterior probabilities given that each of the possible predictions has taken place. It can analyze up to 10 states of nature and 10 predictions of these states of nature. These revised probabilities are then used as input to the second part of the program.

The second part of the program determines the optimal alternative for every decision node in the decision tree. The program also computes the expected payoff if the optimal alternatives are selected each time you go through the decision tree. The program can handle decision trees with up to 100 nodes.

## 1.9  Markov Models

This program analyzes either recurrent state or absorbing state Markov problems. The program can handle problems with up to 12 different states. Any number of these may be absorbing states.

If the problem has no absorbing states, the program can be used to predict long-run (or steady state) market share from the transition probability matrix. It can also use the transition probability matrix and the current market share to predict the market share in either any specified future period or all periods from the current period to any specified future period. This program also computes mean first passage times, first passage time variances, and expected recurrence times.

If the problem has at least one absorbing state, the program determines the mean number of periods that one will remain in each transient state prior to absorption, the mean time to absorption given that one begins in any transient state, and the probability of being absorbed into each of the absorbing states.

## 1.10  Inventory Models

This program solves the EOQ model (with or without shortages) and optimal production lot size model (with or without shortages). Output includes the order quantity, reorder level, order costs, holding costs, total cost, and maximum required inventory levels.

The program can also solve problems where demand is stochastic. Output from the program includes both the optimal order quantity and reorder level. If the shortage cost rate is known, the program computes both the safety stock level, safety stock cost, and total shortage costs. If the shortage cost rate is unknown, then the program requires an estimate of the highest acceptable shortage probability.

## 1.11 Queuing Models

This program analyzes any one of the following seven queuing models:

1. Single server.
2. Single server with finite queue length.
3. Single server with finite calling population.
4. Single server with arbitrary service time distribution.
5. Multiple server.
6. Multiple server with finite queue length.
7. Multiple server with finite calling population.

For each model, the program computes the mean number of customers in the system and in the queue, and the mean wait time in the system and the queue. In addition, the balking percentage is determined for alternatives 2 and 6, and the percentage of time that the server is idle is determined for alternatives 4 and 6.

The multiple server models are restricted to 30 or fewer servers. Unless otherwise specified in the preceding list, each of these seven alternatives finds the steady state solution for a queuing environment with an infinite calling population whose arrival rate is Poisson. Service times are exponential, and queue lengths are unbounded. All customers wait in a single queue in all models, and the customer at the head of the queue goes to the first available server as soon as the server has finished processing the previous customer. All customers enter the queue (no balking), and no customers leave the queue once it is entered. No priorities are used; therefore all customer service is on a first-come, first-served basis.

An economic analysis option is available for any of the seven alternatives. If this option is selected, the program computes the system operating cost, the customer waiting cost, and the total cost. Multiple server models have an additional option that eases the task of determining the optimal number of servers. If this option is selected, the program will request an upper and lower limit for the number of servers. For every number of servers between these limits, the program will output the mean system wait time, the mean number of customers in the system, and the total cost.

# 2

# *How to Use the Programs*

All programs in this package have been designed for first-time users, but they also meet the needs of experienced users. These goals are difficult to achieve simultaneously. First-time users prefer programs with a minimum of options and a maximum of guidance. Experienced users prefer a maximum of options (so they can tailor the program to their needs) and a minimum of guidance (because it slows them down). To meet these conflicting goals, much of the first-time user material appears in this and the remaining chapters. The menus and prompts that are common to all programs are described in this chapter. Anything that is unique to a particular program is described in the chapter for that program. Examples (which are usually illustrated by a copy of a screen image) are included for every program and every major option within each program.

This chapter has been written under the assumption that the reader has not previously used a computer. This does not mean, however, that experienced users should ignore the chapter; those at all levels of experience will find some of its information helpful. The only difference is that the more experienced will be able to skim through much of the material that describes computer operations.

## 2.1 Operations Overview

It is virtually impossible to explain all the operating procedures for all configurations of all computers that can run this package. What we have done, however, is explain the general procedures that are common to all IBM PC and compatible computers and note when you should find out details regarding your computer.

To run this package, your computer must have at least one disk drive, but two disk drives are recommended to reduce the amount of time spent switching diskettes. The program will output a message whenever any disk switching is required.

You need the CMMS program diskette, and you should also have one of your own formatted diskettes if you intend either to save problem data or results for later use or to use data that have previously been saved. *Never* use the program diskette to save data or results.

Copyright restrictions prevent the inclusion of DOS on the CMMS diskette. To run the IBM PC program diskette you must first insert the DOS diskette that came with your computer into drive A and turn on the computer (see your computer manual for details). Then remove the DOS diskette and insert the CMMS program diskette into drive A. Type "CMMS" after the A> prompt that appears on the screen. Once the CMMS program begins, all input is guided by menus and prompts from the programs. It is important to remember that one special key must usually be pressed to send data input or a response to the computer. The IBM PC uses a key that has a left-pointing arrow with a right-angled bend in the arrow's shaft that points upward. This is called the ENTER key on the IBM PC and its compatibles.

The CMMS diskette is formatted at 360K bytes for MS DOS or PC DOS version 2.0 or above. The CMMS diskette is not copy-protected, and we recommend that you make a copy of the full diskette for your own normal use of the package and keep the original diskette as a backup copy. All the CMMS programs may be copied onto another 5-1/4 inch diskette, a hard disk, a 3-1/2 inch diskette, or a high-density diskette of any size. In general, you will minimize problems if you copy the CMMS programs onto a diskette that is formatted at the same density as your drive. See your computer manual for details regarding the copying procedure.

## 2.2 How to Run the Package

If you are running this package on your own computer, and have nobody to ask, use the following procedure. This is not the only way to load and run a program, but it is among the simpler methods and has the advantage of working on most systems.

1. Turn off the computer.

2. Open the disk drive door. If the system has two disk drives, use drive A. In most systems, this is the drive in the left or on top.

3. Remove the computer's DOS diskette from its envelope and insert it into the disk drive slot. Push it in as far as it will go, but do not force it.

   a) Make sure that the diskette label is facing up when it is inserted into the slot. The programs will not run if the diskette is upside down.
   b) Do not touch any part of the diskette that was inside the envelope.
   c) Do not bend the diskette. (Violating either of these latter rules may result in destruction of some or all of the programs on the diskette.)

4. Close the disk drive door. (The door must not "crunch" the diskette.)

5. Turn on the monitor, the computer, and (if you intend to use printed output), the printer. There will be a pause of about a minute on the IBM PC. The red light on the disk drive will then glow, and the disk drive will make several different types of strange noises. The light will go out and the noises will stop after about 10 seconds. The screen should display the system prompt (the "A>" on the IBM PC).

6. Remove the DOS diskette from the drive and replace it with the CMMS program diskette.

7. Type CMMS, and then press the RETURN (or ENTER) key.

8. The red light will again glow, and the disk drive will spin. When the red light goes out, the screen will display the title of this book, the copyright notice, and disclaimer. This will be followed by a series of questions asking which drive is to be used for the program and which drive for data. After these questions are answered, the main menu (Fig. 2.1) will be displayed.

## 2.3  What to Do if It Doesn't Work

If the MAIN MENU did not appear on the screen as described in the previous section, try the following to correct the problem:

1. Go through the procedure from the beginning. Be sure to do each step in the proper sequence.

2. Check to make sure that the proper program diskette is being used, and that it is inserted with the label up (or to the left).

**FIGURE 2.1**   CMMS main menu

```
                -=*=-  M A I N   M E N U  -=*=-


         1  =  LINP ...  LINEAR PROGRAMMING
         2  =  INTP ...  INTEGER PROGRAMMING
         3  =  TRAN ...  TRANSPORTATION MODEL
         4  =  ASGT ...  ASSIGNMENT MODEL
         5  =  PERT ...  PROJECT SCHEDULING
         6  =  NETW ...  NETWORK MODELS
         7  =  DECS ...  DECISION MODELS
         8  =  DTRE ...  DECISION TREE MODEL
         9  =  MRKV ...  MARKOV MODELS
        10  =  INVN ...  INVENTORY MODELS
        11  =  QUES ...  QUEUEING MODELS
        12  =  DATA ...  DISKETTE MANAGEMENT
        13  =  QUIT ...  (EXIT TO DOS)



Enter a number for your selection from this menu & press ↵
```

3. If the system does not respond to any key, wait a minute or so. If it still does not respond, remove all diskettes from the drives, turn off the computer, and begin again. Do *not* open the disk drive door if the red light is on! The end of this chapter explains what to do to fix this situation.

## 2.4 The Main Menu

The MAIN MENU for this package is shown in Fig. 2.1. This is what will be displayed on the screen after you have successfully loaded and run the CMMS program. Thirteen options are available. Selecting one of the first 11 options allows you to solve problems using the management science model named after the program number. Selecting option 12 allows you either to list the contents of a data diskette or delete previously saved problem data. The thirteenth option is used to QUIT and return to DOS.

When option 12 is selected, the screen displays the DATA FILE MANAGE-MENT menu (see Fig. 2.2). Only five options are available on this menu:

- The first option is DELETE FILE. It is recommended that you delete files whenever you have no further use for them. They have a tendency to proliferate.

- The second option is to VIEW DATA DISK DIRECTORY. This option works in the same way as the same option on the PROGRAM OPTIONS menu. It is included here as a convenience for those who wish to see a list of the files on their data diskette.

**FIGURE 2.2**    Data file management menu

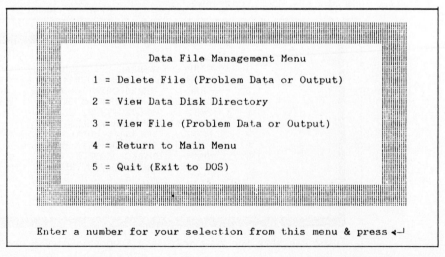

```
               Data File Management Menu

     1 = Delete File (Problem Data or Output)

     2 = View Data Disk Directory

     3 = View File (Problem Data or Output)

     4 = Return to Main Menu

     5 = Quit (Exit to DOS)


 Enter a number for your selection from this menu & press ↵
```

- The third option (VIEW FILE) allows you to see the contents of any file.
- The fourth option is used to return to the MAIN MENU.
- The fifth option is used to QUIT and return to DOS.

## 2.5 The Program Options Menu

If any of the programs (1–11) are selected from the MAIN MENU, the PRO-
GRAM OPTIONS menu will be displayed on the screen. This menu (see Fig.
2.3) is identical for all programs in this package (except for the name of the
model at the top of the menu), and each of the nine options works the same way
in each program. Each option will be fully explained in this section, but will not
be repeated in the chapter describing each program.

1. ENTER PROBLEM FROM KEYBOARD.  Select this option to enter a
complete set of problem data. The data entry sequence and the prompts are
different for each program, and they are fully explained in each chapter.

The first part of the data entry is used to enter the problem structure (e.g.,
the structure of a transportation problem is defined by the number of rows, the
number of columns, and whether it is to be maximized or minimized). After
this is entered, the program will ask if you want to change the problem
structure. Type "Y" if any of the problem structure values are incorrect. The
program will then repeat all the problem structure prompts to allow the correct
data to be entered. Models that require only one number to to define the
problem structure (e.g., queuing) do not have the CHANGE PROBLEM
STRUCTURE option.

**FIGURE 2.3**   Program options menu

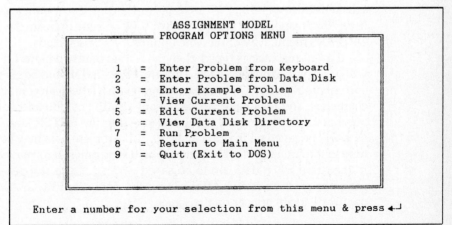

```
                        ASSIGNMENT MODEL
                 ===== PROGRAM OPTIONS MENU =====


             1   =   Enter Problem from Keyboard
             2   =   Enter Problem from Data Disk
             3   =   Enter Example Problem
             4   =   View Current Problem
             5   =   Edit Current Problem
             6   =   View Data Disk Directory
             7   =   Run Problem
             8   =   Return to Main Menu
             9   =   Quit (Exit to DOS)



     Enter a number for your selection from this menu & press ←┘
```

The data entry sequence is often difficult to describe. A level of detail that is appropriate for one person may be too detailed or too brief for someone else. We have attempted to resolve this dilemma in the following way: Beginning with Chapter 3, each chapter contains two sections called Data Input Overview and Data Input Details. The Data Input Overview presents a general description of the data entry sequence, then the Data Input Details describe the data entry sequence step by step, stating just what data should be entered. Note that in the detailed statements (1) everything that is not in a box must be typed exactly as shown and (2) everything that is in a box describes the information that must be typed in at that point. Data values that logically belong together are placed on one line in this section, but are almost always input one item at a time in actual data entry.

An example problem is used for the last two descriptions of the data entry sequence. First, the full set of problem data values are listed in the same format used in the Data Input Details section. Finally a copy of the complete prompted input sequence (as it would appear on the screen) is shown.

Most of the CMMS models use a spreadsheet-type input procedure (that the program explains at the bottom of the screen). The data for a problem are entered into the cells of an on-screen table (where each cell is defined by the intersection of a row and column), and the arrow keys are used to move from cell to cell to edit previously entered data. This data entry procedure is used in linear programming, integer programming, transportation, assignment, decision analysis, decision trees (for Bayesian analysis only), inventory models, and queuing models. Network analysis uses a similar tabular data entry procedure, but the arrow keys cannot be used to edit previously entered data. The Markov model also uses a tabular display of the data, but all data entry and editing occurs in response to prompts at the bottom of the screen. Only the PERT program does not yet have any spreadsheet-type data entry and editing features.

After entering all data for a problem, the full set of data may be saved on a diskette by responding "Y" to the prompt asking if you want to save the data. If an "N" response is typed, control will be sent back to the PROGRAM OPTIONS menu. Any of the nine options may be selected.

If a "Y" response is typed, then the full set of instructions for saving data will be displayed on the screen. Type the name that should be used to save the current problem data. Names must begin with a letter, can contain up to eight characters, and may be composed of any desired combination of letters and numbers. After typing the name and pressing the ENTER key, the problem data will be saved on the data diskette. This problem data may be used at any time in the future. *Note:* The program will stop unless a formatted diskette is in the drive when data are to be saved or read. Once stopped, the CMMS program must be rerun. After saving the data, the PROGRAM OPTIONS menu will again appear on the screen.

2. ENTER PROBLEMS FROM DATA DISKETTE.   Select this option to enter problem data that have previously been saved on the data diskette. Type the name of one of the previously saved problem data sets, and these data will be entered. This problem data set is now the current problem, and it may be viewed, run, or edited.

3. ENTER EXAMPLE PROBLEM.   Selecting this option enters the problem data for the first example problem described in this chapter. This option should be selected the first time that you run each program to familiarize yourself with its operations. This option should also be selected if you believe that something is wrong with a program. It provides a quick check to determine if the program is working correctly.

4. VIEW CURRENT PROBLEM.   This option is used to check the values of all variables in the current problem. When selected, this option displays the OUTPUT OPTIONS menu on the screen. If "S" is typed, the current problem data values will be displayed on the screen, and if "P" is typed, they will be printed. Make sure that the printer is turned on prior to selecting the "P" option. When you have finished viewing or printing the problem, type "R" to return to the program menu.

5. EDIT CURRENT PROBLEM.   Select this option to change one (or more) of the current problem values. The prompts for this option are different for every program, and are fully explained in each chapter. The problem structure cannot be changed with this option. Also, not all data values can be changed in every program. If a data value must be changed, and it is not included in the EDIT CURRENT PROBLEM option, then the full set of data must be entered using the ENTER PROBLEM FROM KEYBOARD option. In general, each program will display the current value of each variable prior to requesting a new value. Type the new value and then press the RETURN key.

After editing a problem, you have the option of saving the current problem data on the data diskette. This is done by following the same data-saving prompts and procedures described in option one.

6. VIEW DATA DISK DIRECTORY.   Select this option to check which sets of problem data values are stored on the data diskette. The output from this option is a list of all problems stored on the data diskette. (This is what would be output after typing FILES or DIR on the IBM PC.)

7. RUN PROBLEM.   Selecting this option runs the program with the current problem data values. The first output is the OUTPUT OPTIONS menu (see Figure 2.4).

If "S" or "P" is typed, the INFORMATION ENTERED and RESULTS (as described in each chapter) will be displayed on the screen or printed on the printer. Thus the results can be viewed on the screen prior to printing or saving them on a disk. These options may be selected or repeated in any order without rerunning the problem.

**FIGURE 2.4**   Output options menu

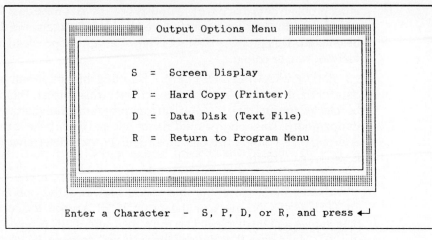

```
|||||||||||||||||||||    Output Options Menu    |||||||||||||||||||||


            S  =   Screen Display

            P  =   Hard Copy (Printer)

            D  =   Data Disk (Text File)

            R  =   Return to Program Menu




        Enter a Character  -  S, P, D, or R, and press ↵
```

If "D" is typed, the INFORMATION ENTERED and RESULTS will be saved on a diskette. These data can then be modified with a word processor for use in reports, exams, slides, and so on. After typing "D," the screen will ask what name you want to use for the file. Respond by typing the name under which the output is to be saved. (Be careful with file names. If a name is used that is the same as a previously used file name, the new data will be saved, and all the old data will be erased.)

Also, *do not save any data on the program diskette*. There is only a limited amount of space on the program diskette, and it must remain blank to ensure proper operation of the programs.

The program will again display the OUTPUT OPTIONS menu after the output data are displayed, printed, or saved. Any of the four options on this menu may be selected in any order. Select "R" to return to the PROGRAM MENU if no more output is desired.

8. RETURN TO MAIN MENU.   Select this option to exit from this program and return to the MAIN MENU. The current problem data is lost when this option is selected, so be sure to save it on the data diskette if it is to be used again.

9. QUIT.   Select this option to quit and return to DOS. Remove the program and data diskettes from the drives. Other programs may now be loaded and run, or you may turn off the computer.

## 2.6  First Use of a Program

This section contains a few examples of the procedures to follow for some frequently occurring tasks. The assignment model is used in these examples, but similar procedures are used for all other programs.

This example begins after the program diskette has been placed into the disk drive and the start-up procedure (as discussed earlier in the How to Run the Package section). The MAIN MENU (see Fig. 2.1) will be displayed on the screen.

Type the number "4" as your selection from the main menu, and then press the ENTER key. The PROGRAM OPTIONS menu (see Fig. 2.3) for the assignment model will now be displayed on the screen.

Type the number "3" as your selection from the PROGRAM OPTIONS menu, and then press the ENTER key. The example problem data for the assignment model will now be loaded into the computer. Next type the number "4" to view this problem and follow this by typing the letter "S". The program will display the INFORMATION ENTERED for this set of data on the screen. Turn to the assignment model, Chapter 6. The INFORMATION ENTERED that is displayed on the screen should be identical to example problem A1 shown at the beginning of that chapter.

Now press the ENTER key, and the screen will again display the PROGRAM OPTIONS menu. Type the number "7" and press the ENTER key. This runs the assignment model with the current problem data (which is the example problem data that has just been loaded).

The program will respond by displaying the OUTPUT OPTIONS menu. Type the letter "S" and press the ENTER key. The screen will first display the INFORMATION ENTERED and follow it with this message:

PRESS ↵

All output to the screen has built-in pauses that display this message. This prevents the computer from displaying data faster than it can be read. When you have read the output on the screen and want to see more output, press the ENTER key. These pauses are unnecessary and are not included if printer output is selected.

The next section of output is the RESULTS. These should look the same as the results for sample problem A1 in the assignment model chapter.

When the results are all output, the screen will again display the OUTPUT OPTIONS menu. Type the letter "R" and press the ENTER key. The PROGRAM OPTIONS menu will again be displayed. Any of the nine options may be selected.

## 2.7    What to Do if Things Go Wrong

First, make sure that something is really wrong. It is clear that something is wrong if the computer's answers are distinctly different from the correct answer, or if the computer output differs completely from the output described in this book, but nothing is wrong if the output differs slightly from the correct output. This can occur for several reasons:

1. *System variations.*   Each computer uses slightly different rules for printing and spacing output. We can almost guarantee that your computer will use a different font and a different spacing compared to the examples printed in this book.

2. *Large problems.*   The output will sometimes look different if your problem is larger than the example shown in the book.

3. *Large numbers.*   The computer will use a form of scientific notation to print numbers that are large. Thus if the answer is 987654321, most computers will print something like 9.8765E08. This means that 9.8765 must be multiplied by 10 to the eighth power. This shifts the decimal point eight places to the right for an answer of 987650000. In some computers you will only receive five- or six-digit precision, and you will lose the least significant digits, as shown in this example.

4. *Rounding differences.*   The last digit in your answer may be one unit larger or smaller than the answer shown in this book. This is due to different rounding rules used in each computer. Program output is usually rounded to two or three digits after the decimal point.

5. *Program changes.*   We may need to change some of the programs to correct errors. In some cases this may result in slight changes in the output. We will, of course, keep these changes to a minimum.

### 2.7.1   System Check Procedure

It is a good idea to check the system when running any program for the first time. The same check procedure should be used anytime it appears that something is wrong with a program.

1. Run the package by following the start up procedure described earlier in this chapter in the section entitled How to Run the Package.

2. Type the number of the desired program from those listed on the MAIN MENU. The PROGRAM OPTIONS menu should appear.

3. Type the number "3" to load the example problem data for the program.

4. Type the number "7" to run the program. You may type either "S" or "P" when the program displays the OUTPUT OPTIONS menu, but it is recommended that printer output be selected, because this eases the job of checking the output for correctness. Compare the problem data (in the output section labeled "** INFORMATION ENTERED **") and the answers (in the output section labeled ** RESULTS **) with the corresponding data in the first example problem in the chapter. All numbers should be the same (except for the minor differences discussed earlier in this section). If everything matches, you can be sure that the diskette is okay

and that the computer is working properly.

If the output is not the same, either the computer or the diskette may be defective. Neither result is likely, but it is possible. It is also possible that we made a typographical error in the book. This, too, is unlikely (we hope), but can happen. In any case, start from the beginning and try again. If it still does not work properly, check with your instructor or computer center.

5. Next (in response to the "WHICH OPTION (1-9)?" question that was output after the above run of the program), type the number "1." Respond to the prompts by typing the data for the first example problem. A copy of the screen image for this data entry sequence for the first example problem is shown in each chapter.

6. Select option "7" to run the program with the data that you have just input. As in step 4, above, all output regarding the problem data and results should exactly match the figures in the chapter. If some of the input data do not match, use the edit feature (option 5) to correct it, and rerun the problem. Something is probably wrong with the diskette if the ** INFOR- MATION ENTERED ** is correct, but the RESULTS are different. Check with your instructor or your computer center.

7. Other options and program features are not tested by this procedure, but we have encountered no case where the above tests worked properly and other features did not. Naturally, we would like to be informed of situations to the contrary.

### 2.7.2 Correcting Typing Mistakes

There are several different ways to correct mistakes or change part of your input:

1. Corrections can be made to any line *before* the ENTER key is pressed. The backspace key (a key with a left pointing arrow on top) is pressed to move the cursor to the first character to be changed. The correct character is then typed. What you see on the screen after the ENTER key is pressed is what was entered into the computer.

2. Some of the programs have built-in data correction features. These pro- grams output a question that asks if you want to change your data. If you do, all changes are made in response to prompts output by the program.

3. If a mistake is made after data have been entered into the computer, then the EDIT CURRENT PROBLEM option must be used to make the correc- tion. If the structure of a problem is to be changed (e.g., from a 3 row by 2 column transportation problem to a 2 row by 3 column problem), it must be entered as a new problem.

### 2.7.3 Stopping the Computer

Often the fastest way to fix problems is to stop the computer and start from the beginning. This almost always works. The stopping procedure is simple, but as usual there is a right way and a wrong way. The right way is as follows:

1. a) Check to see if the disk's red light is on. If it is, press the CTRL key and simultaneously press the BREAK key (the BREAK key has SCROLL LOCK printed on top, and BREAK printed on the front of the key). If the light does not go out, simultaneously press and hold down the CTRL key, the ALT key, and the DEL key. Under some conditions, the IBM PC will take over a minute before anything happens. Be patient.

   b) In the rare situation where none of these steps stop the disk drive, get help from someone who is familiar with your type of computer.

   c) If nobody is available, and the disk light remains lit, turn off the computer. There is a small possibility that some of the programs on the program diskette may be damaged by this procedure, and there is a greater possibility that the data for the current problem will be destroyed on the data diskette, so try the above steps first.

   d) Never open the disk drive door while the red light is lit.

2. If the disk light is out, open the disk drive door, remove the diskette, and place the diskette in its envelope. It makes no difference what is displayed on the screen at this point.

3. Turn off the computer.

4. Go back to Section 2.2 and begin again.

# 3

## LINP

# *Linear Programming*

The linear programming model is the most widely used of all the models contained in this book. The simplest form of a linear programming problem involves maximizing (or minimizing) a single objective function that is constrained by a set of limited resources and requirements that must be met. A typical problem involves finding the optimal production levels of each item in a company's product line. If the objective is to maximize profits, then the optimal solution would be the production levels that meet all constraints and generate the largest possible profit. Profit maximization is frequently encountered in linear programming problems, but minimizing cost, minimizing the number of defects, minimizing the cost of inventory, maximizing the total number of units produced, and other similar objectives can also be a part of linear programming problems.

The most frequently encountered constraints involve the use of limited amounts of raw materials, labor, and so on. These are important, but business use of linear programming also includes other types of constraints. The constraints simply describe any limitations or requirements that must be met. The only restriction is that they must contain linear terms and be expressed by less-than-or-equal-to ($\leq$), equal to ($=$), or greater-than-or-equal-to ($\geq$) relationships.

## 3.1 Program Description

This program will solve a single objective function, continuous variable, linear programming problem with up to 50 variables and 50 constraints. The program solves for variable values, the objective function value, slack and surplus variable values, shadow prices, right-hand-side ranging, and objective function coefficient ranging.

This is a large program, so be prepared for some time delays. Pauses may occur after selecting the program or after selecting the RUN PROBLEM option. This latter pause may take several minutes for larger problems.

## 3.2  Problem Preparation

Only a few steps are required to prepare a linear programming problem for computer input:

1. Arrange all ≤ constraints first, all = constraints next, and all ≥ constraints last.
2. Arrange all variables in the same sequence in the objective function and in every constraint.
3. All right-hand-side values must be positive or zero.

Do not include any slack, surplus, or artificial variables in the problem. Also do not include any boundary (non-negativity) constraints. All of these are automatically inserted in the appropriate places by the computer.

## 3.3  Data Input Overview

The problem data are entered using either prompted or free-form input. Both input modes begin by requesting entry of the problem structure (the number of variables, the number of less-than-or-equal-to constraints, the number of equality constraints, the number of greater-than-or-equal-to constraints, and whether the objective is to maximize or minimize). This is followed by input of the variable names and the objective function name.

Prompted input requests all remaining data values one at a time. First the coefficients of each variable in the objective function are entered. These are followed by the coefficients of the variables in the first constraint, and the first constraint's right-hand-side value. The coefficients and the right-hand-side values of the remaining constraints are then entered. If a variable does not appear in the objective function or a constraint, a zero *must* be typed as the coefficient.

Free form input uses a spreadsheet structure to enter the objective function coefficients, the constraint coefficients, and the constraint right-hand-side values. Initially, the cursor (a blinking rectangle) will be located at the left side of the upper left cell (corresponding to the coefficient of the first variable in the objective function). After you have typed the complete numerical value, press the ENTER key. The cursor will then move to the next cell. Unlike prompted input, variables with zero coefficients need not be entered. Use the arrow keys to move to the next cell that has a non-zero value and continue entering data. The spreadsheet is arranged so each column contains the coefficients of one variable. The variable names are displayed at the top of each column and highlighted in reverse video.

*Note*: With either format, the largest numerical value that can be entered is ±999,999. If the problem contains numbers larger than this, divide the *entire* row by 1,000.

## 3.4 Data Input Details

The problem structure is defined by entering five data values. The first four describe the size of the problem:

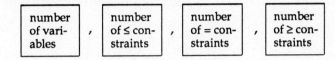

| number of vari-ables | , | number of ≤ con-straints | , | number of = con-straints | , | number of ≥ con-straints |

The last data value in the problem structure is a "1" for maximization problems and a "–1" for minimization problems.

The variable names are entered next. Each name may contain one to four characters, and the first character must be a letter. Do not include spaces in your variable names. If you do not wish to enter variable names, the computer will call your first variable X1, your second variable X2, and so on. The remaining data may be entered as either prompted or free-form input.

### 3.4.1 Prompted Input

If prompted input is used, the next set of data to be input are the coefficients of all variables in the objective function:

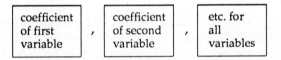

| coefficient of first variable | , | coefficient of second variable | , | etc. for all variables |

Next, you input the coefficients of all variables and the right-hand-side value for all ≤ constraints:

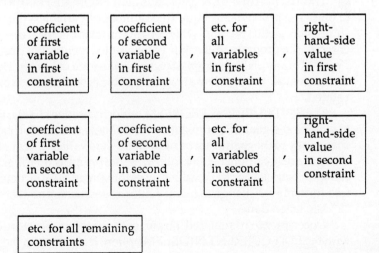

| coefficient of first variable in first constraint | , | coefficient of second variable in first constraint | , | etc. for all variables in first constraint | , | right-hand-side value in first constraint |

| coefficient of first variable in second constraint | , | coefficient of second variable in second constraint | , | etc. for all variables in second constraint | , | right-hand-side value in second constraint |

| etc. for all remaining constraints |

Exactly the same format is then used to input all = constraints. Last, the same format is used to enter all ≥ constraints.

### 3.4.2 Free-Form Input

If free-form input is used, the objective function coefficients are entered on the first line of the spreadsheet:

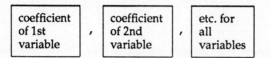

Next, each of the "≤" constraint values are entered using the same format:

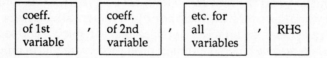

Each "=" constraint is entered next with the same format. Finally, each "≥" constraint is entered with the same format.

## 3.5 Editing the Data

Editing features are a part of both the ENTER PROBLEM FROM KEYBOARD option and the EDIT CURRENT PROBLEM option. The problem structure (but not the problem data values) may be changed in the ENTER PROBLEM FROM KEYBOARD option and the problem data (but not the problem structure) may be changed in the EDIT CURRENT PROBLEM option.

The first part of the ENTER PROBLEM FROM KEYBOARD option is used to enter the problem structure (the number of variables, the number of constraints of each type, and whether the problem is max or min). After it is entered, the program will ask if you want to re-enter the problem structure. Type "Y" if any of the problem structure values are incorrect. The program will then repeat all the problem structure prompts to allow the correct data to be entered.

The EDIT CURRENT PROBLEM option is used to change variable names, to change the goal of optimization from MAX to MIN (or vice versa), or to change any of the coefficient or right-hand-side values. Either of these first two changes are accomplished by following the prompts on the screen. The third change (coefficient or RHV values) uses the spreadsheet structure described in free-form input. Change as many values as you wish, and then press the letter "F" key when done.

Once a problem is entered, no part of the problem structure can be changed with the EDIT CURRENT PROBLEM option. If anything in the problem structure must be changed, all the problem data must be entered as a new problem by using the ENTER PROBLEM FROM KEYBOARD option.

## 3.6 Program Output

The program output includes both answers and some of the data from the original problem (to aid in checking for errors and interpreting the answers). The variable names used in the output are the same user-defined variable names used to input the problem data.

The output for each variable includes its optimal value and its coefficient in the objective function. The program also outputs the objective function coefficient sensitivity (under the heading: COEFF. SENS.). These values (called *reduced costs* in many texts) represent the unit change in the objective function if any of the nonbasic variables is required to enter the solution.

The output for each constraint includes its original right-hand-side value, the amount of slack or surplus (whichever is appropriate), and the shadow price. Some books allow shadow prices to be either positive or negative and use the sign to indicate its effect. Most books require that shadow prices always be positive, and use the problem type (max or min) and the constraint type ($\leq$, $=$, or $\geq$) to determine its effect. This program always outputs positive shadow prices.

The remaining output includes the objective function value, objective function coefficient ranging, and right-hand-side ranging. The original values, upper limits, and lower limits are output for all ranging data. All the ranging data apply only to a single change in the original problem. A new problem must be run to determine the effect of changes in two or more numbers.

*Note:* Strange things happen when linear programming problems have degenerate solutions. The correct values of the objective function and all variables will be obtained in all cases (at least all our test problems worked), but the sensitivity analysis output (shadow prices, ranging, and so on) should be used with caution, because it may not be correct. The program does not test for degeneracy, but the output can be easily checked to see if it exists. The problem is degenerate if any row in the constraint portion of the output simultaneously has a zero value in both the SLACK OR SURPLUS column and the SHADOW PRICE column.

## 3.7 Example Problem LP1

$$\text{MAX } P = X + 2Y$$
$$3X \leq 6$$
$$X + 4Y \leq 8$$
$$Y \leq 3$$

Problem LP1 is a simple maximization problem with three constraints. Its optimal solution is

    X = 2
    Y = 1.5
    P = 5

All of the resources available in the first two constraints are used completely, but there are 1.5 unused units of the third constraint resource. An additional unit of the first constraint resource is worth 0.1666 dollar (if the units of P are in dollars), and an additional unit of the second constraint resource is worth 0.5 dollar. An additional unit of the third constraint resource is not worth anything.

### 3.7.1 Problem Preparation

This problem would look like the following after preparing it for computer input:

$$\text{MAX } P = 1X + 2Y$$
$$3X + 0Y \leq 6$$
$$1X + 4Y \leq 8$$
$$0X + 1Y \leq 3$$

### 3.7.2 Data Input

The following data values must be input to solve this problem:

    2, 3, 0, 0, 1
    1, 2
    3, 0, 6
    1, 4, 8
    0, 1, 3

Figure 3.1 shows how the computer screen looks after the problem structure is input. Figure 3.2 shows the computer screen after the variable names are input. Figure 3.3 shows the screen after all data values are input in response to prompts from the computer.

### 3.7.3 Computer Output

The output from a run of example problem LP1 is shown in Fig. 3.4. The INFORMATION ENTERED section contains a complete statement of the problem that was solved. A minor difference between the original problem and this portion of the output is that the symbol <= is used in place of ≤. If there had been a ≥ constraint, it would have been output as >=.

**FIGURE 3.1** Input of problem structure for example problem LP1

```
               -=*=-  DATA  INPUT  -=*=-


    ENTER NUMBER OF VARIABLES
    ENTER NUMBER IN RANGE ( 2  -  50 ) & press ↵   2

    ENTER NUMBER OF LESS THAN OR EQUAL TO CONSTRAINTS
    ENTER NUMBER IN RANGE ( 0  -  50 ) & press ↵   3

    ENTER NUMBER OF EQUAL TO CONSTRAINTS
    ENTER NUMBER IN RANGE ( 0  -  47 ) & press ↵   0

    ENTER NUMBER OF GREATER THAN OR EQUAL TO CONSTRAINTS
    ENTER NUMBER IN RANGE ( 0  -  47 ) & press ↵   0

    IS THE PROBLEM TYPE MAXIMIZATION (1)  OR  MINIMIZATION (-1)
    Enter a Character ( 1  or  -1 ) & press ↵    -1

    DO YOU WANT TO RE-ENTER PROBLEM STRUCTURE? (Y/N)
    Enter a Character ( Y  or  N ) & press ↵    N
```

**FIGURE 3.2** Computer screen after input of variable names for example problem LP1

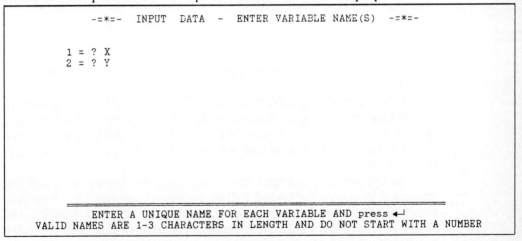

```
        -=*=-  INPUT  DATA  -  ENTER VARIABLE NAME(S)  -=*=-


    1 = ? X
    2 = ? Y




        =====================================================
        ENTER A UNIQUE NAME FOR EACH VARIABLE AND press ↵
  VALID NAMES ARE 1-3 CHARACTERS IN LENGTH AND DO NOT START WITH A NUMBER
```

The first part of the RESULTS section lists all variables and their values. In this problem X equals 2, and Y equals 1.5. Both variables are already in the basis, so the COEFFICIENT SENSITIVITY values are both 0.

The next part of the RESULTS section shows that the first constraint has 0 slack and a shadow price of 0.167. (The true value of this shadow price is 0.16666..., but the program rounds this to 0.167.) The second constraint also has 0 slack but the shadow price equals 0.5. The third constraint has 1.5 units of slack and a shadow price of 0.

**FIGURE 3.3**   Input of data values for example problem LP1

```
                        PROMPTED INPUT

OBJECTIVE FUNCTION

COEFFICIENT FOR VARIABLE # 1  (X) ? 1
COEFFICIENT FOR VARIABLE # 2  (Y) ? 2

CONSTRAINT #  1    - LESS THAN OR EQUAL TO

COEFFICIENT FOR VARIABLE #  1 (X) ? 3
COEFFICIENT FOR VARIABLE #  2 (Y) ? 0
RIGHT HAND VALUE  ? 6


CONSTRAINT #  2    - LESS THAN OR EQUAL TO

COEFFICIENT FOR VARIABLE #  1 (X) ? 1
COEFFICIENT FOR VARIABLE #  2 (Y) ? 4
RIGHT HAND VALUE  ? 8


CONSTRAINT #  3    - LESS THAN OR EQUAL TO

COEFFICIENT FOR VARIABLE # · 1 (X) ? 0
COEFFICIENT FOR VARIABLE #  2 (Y) ? 1
RIGHT HAND VALUE  ? 3
```

The next line shows that the optimal value of the objective function is equal to 5.

The next part of the output contains the objective function ranging data. In this problem, it shows that variable X will remain in the solution with a value of 2 as long as its coefficient is between 0.5 and infinity. Similarly, the variable Y will remain in the solution with a value of 1.5 as long as its coefficient is between 0 and 4.

The last part of the output shows the range of values over which the shadow price of each RHS is valid. Thus the shadow price of 0.167 is valid as long as the RHS of the first constraint varies between 0 and 24. Similarly, the shadow price of 0.5 is valid if the RHS of the second constraint ranges between 2 and 14. Finally, the shadow price of 0 is valid if the RHS of the third constraint remains between 1.5 and infinity.

# 3.8 Example Problem LP2

$$\text{MIN } C = X + 2Y$$
$$3X + 4Y = 12$$
$$5X \geq 10$$

**FIGURE 3.4**   Output from a run of example problem LP1

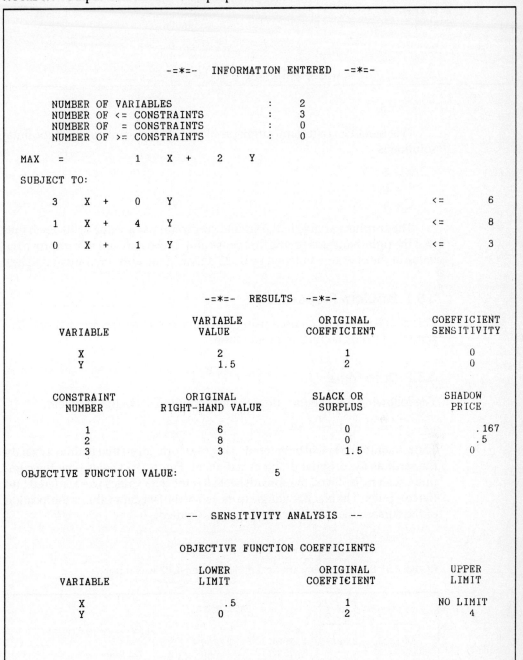

```
                    -=*=-  INFORMATION ENTERED  -=*=-


     NUMBER OF VARIABLES              :     2
     NUMBER OF <= CONSTRAINTS         :     3
     NUMBER OF  = CONSTRAINTS         :     0
     NUMBER OF >= CONSTRAINTS         :     0

MAX  =           1   X  +   2   Y

SUBJECT TO:

    3   X  +   0   Y                                     <=      6

    1   X  +   4   Y                                     <=      8

    0   X  +   1   Y                                     <=      3




                     -=*=-  RESULTS  -=*=-

                        VARIABLE          ORIGINAL        COEFFICIENT
       VARIABLE          VALUE           COEFFICIENT      SENSITIVITY

         X                 2                  1                0
         Y                1.5                 2                0


     CONSTRAINT         ORIGINAL          SLACK OR          SHADOW
      NUMBER         RIGHT-HAND VALUE      SURPLUS           PRICE

         1                 6                  0               .167
         2                 8                  0               .5
         3                 3                 1.5               0

OBJECTIVE FUNCTION VALUE:              5



                  --  SENSITIVITY ANALYSIS  --

              OBJECTIVE FUNCTION COEFFICIENTS

                        LOWER            ORIGINAL           UPPER
       VARIABLE         LIMIT           COEFFICIENT         LIMIT

         X               .5                 1              NO LIMIT
         Y                0                 2                 4
```

(CONT.)

**FIGURE 3.4** *(CONT.)*

|  | RIGHT-HAND-SIDE VALUES | | |
|---|---|---|---|
| CONSTRAINT<br>NUMBER | LOWER<br>LIMIT | ORIGINAL<br>VALUE | UPPER<br>LIMIT |
| 1 | 0 | 6 | 24 |
| 2 | 2 | 8 | 14 |
| 3 | 1.5 | 3 | NO LIMIT |

---------- E N D   O F   A N A L Y S I S ----------

Problem LP2 is a minimization problem with two constraints. Its optimal solution is

X = 4
Y = 0
C = 4

The surplus variable in the second constraint has a value of 10. Each unit that the right-hand-side of the first constraint can be reduced will improve the value of the objective function by 0.333 dollar (if the units of C are in dollars).

### 3.8.1  Problem Preparation

This problem will be entered using free-form input, so the original problem statement needs no further preparation.

### 3.8.2  Data Input

The following initial data values must be input to solve this problem:

2, 0, 1, 1, −1

The remaining data will be entered using free-form input that is almost exactly the same as the original problem statement. Figure 3.5 shows how the computer screen displayed the spreadsheet after the data values were entered into the computer. The black rectangle to the left of the last data value is the location of the cursor when this screen image was printed.

**FIGURE 3.5**  Screen display after example problem LP2 was input

|  | | DATA ENTRY | | |
|---|---|---|---|---|
|  | X | Y | | RHV |
| OF= | 1.000 | 2.000 | | |
| 1 | 3.000 | 4.000 | = | 12.000 |
| 2 | 5.000 | 0 | >= ▮ | 10.000 |

### 3.8.3 Computer Output

Figure 3.6 contains the output from a run of this problem. The output shows that

$$X = 4$$
$$Y = 0$$

Constraint 1 has 0 slack or surplus and a shadow price of 0.333. Constraint 2 has 10 units of surplus and a shadow price of 0. The objective function (C) equals 4.

The COEFFICIENT SENSITIVITY shows that the objective function will be 0.667 unit worse if Y enters the solution with a value of 1. This means that if we really wanted Y to equal 1, then the new optimal solution would be 4.667 instead of 4. Alternatively, we can say that the Y coefficient must be improved by at least 0.667 units (to a value of 1.333 or less) for this variable to enter the solution.

**FIGURE 3.6**   Output from a run of example problem LP2

```
                    -=*=-   INFORMATION ENTERED   -=*=-


    NUMBER OF VARIABLES            :    2
    NUMBER OF <= CONSTRAINTS       :    0
    NUMBER OF  = CONSTRAINTS       :    1
    NUMBER OF >= CONSTRAINTS       :    1

 MIN  =         1   X  +    2   Y

 SUBJECT TO:

    3   X  +   4   Y                              =      12

    5 · X  +   0   Y                              >=     10



                    -=*=-   RESULTS   -=*=-

                      VARIABLE          ORIGINAL         COEFFICIENT
        VARIABLE        VALUE          COEFFICIENT       SENSITIVITY

          X               4                1                0
          Y               0                2                .667


     CONSTRAINT          ORIGINAL          SLACK OR          SHADOW
       NUMBER         RIGHT-HAND VALUE      SURPLUS           PRICE

          1                12                 0               .333
          2                10                10               0

 OBJECTIVE FUNCTION VALUE:              4
```

(CONT.)

**FIGURE 3.6** *(CONT.)*

```
              --  SENSITIVITY ANALYSIS  --

              OBJECTIVE FUNCTION COEFFICIENTS

                    LOWER           ORIGINAL          UPPER
   VARIABLE         LIMIT          COEFFICIENT        LIMIT

      X          NO LIMIT              1               1.5
      Y             1.333              2            NO LIMIT


              RIGHT-HAND-SIDE VALUES

  CONSTRAINT        LOWER           ORIGINAL          UPPER
   NUMBER           LIMIT            VALUE            LIMIT

      1               6               12           NO LIMIT
      2           NO LIMIT            10               20



      ----------  E N D   O F   A N A L Y S I S  ----------
```

## 3.9    Example Problem LP3

$$MAX\ P = X_1 + 2X_2$$
$$X_1 + X_2 \geq 1$$
$$X_1,\ X_2 \geq 0$$

The objective function in this problem is unbounded, so there is no optimal solution. This example problem is included to show you how the program treats this special case.

### 3.9.1 Problem Preparation

$$MAX\ P = 1X_1 + 2X_2$$
$$1X_1 + 1X_2 \geq 1$$

### 3.9.2 Data Input

The following data values must be input to solve this problem:

2, 0, 0, 1, 1
1, 2
1, 1, 1

### 3.9.3 Computer Output

When this problem is run, the only output will be the message: UNBOUNDED SOLUTION!

## 3.10  Example Problem LP4

$$\text{MAX } P = X_1 + X_2$$
$$X_1 + X_2 \leq 1$$

There is more than one correct solution to any problem where the objective function is parallel to a binding constraint. However, the program will identify only one solution.

Some students find it confusing if they compare the results of two different programs and see different values of the variables given as the solution. Others find similar confusion when they compare a graphical solution to the computer printout. In either case, check to see if the objective function has the same value in both of your solutions. If so, it is likely that there are multiple optimal solutions.

The example shown above has valid solutions at the points:

$$X_1 = 1$$
$$X_2 = 0$$

and,

$$X_1 = 0$$
$$X_2 = 1$$

and any point between these two on the line:

$$X_1 + X_2 = 1$$

You should simply be aware of the potential of more than one solution, particularly for business problems where one solution may have additional benefits not described in the model.

### 3.10.1 Problem Preparation

$$\text{MAX } P = 1X_1 + 1X_2$$
$$1X_1 + 1X_2 \leq 1$$

### 3.10.2 Data Input

The following data values must be input to solve this problem:

        2, 1, 0, 0, 1
        1, 1
        1, 1, 1

### 3.10.3 Computer Output

Figure 3.7 contains the output from a run of this problem. The output for this problem shows that

$$X_1 = 1$$
$$X_2 = 0$$
$$P = 1$$

The output also shows that variable $X_2$ has a value of 0 and a COEFFICIENT SENSITIVITY of 0. This means that the value of the objective function will not change if variable $X_2$ is forced to enter the solution. This, of course, is another way of saying that there are multiple optimal solutions.

**FIGURE 3.7**   Output from a run of example problem LP4

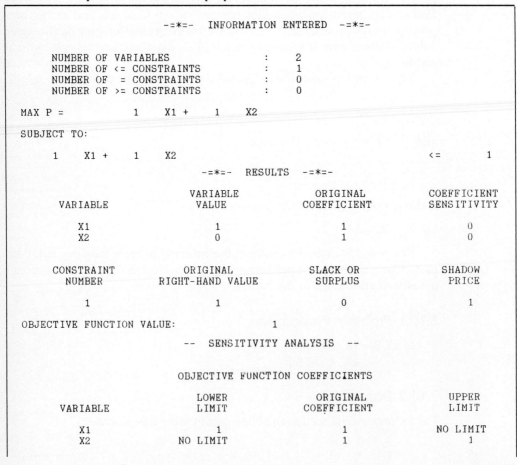

```
                    -=*=-   INFORMATION ENTERED   -=*=-


        NUMBER OF VARIABLES              :    2
        NUMBER OF <= CONSTRAINTS         :    1
        NUMBER OF  = CONSTRAINTS         :    0
        NUMBER OF >= CONSTRAINTS         :    0

MAX P =            1    X1 +    1    X2

SUBJECT TO:

    1    X1 +    1    X2                                <=        1
                    -=*=-   RESULTS   -=*=-

                        VARIABLE          ORIGINAL          COEFFICIENT
        VARIABLE          VALUE          COEFFICIENT        SENSITIVITY

          X1                1                1                   0
          X2                0                1                   0


      CONSTRAINT          ORIGINAL          SLACK OR           SHADOW
       NUMBER          RIGHT-HAND VALUE      SURPLUS            PRICE

         1                  1                  0                  1

OBJECTIVE FUNCTION VALUE:              1
                -- SENSITIVITY ANALYSIS  --


                    OBJECTIVE FUNCTION COEFFICIENTS

                        LOWER             ORIGINAL            UPPER
        VARIABLE        LIMIT           COEFFICIENT           LIMIT

          X1              1                 1               NO LIMIT
          X2           NO LIMIT             1                  1
```

(CONT.)

**FIGURE 3.7**   *(CONT.)*

```
                        RIGHT-HAND-SIDE VALUES

      CONSTRAINT            LOWER            ORIGINAL            UPPER
      NUMBER                LIMIT            VALUE               LIMIT

         1                    0                 1             NO LIMIT




          ----------   E N D   O F   A N A L Y S I S   ----------
```

## 3.11  Example Problem LP5

$$\text{MAX } P = X_1 + 2X_2$$
$$X_1 + X_2 \leq 1$$
$$X_1 + X_2 \geq 2$$

This problem has no feasible solution and the output will indicate "IN-FEASIBLE SOLUTION."

### 3.11.1 Problem Preparation

$$\text{MAX } P = 1X_1 + 2X_2$$
$$1X_1 + 1X_2 \leq 1$$
$$1X_1 + 1X_2 \geq 2$$

### 3.11.2 Data Input

The following data values must be input to solve this problem:

2, 1, 0, 1, 1
1, 2
1, 1, 1
1, 1, 2

### 3.11.3 Computer Output

The only output from a run of this problem will be a message stating: INFEASIBLE SOLUTION!

## 3.12 Linear Programming Problems

1. Solve the following problem (which is example problem LP1 with the constraints in reverse order):

$$MAX\ P = X + 2Y$$
$$Y \le 3$$
$$X + 4Y \le 8$$
$$3X \le 6$$

a) Compare your answers for X, Y, and P with the answers previously given for example problem LP1.
b) Compare your answers for the amount of slack in each constraint with the answers previously given for example problem LP1.

2. Variables can be in any order, but the same sequence must be used in the objective function and in every constraint. Run the following problem (which is example problem LP1 with the variables in reverse order) to test this:

$$MAX\ P = 2Y + 1X$$
$$0Y + 3X \le 6$$
$$4Y + 1X \le 8$$
$$1Y + 0X \le 3$$

a) Compare your answers for X, Y, and P with the answers previously given for example problem LP1.
b) Compare your answers for the amount of slack in each constraint with the answers previously given for example problem LP1.

3. In the discussion of example problem LP2, it was stated that forcing variable $X_2$ to equal 1 would cause the optimal value of C to equal 4.667 instead of 4. Test this assertion by running the following problem:

$$MIN\ C = X + 2Y$$
$$3X + 4Y = 12$$
$$Y = 1$$
$$5X \ge 10$$

As you can see, this new problem is the same as example problem LP2, except for the second constraint. This new constraint forces the value of Y to be equal to 1. What are the new values of X, Y, and C?

4. Find the values of X, Y, and P by using the computer, and then check your results by solving the problem graphically:

$$MAX\ P = X + 2Y$$
$$2X + Y \le 4$$
$$X \ge 1$$

5. By how much will the value of P change if the RHS of the first constraint in the previous problem is changed from 4 to 5? Answer this question by using data contained in the computer output from the previous problem. Check your answer by solving the new problem graphically.

6. Find the values of X, Y, and P by using the computer, and then check your results by solving the problem graphically:

$$MAX\ P = X - 2Y$$
$$X + \ Y \geq 4$$
$$X + 2Y = 6$$

7. By how much will the value of P change if the RHS of the first constraint in the previous problem is changed from 4 to 5? Answer this question by using data contained in the computer output from the previous problem. Check your answer by solving the new problem on the computer.

8. Find the values of X, Y, and C by using the computer, and then check your results by solving the problem graphically:

$$MIN\ C = \ X + \ Y$$
$$X + 2Y \geq 4$$
$$2X + \ Y \leq 6$$

9. By how much will the value of C change if the RHS of the second constraint in the previous problem is changed from 6 to 3? Answer this question by using data contained in the computer output from the previous problem. Check your answer by solving the new problem graphically.

10. Find the values of X, Y, and C by using the computer, and then check your results by solving the problem graphically:

$$MIN\ C = 3X - 2Y$$
$$X + \ Y \geq 4$$
$$X \leq 3$$
$$Y \leq 2$$

11. By how much will the value of C change if the RHS of the third constraint is changed from 2 to 3? Answer this question by using data contained in the computer output from the previous problem. Check your answer by solving the new problem on the computer.

12. Solve for the optimal value of X, Y, Z, and P:

$$MAX\ P = 3X + \ 2Y \ - Z$$
$$4X + \ 5Y \geq 6$$
$$7Z - \ 8Y = 9$$
$$10X \leq 11$$

13. Solve for the optimal values of X, Y, Z, W, and C:

$$
\begin{aligned}
\text{MIN } C = 2X + 3Y + 4Z + \ &W \\
3X + 4Y + Z + \ &W \geq 10 \\
X + \ &W = 8 \\
2X + 3Z \ &\geq 15 \\
Y + 3W \ &\geq 12
\end{aligned}
$$

14. The objective function coefficient of X in the previous problem has changed from 2 to 3.

    a)  What are the new optimal values of X, Y, Z, and W?
    b)  What is the new optimal value of C?

    Answer these questions by using data contained in the computer output from the previous problem. Check your answer by solving the new problem on the computer.

15. Solve for the optimal values of $X_1$, $X_2$, $X_3$, and Z:

$$
\begin{aligned}
\text{MAX } Z = 3X_1 + 2X_2 + X_3 \\
X_1 + 2X_2 + X_3 \leq 8 \\
2X_1 + 3X_3 \leq 14
\end{aligned}
$$

16. The objective function coefficient of $X_3$ in the previous problem has changed from 1 to 3. Will $X_3$ still have a value of 0 in the optimal solution? Answer this question by using data contained in the computer output from the previous problem. Check your answer by solving the new problem on the computer.

17. Solve for the optimal values of $X_1$, $X_2$, $X_3$, $X_4$, and Z:

$$
\begin{aligned}
\text{MIN } Z = X_1 + 4X_2 + 3X_3 + X_4 \\
2X_1 + X_2 + 3X_3 + 5X_4 \geq 200 \\
5X_1 + 2X_2 + 10X_3 + 4X_4 \geq 300 \\
6X_1 + X_2 + 8X_3 + 3X_4 \geq 180
\end{aligned}
$$

18. The objective function coefficient of $X_2$ in the previous problem has changed from 4 to 1. Will $X_2$ still have a value of 0 in the optimal solution? Answer this question by using data contained in the computer output from the previous problem. Check your answer by solving the new problem on the computer.

19. Solve for the optimal values of $X_1$, $X_2$, $X_3$, and Z:

$$
\begin{aligned}
\text{MAX } Z = 2X_1 + 3X_2 + 5X_3 \\
X_1 + 2X_2 + 4X_3 \leq 25 \\
2X_1 + 5X_2 + 8X_3 = 60 \\
3X_1 + 4X_2 + 2X_3 \geq 10
\end{aligned}
$$

20. What is the smallest value of the objective function coefficient of $X_3$ in the previous problem that will cause $X_3$ to enter the solution? Answer this question by using data contained in the computer output from the previous problem. Check your answer by solving the new problem on the computer.

21. Solve for the optimal values of $X_1$, $X_2$, $X_3$, $X_4$, and Z:

$$MIN\ Z = 5X_1 + 4X_2 + 3X_3 + 7X_4$$
$$2X_1 + 5X_2 + \quad X_4 \geq 100$$
$$X_2 + 3X_3 = 75$$

22. What is the smallest value of the objective function coefficient of $X_4$ in the previous problem that will cause $X_4$ to enter the solution? Answer this question by using data contained in the computer output from the previous problem. Check your answer by solving the new problem on the computer.

23. Determine whether the following problems result in multiple optimal, unbounded, or infeasible solutions. Check the computer answers by solving graphically.

a) $MAX\ P = 3X_1 + 4X_2$ 　　　　 c) $MIN\ C = 4X_1 + 3X_2$
　　　　　 $X_1 \leq 6$ 　　　　　　　 $8X_1 + 6X_2 \geq 24$
　　 $2X_1 - X_2 \leq 14$ 　　　　　 $2X_1 + X_2 \leq 6$
b) $MIN\ C = X_1 + X_2$ 　　　　 d) $MAX\ P = X_1 + X_2$
　　 $2X_1 + 3X_2 = 0$ 　　　　　　 $5X_1 - X_2 \leq 6$
　　 $X_1 + X_2 \geq 3$ 　　　　　　 $X_1 - 3X_2 = 5$

24. Introduce and identify all slack and surplus variables that are needed to solve the following problem:

$$MAX\ P = 3X - 2Y$$
$$4X + 5Y \geq 6$$
$$7X - 8Y = -9$$
$$10X \leq 11$$

What are the optimal values of X, Y, and P?

25. Introduce and identify all slack and surplus variables that are needed to solve the following problem:

$$MIN\ P = 3X - 2Y$$
$$4X + 5Y \geq 6$$
$$7X - 8Y = -9$$
$$10X \leq 11$$

What are the optimal values of X, Y, and P?

26. A company has the capacity to manufacture a maximum of 240 radios per day. The three kinds they manufacture require, respectively, 9 ounces, 6

ounces, and 2 ounces of copper wire, and they yield profits of $6, $2, and $2. If 900 ounces of copper wire are available on a certain day, how many radios of each kind should they produce to maximize their profit?

27. A cement manufacturer has 150,000 pounds of sand and 50,000 pounds of cement. It can sell two kinds of products: pure cement or a concrete mix that has 80% sand and 20% cement. If it can sell the pure cement at 8¢ a pound and the concrete mix at 5¢ a pound, how many pounds of each should be made in order to maximize revenue? Solve this problem using both the graphical method and the computer.

28. A confectioner manufactures two kinds of candy bars: Ergies (packed with energy) with a 40¢ profit per bar and Nergies (the "low-cal" nugget) with a 50¢ profit per bar. The company has 12 hours of blending time, 30 hours of cooking time, and 15 hours of packaging time available. The average processing time required per bar is as follows:

| | Blending | Cooking | Packaging |
|---|---|---|---|
| Ergies | 1 Min. | 5 | 3 |
| Nergies | 2 | 4 | 1 |

Determine the optimal mix of candy bars that will maximize profit.

29. The Nutola Candy Company produces two types of bars (Ergies and Nergies) from premixed chocolate and caramel solutions (Type X and Type Y). Type X contains 80% chocolate and 20% caramel, and type Y contains 30% chocolate and 70% caramel. Ergies sell for 50¢ per bar and Nergies for 60¢ per bar. Ergies, which require 0.06 liters of premix, must consist of at least 30% chocolate and 40% caramel. Nergies, which require 0.05 liters of premix, must consist of no more than 40% chocolate and at least 40% caramel. If 200 liters of the Type X solution and 100 liters of the Type Y solution are on hand, determine the number of bars that maximize revenue.

30. Professor Grade has given his class three lists of problems:

   a) 1-point problems that require 1.5 minutes (a maximum of 50 problems).
   b) 2-point problems that require 4 minutes (a maximum of 20 problems).
   c) 5-point problems that require 12 minutes (a maximum of 10 problems).

   A student can attempt no more than 100 points of problems and has 2 hours to complete the examination. A maximum of 60 minutes are available for 5-point problems. Determine the optimal mix of problems the student should try in order to maximize his or her score.

31. Leisure Time Inc. is considering three different items to stock in its stores. Hi-fi systems cost $50, sell for $150, weigh 20 pounds, and use 3 square feet

of shelf space. Boat anchors cost $2, sell for $8, weigh 50 pounds, and use 1 square foot of shelf space. Sails cost $90, sell for $200, weigh 22 pounds, and use 10 square feet of shelf space. Each store has a purchasing budget maximum of $500. At least 20% of its purchasing dollars must be spent on hi-fi systems. Each store has 75 square feet of shelf space that can carry a total load of no more than 1000 pounds. It can sell up to 20 sails and 10 anchors per month and as many hi-fi systems as it can stock. How many of each item should a store order each month if it wants to maximize profit?

32. Grandma's Luscious Old-Fashioned Bread, Inc. (GLOB) makes Ten-Grain Bread and Health Bread. Grandma sells her bread to a distributor and gets 47¢ for a Ten-Grain loaf and 43¢ for a Health loaf. Each kind of bread can be made from a commercial mix of ingredients or from ingredients that are purchased separately and mixed at the plant. The Ten-Grain commercial mix costs 18¢ per loaf, and the Health commercial mix costs 13¢ per loaf. If mixed at the plant, the Ten-Grain ingredients cost 10¢, but an employee must take an average of 12 seconds per loaf to mix the ingredients. If the commercial mix is purchased, no employee time is required for mixing. Similarly, the Health loaf ingredients cost 7¢ and require 9 seconds per loaf when mixed at the plant. Each loaf of each kind of bread requires an average of 19 seconds of employee time for baking, wrapping, etc. There are 10 employees who work a full 8-hour day. If grandma wants to maximize profit:

    a) How much of each kind of bread should be baked each day?
    b) How much of each kind of commercial mix should be purchased each day?

33. An investor has $100,000 in cash available. The investor can put up to $60,000 in a new company that will return a one-year profit of 40% on all money invested. Another investment alternative is stock (no dollar limit) that pays 10% per year. Up to $150,000 can be borrowed at an interest rate of 15% per year. If all projections are true, and if at least 40% of the investment (cash plus borrowed money) must be in stock, then what should the full investment portfolio look like to maximize a one-year return?

34. Go heavily Farms has just purchased four new sites, and now they must decide how much of each of four different crops (cotton, alfalfa, walnuts, and avocados) should be planted at each site to maximize net profit. Each site has a fixed limit to the total amount of irrigation water that can be used over each growing season, and each crop requires a minimum amount of water per acre. There is also a limit to the amount of each crop that can be successfully marketed. A summary of their crop data is as follows:

| Crop | Acre-Feet of Water Required per Acre | Maximum Acreage That Can Be sold | Net Profit ($ per Acre) |
|---|---|---|---|
| Cotton | 4 | 500 | 100 |
| Alfalfa | 6 | 900 | 50 |
| Walnuts | 3 | 400 | 150 |
| Avocados | 3 | 200 | 200 |

A summary of their site data is as follows:

| Site | Water Use Limit (Acre-Feet) | Total Area (Acres) |
|---|---|---|
| 1 | 2500 | 1000 |
| 2 | 1500 | 600 |
| 3 | 1200 | 800 |
| 4 | 200 | 500 |

How much of each crop should be planted at each site?

35. A vitamin retailer produces its own line of vitamins from bulk vitamin powder obtained from pharmaceutical companies. It uses a mixture of M1 (a multivitamin) and E3 (a combination of vitamins E and C) to produce its ACE line of vitamins. Data for this situation include the following:

| Bulk Vitamin | Cost $/Lb. | Guaranteed Contents per Pound | | |
|---|---|---|---|---|
| | | A (1,000,000 IU) | C (1,000 Mg) | E (1,000 IU) |
| M1 | 5 | 10 | 50 | 2 |
| E3 | 8 | 0 | 20 | 40 |

Each ACE pill (100 per bottle) must contain at least 5000 IU of vitamin A, 60 mg of C, and 30 IU of E. How many pounds of each bulk vitamin must the retailer purchase if it wants to produce 5000 ACE bottles at minimum cost?

36. A computer manufacturer makes three models: the PC-100 (with 64K RAM and one built-in diskette drive), the PC-200 (with 128K RAM and two built-in diskette drives), and the PC-500 (with 256K RAM, one built-in diskette drive, and one built-in hard disk drive). It currently has a sufficient supply of all items except 64K RAM chips (10,000 in stock) and diskette drives (3000 in stock). All its computers use the 64K RAM chips, but the PC-200 requires two of them, and the PC-500 requires four. Deliveries of the RAM chips and the diskette drives are scheduled for next month, but none can be obtained sooner. The manufacturer has decided to

maximize the total number of computers produced this month, because this will keep its assembly employees as productive as possible and will also allow the maximum number of units to be shipped to distributors.

a) How many of each computer should be assembled?
b) Orders for 1000 units of the PC-200 have been guaranteed. If the company decides to meet these guarantees, how many of each computer should be assembled?

37. A health food chain blends its food supplements from ingredients supplied by health food store wholesalers. The chain sells the HiPro mix for $3 per pound, VitaPro for $4 per pound, and Health for $2 per pound. Other data for these three products are as follows:

| Product | Sales lb/Month | Protein (%) | Vitamin A (IU/lb) | Vitamin C (mg/lb) |
|---------|---------|---------|---------|---------|
| HiPro | 1000 | 10 | 200 | 300 |
| VitaPro | 1500 | 10 | 10000 | 600 |
| Health | 4000 | 2 | 300 | 500 |

Four different ingredients are used to blend these products. Data for the ingredients are as follows:

| Ingredient | Cost $/Lb | Protein (%) | Vitamin A (IU/lb) | Vitamin C (Mg/lb) |
|---------|---------|---------|---------|---------|
| Protein Mix | .70 | 20 | 100 | 50 |
| Powdered A | .85 | 0 | 40000 | 0 |
| Powdered C | .90 | 0 | 0 | 5000 |
| Organic Filler | .05 | 1 | 20 | 10 |

a) How many pounds of each ingredient should the chain buy each month to maximize profit?
b) How much profit will it make per month on all three products?

---

CASE STUDY **The Napa Winery**

The Napa Winery was one of the first wineries to use linear programming to help make blending decisions for its wine products. The blending decisions take place in several stages. First, a computer analysis is

(CONT.)

CASE STUDY **The Napa Winery**   *(CONT.)*

conducted to determine how each wine should be used to maximize profit. The analysis considers winery objectives, grape characteristics, and government regulations. Each of the blends that results from this analysis is then run through a series of subjective taste tests. Often some of the proposed blends are unacceptable. In these cases, a revised computer analysis is made using the results of the taste testing. This process continues until the tasters agree that all blends are acceptable. At that point, bottling begins.

Napa is using linear programming to determine the optimal blends for the coming year. The model must meet the following winery objectives and government regulations.

## Winery Objectives

- The winery prefers to use all available wine, but if greater profit will result by not using some of the wine this season, then the unused wine will be stored for use next year.
- No Cabernet Sauvignon may contain more than 0.75 gm acid per 100 ml.
- The vintage Cabernet Sauvignon will be their driest wine. It must not contain more than 0.2% sugar. The non-vintage Cabernet Sauvignon will also be dry. It must not contain more than 0.3% sugar.

## Government Regulations

- If a wine is labeled as a varietal (e.g., Cabernet Sauvignon) then the blend must contain 51% of the named wine.
- If a wine is vintage dated, then 100% of the wine must be from the vintage year stated on the label. The viticultural area must also be stated on the label, and at least 75% of the wine must come from that area.
- All table wine must contain at least 10% and at most 14% alcohol.

The following table shows the wines that are available for blending. Each of these wines are produced from a single variety of grape. The cost per bottle includes all variable costs of production, aging, bottling, and shipping. Fixed costs (overhead, etc.) are not included. When different wines are blended, the physical and cost characteristics remain in direct proportion to the amount of each wine used.

(CONT.)

## CASE STUDY The Napa Winery *(CONT.)*

| Grape | Viti-cultural Area | Vintage Year | Acid (gm/100ml) | Sugar (%) | Alcohol (%) | Quantity (bottles) | Cost ($/bottle) |
|---|---|---|---|---|---|---|---|
| Cabernet Sauvignon | Napa | 89 | 0.65 | 0.11 | 13.5 | 50,000 | 1.10 |
| Cabernet Sauvignon | Napa | 88 | 0.72 | 0.27 | 15.1 | 40,000 | 1.15 |
| Cabernet Sauvignon | Sonoma | 89 | 0.55 | 0.37 | 11.9 | 60,000 | 0.93 |
| Carignane | Napa | 89 | 0.82 | 0.10 | 13.8 | 150,000 | 0.52 |

The winery has three different wines that can be produced from these blending wines. There is a 1989 vintage Cabernet Sauvignon that wholesales for $3.10, a non-vintage Cabernet Sauvignon that wholesales for $2.00 per bottle, and a non-vintage burgundy that wholesales for $1.05 per bottle.

Specifically, Napa management wants to know:

a) How much of each wine should be produced?

b) What profit will result from this solution?

c) How much of each blending wine is not used?

d) There was a mistake in the original data. There are actually 61,000 bottles of the 1989 Sonoma Cabernet Sauvignon on hand (instead of the 60,000 bottles originally reported). By how much will profits change as a result of this?

# 4

## INTP

# *Integer Programming*

Integer programming is an important special case of linear programming. Several different forms of integer programming models exist, but the one contained in this package is most frequently referred to as the zero-one (or 0-1) programming model. It is used to solve problems in which all variables must be equal to either zero or one.

The zero-one programming model can be applied to a variety of business problems that include selection of the following:

- Investment alternatives.
- People to staff positions.
- Plant location sites.
- The size of a facility.
- Items to be included in shipping containers.
- Projects to be funded.

The objective function, constraints, and so on in a zero-one programming model all follow the same rules and structure as a linear programming model.

## 4.1 Program Description

This program will solve any single objective function, zero-one integer programming problem with up to 50 variables and 50 constraints. The program solves for variable values, the objective function value, and slack and surplus variable values. Unlike the linear programming model, this integer programming model does not output shadow prices, right-hand-side ranging, or objective function coefficient ranging.

Integer programming models tend to require more computer time than linear programming models, so be prepared for some time delays. Pauses may occur after selecting the program or after selecting the RUN PROBLEM option. This latter pause may take several minutes for large problems.

Fast solutions are obtained on most computers if the problem contains fewer than ten variables. If there are ten or more variables, the computer will use a heuristic to solve the problem. The exact solution is not guaranteed for these larger problems, but all test problems have either found the exact solution or have been close to it.

## 4.2 Problem Preparation

The problem preparation for integer programming problems is exactly the same as for linear programming problems; however, there are also a few "don'ts":

1. Do not include any boundary (non-negativity) constraints.
2. Do not include any slack, surplus, or artificial variables.
3. Do not include any zero-one constraints.

Everything listed in the "don't" section is automatically included by the program.

## 4.3 Data Input Overview

The data input overview is exactly the same as in linear programming. See the Data Input Overview section in the previous chapter.

## 4.4 Data Input Details

Data input details are exactly the same as in linear programming. See the Data Input Details section in the previous chapter.

## 4.5 Editing the Data

Editing features are exactly the same as in linear programming. See the Editing the Data section in the previous chapter.

## 4.6 Program Output

The program output includes both answers and some of the data from the original problem (to aid in checking for errors and interpreting the answers). The variable names used in the output are the same user-defined variable names used to input the problem data.

The output for each variable includes its optimal value and its coefficient in the objective function. Unlike linear programming, the program does not output the objective function coefficient sensitivity (reduced costs). The output for each constraint includes its original right-hand-side value, and the amount of slack or surplus (whichever is appropriate). Unlike linear programming, neither shadow prices nor ranging data are output.

## 4.7  Example Problem IP1

Six proposals have passed all screening criteria of a venture capital firm. Each proposal has a required investment, and an estimated return. The firm's owners want to select all proposals that collectively maximize their return and do not exceed the $500,000 available as investment capital. A summary of the investment and return data are as follows:

| Proposal | Investment | Return |
|----------|-----------|--------|
| 1 | 100,000 | 150,000 |
| 2 | 200,000 | 270,000 |
| 3 | 90,000 | 130,000 |
| 4 | 170,000 | 250,000 |
| 5 | 180,000 | 280,000 |
| 6 | 125,000 | 160,000 |

### 4.7.1  Problem Preparation

The formulated problem is (with all coefficients in thousands of dollars):

$$MAX\ R = 150P1 + 270P2 + 130P3 + 250P4 + 280P5 + 160P6$$
$$100P1 + 200P2 + 90P3 + 170P4 + 180P5 + 125P6 \leq 500$$

### 4.7.2  Data Input

The following data values must be input to solve this problem:

    6, 1, 0, 0, 1
    150, 270, 130, 250, 280, 160
    100, 200, 90, 170, 180, 125, 500

Figure 4.1 shows how the first five of these data values should be input in response to prompts from the computer. As in linear programming, these first five values define the structure of the problem. Figure 4.2 shows how the remaining data is input in response to prompts. As in linear programming, these data values can also be input in a spreadsheet-like structure by selecting the free-form input option.

**FIGURE 4.1**    Data input of problem structure for example problem IP1

```
                -=*=-   DATA   INPUT   -=*=-

    ENTER NUMBER OF VARIABLES
    ENTER NUMBER IN RANGE ( 2  -  50 ) & press ↵   6

    ENTER NUMBER OF LESS THAN OR EQUAL TO CONSTRAINTS
    ENTER NUMBER IN RANGE ( 0  -  50 ) & press ↵   1

    ENTER NUMBER OF EQUAL TO CONSTRAINTS
    ENTER NUMBER IN RANGE ( 0  -  49 ) & press ↵   0

    ENTER NUMBER OF GREATER THAN OR EQUAL TO CONSTRAINTS
    ENTER NUMBER IN RANGE ( 0  -  49 ) & press ↵   0

    IS THE PROBLEM TYPE MAXIMIZATION (1)  OR  MINIMIZATION (-1)
    Enter a Character ( 1  or  -1 ) & press ↵    1

    DO YOU WANT TO RE-ENTER PROBLEM STRUCTURE? (Y/N)
    Enter a Character ( Y  or  N ) & press ↵    N
```

**FIGURE 4.2**    Input of problem data for example problem IP1

```
                     PROMPTED INPUT

        OBJECTIVE FUNCTION

            COEFFICIENT FOR VARIABLE # 1  (P1) ? 150
            COEFFICIENT FOR VARIABLE # 2  (P2) ? 270
            COEFFICIENT FOR VARIABLE # 3  (P3) ? 130
            COEFFICIENT FOR VARIABLE # 4  (P4) ? 250
            COEFFICIENT FOR VARIABLE # 5  (P5) ? 280
            COEFFICIENT FOR VARIABLE # 6  (P6) ? 160


        CONSTRAINT # 1   - LESS THAN OR EQUAL TO

            COEFFICIENT FOR VARIABLE #  1 (P1) ? 100
            COEFFICIENT FOR VARIABLE #  2 (P2) ? 200
            COEFFICIENT FOR VARIABLE #  3 (P3) ? 90
            COEFFICIENT FOR VARIABLE #  4 (P4) ? 170
            COEFFICIENT FOR VARIABLE #  5 (P5) ? 180
            COEFFICIENT FOR VARIABLE #  6 (P6) ? 125
            RIGHT HAND VALUE  ? 500
```

## 4.7.3 Computer Output

The output from a run of example problem IP is shown in Fig. 4.3. The INFORMATION ENTERED section contains a complete statement of the problem that was solved.

The first part of the RESULTS section lists all variables and their values. In this problem, only proposals, 1, 3, 5, and 6 should be funded. This will produce a total return of $720,000.

**FIGURE 4.3**    Output from a run of example problem IP1

```
                    -=*=-   INFORMATION ENTERED   -=*=-


       NUMBER OF VARIABLES           :    6
       NUMBER OF <= CONSTRAINTS      :    1
       NUMBER OF  = CONSTRAINTS      :    0
       NUMBER OF >= CONSTRAINTS      :    0

   MAX R =          150    P1 +  270    P2 +  130    P3 +  250    P4 +  280    P5
                 +  160    P6

   SUBJECT TO:

      100    P1 +  200    P2 +   90    P3 +  170    P4 +  180    P5
   +  125    P6                                                     <=     500



                    -=*=-   RESULTS   -=*=-

                                                    ORIGINAL
            VARIABLE              VALUE            COEFFICIENT

              P1                    1                   150
              P2                    0                   270
              P3                    1                   130
              P4                    0                   250
              P5                    1                   280
              P6                    1                   160


            CONSTRAINT            ORIGINAL            SLACK OR
             NUMBER          RIGHT-HAND VALUE         SURPLUS

                1                   500                  5

   OBJECTIVE FUNCTION VALUE:           720

            ---------  E N D   O F   A N A L Y S I S  ---------
```

# 4.8 Integer Programming Problems

1. Solve the following integer programming problem:

$$MAX\ P = 3X + 4Y + 8Z$$
$$X + 2Y + 4Z \leq 7$$
$$2X + 4Y + 6Z \leq 11$$
$$7X + 9Y + 6Z \leq 14$$

2. Solve the following integer programming problem:

$$MIN\ C = 3X + 4Y + 8Z$$
$$X + 2Y + 4Z \geq 5$$
$$2X + 4Y + 6Z \geq 6$$
$$7X + 9Y + 6Z \geq 16$$

3. Solve the following integer programming problem:

$$MIN\ C = 3X + 4Y + 8Z$$
$$X + 2Y + 4Z \geq 5$$
$$2X + 4Y + 6Z \geq 6$$
$$7X + 9Y + 6Z \geq 14$$

4. The Esterly Corp. needs to build two Western region warehouses to better serve its customers in that area. The construction cost (in millions of dollars) and the average yearly delivery delay cost (in thousands of dollars per year) are shown in the following table:

| Warehouse Location | Construction Cost | Delivery Delay Cost |
|---|---|---|
| Denver | 4.1 | 150 |
| Los Angeles | 4.9 | 100 |
| Phoenix | 3.2 | 170 |
| San Francisco | 5.1 | 110 |
| Seattle | 3.6 | 180 |

Which two locations should be selected to minimize the total yearly delivery delay cost and not exceed a construction budget of $9 million?

5. The Eastern sales region must assign three sales managers to three sales offices. Its objective is to find the assignments that maximize the total yearly sales of all three offices. Naturally, only one person can be assigned to each sales office. The expected yearly sales (in millions of dollars) if each individual is assigned to each office are as follows:

| | Sales Office | | |
|---|---|---|---|
| | Albany | Boston | Chicago |
| Smith | 20 | 23 | 17 |
| Turner | 15 | 16 | 14 |
| Unger | 17 | 19 | 16 |

The relocation expense budget for all three moves is $200,000. The costs (in thousands of dollars) of relocating each individual to each location are as follows:

| | Sales Office | | |
|---|---|---|---|
| | Albany | Boston | Chicago |
| Smith | 65 | 50 | 40 |
| Turner | 80 | 65 | 70 |
| Unger | 90 | 70 | 80 |

a) Which individual should be relocated to which sales office to keep within the relocation expense budget?

    b) What are the total yearly sales in this case?

    c) What would total yearly sales be if there were no relocation expense budget limitations?

6. Five new products have been suggested for introduction next year. Each has a different cost of introduction (including production, advertising, etc.) and a different estimated yearly return. The relevant data for each of these five products (code named, A, B, etc.) are as follows:

| Product | Introduction Cost($Million) | Return ($Thousands) |
|---------|------------------------------|----------------------|
| A | 2 | 300 |
| B | 7 | 800 |
| C | 5 | 600 |
| D | 3 | 400 |
| E | 4 | 500 |

    a) Which products should be introduced to maximize total yearly return but not exceed a $14 million budget for new product introduction costs?

    b) What is the total expected yearly return if this decision is implemented?

7. The company has decided to use a different approach to make its new product introduction decisions. It believes that the use of one number for yearly return tends to mask the level of certainty in these estimates. Therefore it will use estimates of the maximum and minimum yearly percentage return on investment (ROI) as the basis for its decision. It wants to maximize the yearly dollar return that results if the Max ROI values are correct, but it also wants the minimum average ROI of all selected products to be no less than 8%. The $14 million introduction cost limit still exists. The relevant data are as follows:

| Product | Introduction Cost($Million) | Max ROI | Min ROI |
|---------|------------------------------|---------|---------|
| A | 2 | 20 | 5 |
| B | 7 | 15 | 10 |
| C | 5 | 12 | 8 |
| D | 3 | 14 | 10 |
| E | 4 | 20 | 7 |

    a) Which products should be introduced?

    b) What is the total expected yearly return if this decision is implemented?

8. A presidential candidate must decide which states to visit in the last 10 days before the election. Naturally the goal is to increase the number of votes by the largest possible amount. The relevant data are as follows:

| State | Vote Increase by Visit | Days Required for Visit |
|-------|-----------------------|-------------------------|
| A | 100,000 | 4 |
| B | 20,000 | 3 |
| C | 40,000 | 3 |
| D | 90,000 | 4 |
| E | 30,000 | 3 |
| F | 10,000 | 1 |

a) Which states should be visited?

b) How many votes will be generated by these visits?

9. A presidential candidate is down to the last five days of the campaign, and the race is close. Only $300,000 remains in the campaign budget. Three key states appear likely to swing the election one way or the other. Each state can be visited, or a saturation TV ad series can be purchased. The candidate's staff has made up the following estimates:

| State | Action | Vote Increase | Days Required | Cost |
|-------|--------|---------------|---------------|------|
| J | Visit | 100,000 | 4 | 200,000 |
| J | Ads | 50,000 | 0 | 100,000 |
| K | Visit | 80,000 | 4 | 150,000 |
| K | Ads | 40,000 | 0 | 90,000 |
| L | Visit | 20,000 | 1 | 45,000 |
| L | Ads | 15,000 | 0 | 30,000 |

In no case will both the ad series and a visit be scheduled in the same state.

a) Which states should be visited?

b) In which states should the ad series be purchased?

c) How many votes will be generated by these visits and ads?

10. Three people are available for assignment to two machines. Only one person can be assigned to each machine. When assigned to a machine, each person gets paid on a piece-rate basis of 1¢ per item produced. If not assigned to a machine, each person is paid his or her base hourly rate. Data for this problem are as follows:

| Person | Production Rate (Items/Hr) on Each Machine | | Base Hourly Rate ($/Hr) |
|--------|------|------|-------------------------|
| | J | K | |
| Adams | 800 | 700 | 7.00 |
| Baker | 850 | 800 | 8.00 |
| Cabot | 900 | 850 | 8.25 |

a) What are the assignments that minimize total daily (8-hour) cost and produce at least 13,000 units?
b) How many items are produced?
c) What are the total daily costs with these assignments?

11. Management is concerned about the high scrap rates resulting in the current piece-rate system, so it has changed the payment schedule to 1.1¢ for each *good* item. Data for this problem are as follows:

| Person | Production Rate (Items/Hr) on Each Machine | | Base Hourly Rate ($/Hr) |
|---|---|---|---|
| | J | K | |
| Adams—Good | 725 | 620 | 7.00 |
| Adams—Scrap | 75 | 80 | 7.00 |
| Baker—Good | 760 | 710 | 8.00 |
| Baker—Scrap | 90 | 90 | 8.00 |
| Cabot—Good | 800 | 770 | 8.25 |
| Cabot—Scrap | 100 | 80 | 8.25 |

a) What are the assignments that minimize total daily (8-hour) cost and produce at least 11,600 good items and no more than 1400 scrap items?
b) How many good items are produced?
c) How many scrap items are produced?
d) What are the total daily costs with these assignments?

12. An oil company exploration team is ready to return from its Arctic mission, but one of its aircraft is disabled. Some equipment must be abandoned at the site, but the team wants to fly out with as much of the most valuable equipment as possible. The cargo bay of the aircraft has room for 250 cubic feet of cargo weighing up to 8000 pounds. Items that the team would like to bring back include the following:

| Equipment Category | Volume (Cu Ft) | Weight (Lbs) | Replacement Cost ($1000) |
|---|---|---|---|
| Computer | 30 | 200 | 50 |
| Seismic | 100 | 5000 | 40 |
| Shelter-1 | 150 | 3000 | 30 |
| Shelter-2 | 80 | 1500 | 20 |
| Supplies | 40 | 3000 | 10 |
| Life Support | 50 | 500 | 25 |

a) Which equipment should the team bring back if it wants to maximize its total dollar value?

b) What is the total dollar value of the equipment brought back?

---

CASE STUDY **Anderson Industries**

Anderson Industries, a leading manufacturer of car stereo components, is considering locating several new assembly plants in the Southwest. These new plants must have a combined production capacity of at least 450,000 units per year and must have a combined operating cost that does not exceed $7.5 million per year. The selection team has narrowed the list to four sites in Phoenix, Tucson, Santa Fe, and El Paso. Anderson's management has established a construction cost limit of $45 million for the project. This money will be used to build the combination of plants that provides the maximum yearly profit.

Any one of three different-sized plants can be built on the Phoenix site, but only one size plant can be built on each of the other sites. All estimates of production capacity, yearly operating cost, yearly profit, and construction cost are as follows:

| Plant Site Location | Production Capacity (units/yr) | Operating Cost ($/yr) | Yearly Profit ($/yr) | Construction Cost ($) |
|---|---|---|---|---|
| **Phoenix** | | | | |
| Size 1 | 250,000 | 4,000,000 | 400,000 | 25,000,000 |
| Size 2 | 225,000 | 3,500,000 | 350,000 | 22,000,000 |
| Size 3 | 200,000 | 3,000,000 | 300,000 | 19,000,000 |
| **Tucson** | 200,000 | 3,000,000 | 325,000 | 22,000,000 |
| **Santa Fe** | 200,000 | 2,500,000 | 325,000 | 20,000,000 |
| **El Paso** | 225,000 | 3,000,000 | 275,000 | 23,000,000 |

a) Which sites should be selected?

b) If the Phoenix site is selected, which size plant should be constructed?

c) How much yearly profit results from this solution?

# 5

## TRAN

# *Transportation Model*

The classic transportation model solves the problem of scheduling the shipment of goods from warehouses to customers in such a way that the total shipping costs are minimized. In this problem, the total number of items in the warehouses is exactly equal to the total number of items required by customers. Each item shipped between any two points costs the company a fixed amount of money. All items are identical, so no customer prefers one warehouse over another.

The model is not restricted to warehouses and customers, and can be used for any problem where groups of items must be matched with other groups of items. Shipping problems of some type are the most common application, but a wide variety of production problems can also be solved with the transportation model.

Any transportation problem can also be solved as a linear programming problem, but the formulation and solution are always much simpler with the transportation model.

## 5.1 Program Description

This program solves the classic transportation model by finding either the maximum or minimum total payoff that results when items are shipped from a set of sources to a set of destinations. The number of items to be shipped between each source and each destination is also output by the program. Problems with up to 20 sources and 20 destinations may be solved.

## 5.2 Problem Preparation

The total number of items available from the sources must be exactly equal to the total number of items required at the destinations. If these totals are not equal, then an extra row or column must be added to make up the difference. Unless other data are available, the cost of shipping any item to or from this extra column or row should be set at zero.

Another adjustment should be made if shipments between any two points cannot be made for any reason. In such a case, the unit shipping cost should be set to a large number for minimization problems and to a large magnitude negative number for maximization problems. When this is done, the computer will avoid making any shipments between these "unattractive" points.

In most cases, it is sufficient to use a payoff with a magnitude 10 to 100 times larger than the largest payoff in the problem. If the problem results show no shipments in any of the adjusted cells, then the numbers were sufficiently large. If some shipments are assigned to these adjusted cells, then simply use a larger magnitude number and rerun the problem. If assignments are again made to these adjusted cells, the problem may be the special case discussed next.

## A Special Case

There is one special case where an illegal cell will have items assigned to it even if extremely large values for cost are entered for that cell. This will occur if no feasible solution exists without assigning items to the "illegal" cell. Consider the following simple example minimization problem:

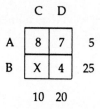

Adjusting this for input into the computer:

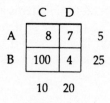

A computer run of this problem will always result in 5 units being assigned to cell B C. This result occurs because destination C needs 10 units and source A has only 5 units available. Thus 5 units must be shipped from B to C if there is to be a feasible solution.

## 5.3  Data Input Overview

Once the problem is properly adjusted, data may be entered into the computer. First, you enter the problem structure. The first values are the number of rows (sources, warehouses, and so on) and then the number of columns (destinations, customers, and so on). These numbers are followed by a –1 for minimization problems or by a 1 for maximization problems.

Next you input the first row of payoffs from the table, followed by the total number of items available from that source. Each of these values is input into one cell of a spreadsheet-like table. Data for all the other rows in the problem are input in the same way.

The last values input are the number of items required at each destination.

## 5.4  Data Input Details

The first set of data (the problem structure) is as follows:

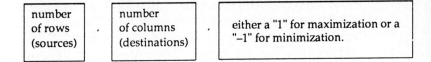

The next set of data should be as follows:

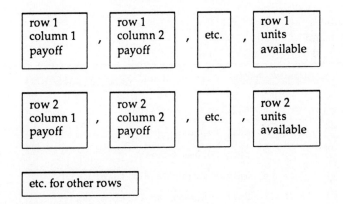

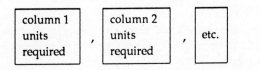

The last set of data should contain the following:

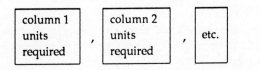

## 5.5  Editing the Data

Editing features are a part of both the ENTER PROBLEM FROM KEYBOARD option and the EDIT CURRENT PROBLEM option. The problem structure may be changed in the ENTER PROBLEM FROM KEYBOARD option. The problem data (but not the problem structure) may be changed in the EDIT CURRENT PROBLEM option.

The first part of the ENTER PROBLEM FROM KEYBOARD option is used to enter the problem structure (the number of rows, the number of columns, and whether it is a max or min problem). After the data are entered, the program will ask if you want to re-enter the problem structure. Type "Y" if any of the problem structure values are incorrect. The program will then repeat all the problem structure prompts to allow the correct data to be entered.

The EDIT CURRENT PROBLEM option is used to change any value of the payoff for shipments between two points, the unit available (supply), of units required (demand). This option is also used to edit row labels, edit column labels, or switch from MAX to MIN (or vice versa). After you select the EDIT CURRENT PROBLEM option, the program will display the Editing Menu (as shown in Figure 5.1). If Edit option 1 (Edit All Data Values) is selected, the screen will display the same spreadsheet structure that was used for the original data input. Use the arrow keys to move the cursor to the left of the number you want to change and then type the new value. Any number of values may be changed in one editing session. As in the original data input, type "F" when you are finished.

**FIGURE 5.1**  Editing menu

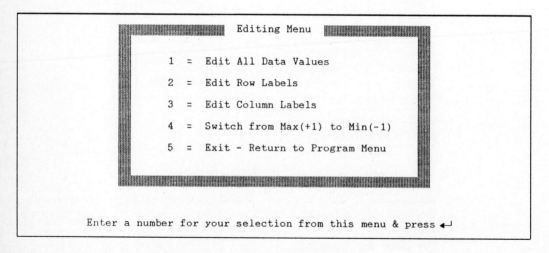

```
                      Editing Menu

        1  =  Edit All Data Values

        2  =  Edit Row Labels

        3  =  Edit Column Labels

        4  =  Switch from Max(+1) to Min(-1)

        5  =  Exit - Return to Program Menu



   Enter a number for your selection from this menu & press ↵
```

## 5.6 Program Output

The program output indicates the number of items to be shipped between each source and each destination. The optimal value of the object function is also output.

The portion of the output that contains the information that was entered looks similar to the original matrix where the amounts available are printed to the right of the matrix and the amounts needed are printed below the matrix. The names (or variables) used for the sources and the destinations are included in the output.

One exception to this statement about data arrangement occurs when you have large problems. When there is insufficient space to print one row of numbers on one line, the computer will split the spreadsheet into two or more blocks of data. All rows and columns are labeled in each block.

Some problems may have multiple optimal solutions. When this occurs, a different shipping schedule will have the same optimal value of the objective function. This program does not indicate if multiple optimal solutions exist.

## 5.7 Example Problem T1

Minimize the total cost of shipping 60 items from sources A and B to destination C, D, and E. The cost of shipping one item between each pair of points is given inside the matrix. The number of items available at each of the sources is given to the right of the matrix, and the number of items needed at each destination is given in the row below the matrix.

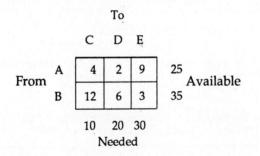

### 5.7.1 Problem Preparation

No adjustments are required for this problem, because shipments are possible between every pair of points, and the number of items available (60) is exactly equal to the number of items needed (60).

## 5.7.2 Data Input

The following data values must be input prior to a run of the program:

        2, 3, -1
        4, 2, 9, 25
        12, 6, 3, 35
        10, 20, 30

Figure 5.2 shows how the problem structure should be input. Figure 5.3 shows how the screen appears after all data values have been input.

## 5.7.3 Computer Output

Figure 5.4 contains the output from a run of this problem. Each row of the matrix in the INFORMATION ENTERED section contains the same data as the corresponding row of the original problem. As with all programs, it is a good idea to check this section to make sure that the correct data were entered.

The RESULTS for this problem show the number of items that should be shipped between locations:

**FIGURE 5.2**    Input of problem structure for example problem T1

```
                    -=*=-   DATA   INPUT   -=*=-


    ENTER NUMBER OF SOURCE ROWS
    ENTER NUMBER IN RANGE ( 2   -   20 ) & press ↵    2

    ENTER NUMBER OF DESTINATION COLUMNS
    ENTER NUMBER IN RANGE ( 2   -   20 ) & press ↵    3

    IS THE PROBLEM TYPE MAXIMIZATION (1)  OR  MINIMIZATION (-1)
    Enter a Character ( 1  or  -1 ) & press ↵      -1



    DO YOU WANT TO RE-ENTER PROBLEM STRUCTURE? (Y/N)
    Enter a Character ( Y  or  N ) & press ↵    N
```

**FIGURE 5.3**    Computer screen after input of all data from example problem T1

```
                            DATA ENTRY

                    C           D           E           UA
        A        4.000       2.000       9.000      25.000
        B       12.000       6.000       3.000      35.000
        UN      10.000      20.000 ▌    30.000
```

**FIGURE 5.4**   Output from a run of example problem T1

```
            -=*=-   INFORMATION ENTERED   -=*=-


    NUMBER OF SOURCE ROWS             :       2
    NUMBER OF DESTINATION COLUMNS     :       3
    PROBLEM TYPE                      :   MINIMIZATION


                    PAYOFF PER UNIT

            C           D           E           UA

    A       4.000       2.000       9.000       25.000
    B      12.000       6.000       3.000       35.000
    UN     10.000      20.000      30.000       60.000


                -=*=-   RESULTS   -=*=-


                OPTIMAL ALLOCATION

            C           D           E           UA

    A      10.000      15.000       0           25.000
    B       0           5.000      30.000       35.000
    UN     10.000      20.000      30.000       60.000

            TOTAL PAYOFF :   190


    ----------   E N D   O F   A N A L Y S I S   ----------
```

10 items are shipped from A to C

15 items are shipped from A to D

 5 items are shipped from B to D

30 items are shipped from B to E

and nothing is shipped between the remaining locations.

The value of the objective function (or total shipping cost) in this problem is 190.

## 5.8 Example Problem T2

Maximize profit, where the values in the matrix are the amount of profit that would be received if one item was shipped from each source to each destination. No shipments are allowed between B and F.

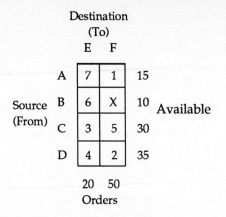

Destination (To)

|  | E | F | Available |
|---|---|---|---|
| A | 7 | 1 | 15 |
| B | 6 | X | 10 |
| C | 3 | 5 | 30 |
| D | 4 | 2 | 35 |

20  50
Orders

### 5.8.1 Problem Preparation

In this problem, no shipments are allowed between locations B and location F. The computer input must be numerical, so we cannot input "X" for the B to F profit. Since this is a maximization problem, we must put a large-magnitude negative number in place of the "X" to ensure that no B to F shipments will be made. We will use –100 in this problem.

This problem is also unbalanced. We have 90 items available and 70 ordered. We must therefore add a column that represents unshipped items. No profits result from these unshipped items, so we set each profit value to "0" in this new column.

The problem that results from these two adjustments is as follows:

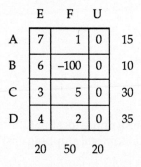

|  | E | F | U |  |
|---|---|---|---|---|
| A | 7 | 1 | 0 | 15 |
| B | 6 | –100 | 0 | 10 |
| C | 3 | 5 | 0 | 30 |
| D | 4 | 2 | 0 | 35 |

20   50   20

### 5.8.2 Data Input

The following data values must be input to solve this problem:

    4, 3, 1
    7, 1, 0, 15
    6, –100, 0, 10

3, 5, 0, 30
4, 2, 0, 35
20, 50, 20

Figure 5.5 shows how the problem structure should be input in response to prompts from the computer. Figure 5.6 shows how the computer screen appears after all data values have been input.

### 5.8.3 Computer Output

Figure 5.7 contains the output from a run of this problem. The results indicate that:

15 items are shipped from A to E

5 items are shipped from B to E

30 items are shipped from C to F

20 items are shipped from D to F

**FIGURE 5.5**    Input of problem structure for example problem T2

```
                    -=*=-   DATA   INPUT   -=*=-


ENTER NUMBER OF SOURCE ROWS
ENTER NUMBER IN RANGE ( 2  -  20 ) & press ↵   4

ENTER NUMBER OF DESTINATION COLUMNS
ENTER NUMBER IN RANGE ( 2  -  20 ) & press ↵   3

IS THE PROBLEM TYPE MAXIMIZATION (1)  OR  MINIMIZATION (-1)
Enter a Character ( 1  or  -1 ) & press ↵    1



DO YOU WANT TO RE-ENTER PROBLEM STRUCTURE? (Y/N)
Enter a Character ( Y  or  N ) & press ↵   N
```

**FIGURE 5.6**    Computer screen after input of all data for example problem T2

```
                          DATA EDIT

               E           F          U          UA
    A  ▌     7.000       1.000       0        15.000
    B        6.000    -100.000       0        10.000
    C        3.000       5.000       0        30.000
    D        4.000       2.000       0        35.000
    UN      20.000      50.000     20.000
```

**FIGURE 5.7** Output from a run of example problem T2

```
              -=*=-   INFORMATION ENTERED   -=*=-


    NUMBER OF SOURCE ROWS              :        4
    NUMBER OF DESTINATION COLUMNS      :        3
    PROBLEM TYPE                       :    MAXIMIZATION


                      PAYOFF PER UNIT

              E             F           U          UA

    A       7.000         1.000        0         15.000
    B       6.000      -100.000        0         10.000
    C       3.000         5.000        0         30.000
    D       4.000         2.000        0         35.000
    UN     20.000        50.000     20.000       90.000


                  -=*=-   RESULTS   -=*=-


                   OPTIMAL ALLOCATION

              E             F           U          UA

    A      15.000         0            0         15.000
    B       5.000         0          5.000       10.000
    C       0           30.000         0         30.000
    D       0           20.000       15.000      35.000
    UN     20.000       50.000       20.000      90.000


              TOTAL PAYOFF :   325

    ----------   E N D   O F   A N A L Y S I S   ----------
```

and nothing is shipped between the remaining locations.

The values in the U column represent available items that remain at the source. Therefore:

5 items remain at B

15 items remain at D

and no items remain at the other two sources.

The value of the objective function (or total profit) is 325.

# 5.9 Transportation Problems

What is the minimum cost shipping schedule for each of the following nine problems?

1. From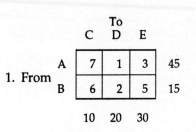

2. From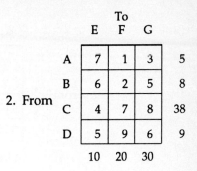

3. From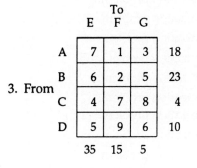

4. From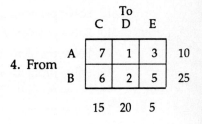

5. From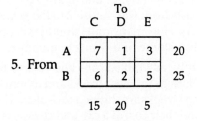

6. From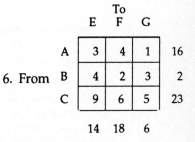

7. From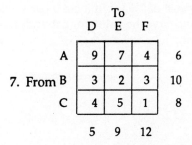

8. From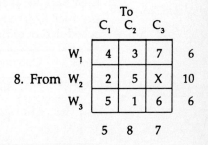

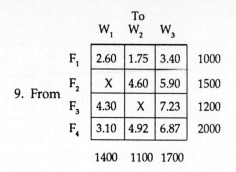

9. From

|  | To | | |  |
|---|---|---|---|---|
|  | $W_1$ | $W_2$ | $W_3$ |  |
| $F_1$ | 2.60 | 1.75 | 3.40 | 1000 |
| $F_2$ | X | 4.60 | 5.90 | 1500 |
| $F_3$ | 4.30 | X | 7.23 | 1200 |
| $F_4$ | 3.10 | 4.92 | 6.87 | 2000 |
|  | 1400 | 1100 | 1700 |  |

10. Solve problem 1 as a maximization problem.

11. Solve problem 2 as a maximization problem.

12. Solve problem 3 as a maximization problem.

13. Solve problem 4 as a maximization problem.

14. Solve problem 5 as a maximization problem.

15. Solve problem 6 as a maximization problem.

16. Solve problem 7 as a maximization problem.

17. Solve problem 8 as a maximization problem.

18. Solve problem 9 as a maximization problem.

19. A company has received three orders for the same item. Customer 1 wants 50 units, customer 2 wants 75, and customer 3 wants 125. They currently have 80 of these items in warehouse 1 and 170 in warehouse 2. Unit shipping costs from warehouse 1 to customers 1, 2, and 3 are $10, $12, and $15 respectively. Unit shipping costs from warehouse 2 to the same customers are $11, $9, and $10 respectively. How many units should the company ship from each warehouse to each customer if it wants to minimize cost?

20. Import Motors imports the fully assembled cabs and chassis for a line of small trucks. They fabricate the beds for these trucks and mount the beds on the cab and chassis. The finished trucks are shipped to dealers. Their full cost of fabricating a bed is $220, and their cost of a cab and chassis is $2000. The final assembly of bed to cab and chassis cannot take place if they are short of either one. Cabs and chassis or beds that cannot be matched are stored in their back lot at an inventory cost of 1% (of unit cost) per week. They can produce 1000 beds per week and have the following cab and chassis arrivals scheduled over the next month:

| Week | Cab and Chassis |
|---|---|
| 1 | 1500 |
| 2 | 0 |
| 3 | 1700 |
| 4 | 0 |

If they currently have nothing stored in the back lot, and if items produced and delivered in the same week incur no inventory cost, how many beds should they produce each week to minimize total four week inventory cost?

21. Same as problem 20 except that the trucks were in two colors: red and blue. Naturally, the color of the bed must be the same as the cab and the chassis. The new details about the next month's scheduled arrivals are as follows:

| Week | Cab and Chassis Red | Blue |
|------|------|------|
| 1 | 1000 | 500 |
| 2 | 0 | 0 |
| 3 | 100 | 1600 |
| 4 | 0 | 0 |

22. Same as problem 21 except that all the blue trucks are in great demand. Therefore management wants all blue trucks to be shipped in the same week that the cab and chassis arrive in port.

23. Same as problem 21, except that their bed production plant is set up to produce beds in 100 bed lots.

24. The Haskins Corporation has warehouses in Los Angeles and Chicago. From the Chicago warehouse, it costs $1 to ship an item to the Chicago distributor, $11 to Seattle, $7 to Denver, and $9 to Los Angeles. The shipping costs from the Los Angeles warehouse are $2 to the Los Angeles distributor, $9 to Chicago, $6 to Denver, and $6 to Seattle. There currently are 1050 items in the Chicago warehouse and 830 in the Los Angeles warehouse. The current need is for 500 items in Seattle, 600 in Denver, 560 in Los Angeles, and 220 in Chicago. What shipping schedule minimizes total shipping costs?

25. Same as problem 24 except that only 120 items are needed in Chicago.

26. Same as problem 25 except that an unshipped item in the Chicago warehouse incurs a cost of $8 and an unshipped item in the Los Angeles warehouse incurs a cost of $3.

27. Same as problem 24 except that 320 items are needed in Chicago.

28. Same as problem 27 except that each unit not shipped to Denver costs $10 in lost good will. Items not shipped to any of the other cities cost only $4 in lost good will. The figure is more in Denver due to the very intense advertising campaign that has been running for the last two months.

29. The Computer Services Division provides the data-processing capability to all divisions of the corporation. It uses its own computer in Kansas City to provide service in Kansas City, Chicago, and New Orleans. If it needs more time than can be provided by its own computer, it buys time from computer service bureaus in each of the three cities.

Tomorrow it will need 15 hours of processing in Kansas City, 12 hours in Chicago, and 8 hours in New Orleans. The computer will be available for only 22 hours. The computer costs $300 per hour; the Kansas City service bureau costs $500 per hour, the Chicago service bureau costs $450 per hour, and the New Orleans service bureau costs $550 per hour. Data transmission costs from the computer to the divisions are $10 per hour to Kansas City, $50 per hour to Chicago, and $70 per hour to New Orleans. The service bureaus can only be used in their own city and their rates include local data transmission costs. There is no limit to the amount of time available at the service bureaus. How much time should be used on each of the computers to minimize cost?

30. Assembling a calculator and shipping it to the United States costs $2.70 in Taiwan, $2.60 in Hong Kong, and $3.20 in Mexico. The assembly capacity is 70,000 units in Taiwan, 40,000 units in Hong Kong, and 50,000 units in Mexico. Each calculator uses one chip.

| | Number of Logic Chips Available | Cost($) per Chip | Cost($) of Shipping 1,000 Chips to | | |
| --- | --- | --- | --- | --- | --- |
| | | | Taiwan | Hong Kong | Mexico |
| Japan | 20,000 | .10 | 10 | 15 | 30 |
| U.S. | 40,000 | .14 | 25 | 35 | 5 |

If the above table contains all other relevant costs and availability, and the company wants to produce 60,000 calculators at minimum cost, how many units should be assembled in each location?

31. A roller skate manufacturer found itself unprepared for the surge in interest in its product. The Indianapolis plant has enough wheel bearings to produce 2000 pairs of skates and the Boston plant has enough to produce 3000 pairs of skates. No new wheel bearing assemblies will be delivered for at least one month. Total manufacturing cost per pair is $7 in Boston and $8 in Indianapolis.

The Western Region distributor wants 4000 pairs of skates, the Central Region distributor wants 2000 pairs, and the Eastern Region distributor wants 7500 pairs. The shipping cost per pair of skates is as follows:

| From | To | | |
| --- | --- | --- | --- |
| | Eastern | Central | Western |
| Indianapolis | 0.40 | 0.20 | 0.90 |
| Boston | 0.10 | 0.35 | 1.20 |

Pairs of skates wholesale for $14 to the Eastern distributor, $15 to the Central distributor, and $18 to the Western distributor. How many pairs of skates should each distributor get if the manufacturer wants to maximize profit?

32. Same as problem 31 except that the manufacturer wants to ship at least 1000 pairs of skates to each distributor.

---

## CASE STUDY   Southern Cabinet Co.

The Southern Cabinet Co. uses ash, birch, and walnut to make kitchen cabinets. Three styles are available: Moderne (which is made only from ash or birch), Classic (which is made only from birch or walnut), and Scandia (which is made from all three types of wood). The wood, trim, and hardware cost $75 for a set of Moderne if made from ash and $84 if made from birch. Similarly, the wood, trim, and hardware cost $100 for a Classic set in birch and $170 in walnut. These same items for a Scandia set cost $90 in ash, $110 in birch, and $163 in walnut.

The wholesale price for an ash Moderne set is $210, a birch Classic set is $250, and an ash Scandia set is $200. The price of a birch set in any style is 10% more than the corresponding ash set, and the price of a walnut set is 20% more than the price for a birch set.

Southern Cabinet's last delivery of wood was not properly dried, and no more wood can be obtained until next week. This week's production schedule must be developed using only the supply of wood that was left after last week's production. Enough ash is available to make 150 sets of any style cabinet, enough birch to make 100 sets, and enough walnut to make 70 sets. The dealers have requested 60 sets of Moderne, 270 sets of Classic, and 300 sets of Scandia. The dealers usually specify both style and wood, but Southern Cabinet's president has decided to respond only to the dealer's style requests this week, and produce the style/wood combinations that result in the maximum total profit. How many sets should be produced in each style with each wood? How much profit will result?

# 6
## ASGT

# *Assignment Model*

The classic assignment model solves the problem of assigning people to machines so that the total costs of production are minimized. In such a problem, each person can be assigned to only one machine and each machine can be assigned to only one person. The number of people must be exactly the same as the number of machines.

The model is not restricted to people/machine assignments, but can be used for any problem where individual items in one group are paired with individual items in another group. The model can solve either maximization or minimization problems.

The assignment model is not used as frequently as many of the other models because it applies to a much narrower range of applications. It is of interest, however, as a special case of a transportation problem. It is an efficient model to use when a problem fits its specific structure.

## 6.1 Program Description

This program finds the minimum or maximum payoff that can be obtained by assigning people to machines (or any one set of items to another set). Problems can be solved with up to 25 rows and 25 columns.

## 6.2 Problem Preparation

If a problem has an unequal number of rows and columns, additional rows or columns must be added. Each added row or column must have a payoff for each person (or machine) that is assigned to it. If no additional information is given in the problem, these values should be set to zero.

If any particular assignment is illegal, impossible, or just not to be considered as part of a solution, then the payoff for that assignment should be given a value that ensures the desired result. If it is a minimization problem, then you should use a large value for this payoff. If it is a maximization problem, you should use a large magnitude negative number. The usual procedure is to use a number with a magnitude that is 10 or 100 times larger than the largest payoff in the matrix. If none of the "illegal" assignments are made, then all numbers are sufficiently large. If any of the "illegal" assignments are made, input a larger magnitude number and run the problem again.

## 6.3 Data Input Overview

First, you enter the problem structure. The first item to be input is the size of the problem. Since the number of rows must equal the number of columns in any assignment problem, only the number of rows is required. This is followed by a 1 for maximization problems and a –1 for minimization problems.

The payoffs that would result from each assignment are entered next. Each of these values is input into one cell of a spreadsheet-like table. These are entered from left to right starting from the top row. The values for each row are entered from the top row to the bottom row.

## 6.4 Data Input Details

The first set of data (the problem structure) should be the following:

| number of rows | , | either a "1" for maximization or a "–1" for minimization. |

The next set of data should be the following:

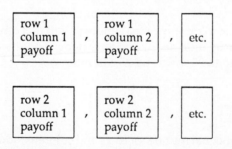

| row 1 column 1 payoff | , | row 1 column 2 payoff | , | etc. |

| row 2 column 1 payoff | , | row 2 column 2 payoff | , | etc. |

## 6.5 Editing the Data

Editing features are a part of both the ENTER PROBLEM FROM KEYBOARD option and the EDIT CURRENT PROBLEM option. The problem structure may be changed in the ENTER PROBLEM FROM KEYBOARD option and the problem data (but not the problem structure) may be changed in the EDIT CURRENT PROBLEM option.

The first part of the ENTER PROBLEM FROM KEYBOARD option is used to enter the problem structure (the number of rows, and whether it is a max or min problem). After these data are entered, the program will ask if you want to re-enter the problem structure. Type "Y" if any of the problem structure values are incorrect. The program will then repeat all the problem structure prompts to allow the correct data to be entered.

The EDIT CURRENT PROBLEM option is used to change any of the payoff values. This option is also used to edit row labels, column labels, or switch from MIN to MAX (or vice versa). After you select the EDIT CURRENT PROBLEM option, the program will display the Editing Menu (as shown in Figure 6.1). If edit option 1 (Edit Payoff Values) is selected, the screen will display the same spreadsheet structure that was used for the original data input. Use the arrow keys to move the cursor to the left of the number you want to change and then type the new value. Any number of values may be changed in one editing session. Type the letter "F" when you are finished.

## 6.6 Program Output

The program output notes which row is assigned to which column by printing the letter "A" in the paired row and column. All other unassigned pairs will be noted by dashes. The minimum (maximum) total value of the assignment is output last.

**FIGURE 6.1**   Assignment model editing menu

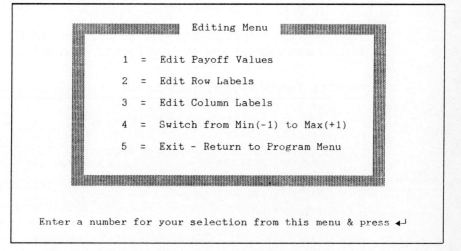

```
                        Editing Menu

         1  =   Edit Payoff Values

         2  =   Edit Row Labels

         3  =   Edit Column Labels

         4  =   Switch from Min(-1) to Max(+1)

         5  =   Exit - Return to Program Menu



    Enter a number for your selection from this menu & press ↵
```

Some problems may have multiple optimal solutions. When this situation occurs, a different set of assignments will generate the same payoff. This program does not indicate if multiple optimal solutions exist.

# 6.7  Example Problem A1

Find the assignment of people to machines that minimizes the total payoff.

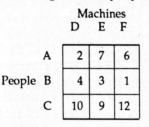

## 6.7.1 Problem Preparation

No preparation is needed for this problem, because the number of rows and the number of columns are equal, and each person can be assigned to each machine.

## 6.7.2 Data Input

The following data values must be input to solve this problem:

    3, -1
    2, 7, 6
    4, 3, 1
    10, 9, 12

Figure 6.2 shows how the problem structure should be input. Figure 6.3 shows how the screen appears after all data values have been input.

**FIGURE 6.2**   Input of problem structure for example problem A1

```
              -=*=-   DATA   INPUT   -=*=-


    ENTER THE MODEL SIZE (NUMBER OF ROWS)
    ENTER NUMBER IN RANGE ( 1  -  25 ) & press ↵   3

    IS THE PROBLEM TYPE MAXIMIZATION (1)   OR   MINIMIZATION (-1)
    Enter a Character ( 1  or  -1 ) & press ↵     -1



    DO YOU WANT TO RE-ENTER PROBLEM STRUCTURE?  (Y/N)
    Enter a Character ( Y  or  N ) & press ↵    N
```

**FIGURE 6.3**   Computer screen after input of all data for example problem A1

```
                          DATA ENTRY

                  D            E            F
          A     2.000        7.000        6.000
          B     4.000        3.000        1.000
          C    10.000        9.000 ▌     12.000
```

### 6.7.3 Computer Output

Figure 6.4 contains the output from a run of this problem. The output shows an "A" in the first row and the first column. This means that person A is assigned to machine D. Similarly, the "A" in the second row, third column, means that person B is assigned to machine F. The third row has the "A" in the second column, so this means that person C is assigned to machine E.

The total payoff from these assignments is 12 (2 for AD plus 1 for BF plus 9 for CD). You can always check yourself to see if you are reading the output correctly by adding the payoffs of all assigned pairs. This is usually necessary only for large problems.

**FIGURE 6.4**   Output from a run of example problem A1

```
            -=*=-   INFORMATION ENTERED   -=*=-


   TOTAL NUMBER OF ROWS              :        3
   TOTAL NUMBER OF COLUMNS           :        3
   PROBLEM TYPE                      :     MINIMIZATION

                    PAYOFF VALUES

                  D            E            F
          A     2.000        7.000        6.000
          B     4.000        3.000        1.000
          C    10.000        9.000       12.000




            -=*=-   RESULTS   -=*=-

                  ROW ASSIGNMENTS

              D  E  F

          A   A  -  -
          B   -  -  A
          C   -  A  -

              TOTAL PAYOFF :   12


 ----------  E N D   O F   A N A L Y S I S  ----------
```

# 6.8  Example Problem A2

Same as problem A1, except maximize.

### 6.8.1  Problem Preparation

Problem preparation is exactly the same as in example problem A1.

### 6.8.2  Data Input

The following data values must be input to solve this problem:

3, 1
2, 7, 6
4, 3, 1
10, 9, 12

These data values could be entered in the same way that example problem A1 was entered, but it is easier to select option 5 (Edit Current Problem) from the ASSIGNMENT MODEL—PROGRAM OPTIONS MENU. When the Editing Menu appears on the screen, press 4 to switch the problem from MIN to MAX. Then return to the Program Menu to run the problem.

### 6.8.3  Computer Output

Figure 6.5 contains the output from a run of this problem. The results show that the following pairs are assigned to each other.

A and E
B and D
C and F

The total payoff from these assignments is 23.

# 6.9  Example Problem A3

Solve the following assignment minimization problem:

|    | M1 | M2 |
|----|----|----|
| P1 | 7  | 10 |
| P2 | 3  | X  |
| P3 | 2  | 8  |

**FIGURE 6.5**  Output from a run of example problem A2

```
            -=*=-   INFORMATION ENTERED   -=*=-



    TOTAL NUMBER OF ROWS              :        3
    TOTAL NUMBER OF COLUMNS           :        3
    PROBLEM TYPE                      :    MAXIMIZATION

                    PAYOFF VALUES

                  D           E           F
        A       2.000       7.000     · 6.000
        B       4.000       3.000       1.000
        C      10.000       9.000      12.000




            -=*=-   RESULTS   -=*=-

               ROW ASSIGNMENTS

           D  E  F

        A   -  A  -
        B   A  -  -
        C   -  -  A

            TOTAL PAYOFF :   23



    ---------  E N D   O F   A N A L Y S I S   ----------
```

## 6.9.1 Problem Preparation

This problem is both unbalanced (three rows, but only two columns) and contains an illegal assignment (row P2 cannot be assigned to column M2).

The balance is corrected by adding a new column (labeled "U," below) that contains all zeros. Any person assigned to this column by the computer will actually be idle. We now have a three-row, three-column problem.

The illegal assignment cell is readied for computer input by replacing the "X" by 100. The resultant problem is as follows:

|    | M1 | M2  | U |
|----|----|-----|---|
| P1 | 7  | 10  | 0 |
| P2 | 3  | 100 | 0 |
| P3 | 2  | 8   | 0 |

### 6.9.2 Data Input

The following data values must be input to solve this problem:

```
3, -1
7, 10, 0
3, 100, 0
2, 8, 0
```

### 6.9.3 Computer Output

Figure 6.6 contains the output from a run of this problem. The results show that the following pairs are assigned to each other:

**FIGURE 6.6**   Output from a run of example problem A3

```
            -=*=-  INFORMATION ENTERED  -=*=-


    TOTAL NUMBER OF ROWS              :       3
    TOTAL NUMBER OF COLUMNS           :       3
    PROBLEM TYPE                      :    MINIMIZATION

                    PAYOFF VALUES

                    M1          M2          U
          P1        7.000       10.000      0
          P2        3.000       100.000     0
          P3        2.000       8.000       0




            -=*=-  RESULTS  -=*=-

                ROW ASSIGNMENTS

          M1 M2 U

          P1   -   -   A
          P2   A   -   -
          P3   -   A   -

                TOTAL PAYOFF :   11


    ----------  E N D   O F   A N A L Y S I S  ----------
```

P1 and U

P2 and M1

P3 and M2

Therefore person 1 is unassigned, person 2 is assigned to machine 1, and person 3 is assigned to machine 2. The total payoff from these assignments is equal to 11.

## 6.10 Assignment Problems

1. Find the minimum value assignment:

|   | D | E | F |
|---|---|---|---|
| A | 7 | 3 | 6 |
| B | 4 | 2 | 5 |
| C | 8 | 4 | 9 |

2. Find the minimum value assignment:

|   | K | L | M | N |
|---|---|---|---|---|
| A | 3.6 | 7.2 | 5.0 | 6.1 |
| B | 5.1 | 6.2 | 7.3 | 8.9 |
| C | 6.6 | 3.4 | 5.7 | 9.1 |
| D | 4.7 | 2.9 | 7.7 | 5.6 |

3. Find the maximum value assignment:

|   | X | Y | Z |
|---|---|---|---|
| A | 11 | 15 | 9 |
| B | 7 | 12 | 13 |
| C | 8 | 14 | 10 |

4. Find the maximum value assignment:

|       | $Y_1$ | $Y_2$ | $Y_3$ | $Y_4$ |
|-------|-------|-------|-------|-------|
| $X_1$ | 3     | 4     | 7     | 8     |
| $X_2$ | 15    | 5     | 6     | 10    |
| $X_3$ | 13    | 1     | 14    | 2     |
| $X_4$ | 16    | 9     | 11    | 12    |

5. Find the maximum value assignment:

|   | E | F | G |
|---|---|---|---|
| A | 1 | 3 | 7 |
| B | 6 | 2 | 9 |
| C | 5 | 4 | 6 |
| D | 3 | 1 | 2 |

6. Find the minimum value assignment:

|   | C | D | E | F |
|---|---|---|---|---|
| A | 1 | 3 | 2 | 4 |
| B | 5 | 7 | 8 | 9 |

7. Find the maximum value assignment if W1 and $X_2$ cannot be assigned to each other:

|       | $X_1$ | $X_2$ | $X_3$ |
|-------|-------|-------|-------|
| $W_1$ | 10    | –     | 11    |
| $W_2$ | 8     | 14    | 6     |
| $W_3$ | 7     | 16    | 4     |

8. Find the maximum value assignment if neither B and D nor C and F can be assigned to each other:

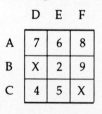

|   | D | E | F |
|---|---|---|---|
| A | 7 | 6 | 8 |
| B | X | 2 | 9 |
| C | 4 | 5 | X |

9. Find the maximum value assignment (where unacceptable assignments are noted by an X):

|     | B₁ | B₂ | B₃ | B₄ |
|-----|----|----|----|----|
| A₁  | 10 | 14 | X  | 9  |
| A₂  | X  | 18 | 17 | 13 |
| A₃  | 11 | X  | 12 | 7  |

10. Find the minimum value assignment (where unacceptable assignments are noted by an X):

|     | D₁ | D₂ | D₃ |
|-----|----|----|----|
| S₁  | 10 | 12 | 9  |
| S₂  | X  | 14 | 13 |
| S₃  | 15 | 16 | X  |
| S₄  | 13 | 15 | 12 |
| S₅  | 12 | X  | 11 |

11. What is the minimum cost of assigning the following three workers (W1, W2, and W3) to the following three machines (M1, M2, and M3)?

|     | M₁ | M₂ | M₃ |
|-----|----|----|----|
| W₁  | 4  | 4  | 3  |
| W₂  | 5  | 6  | 8  |
| W₃  | 10 | 7  | 9  |

12. The number of defective parts produced if an employee works a full day on each machine is given in the following table. Each of the three machines must operate for the full day. What is the minimum number of defective parts that would result from assigning these four employees to three machines for one day?

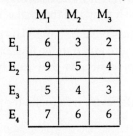

|     | M₁ | M₂ | M₃ |
|-----|----|----|----|
| E₁  | 6  | 3  | 2  |
| E₂  | 9  | 5  | 4  |
| E₃  | 5  | 4  | 3  |
| E₄  | 7  | 6  | 6  |

13. Same as problem 12, except that employee 1 cannot operate machine 3 and employee 3 cannot operate machine 1.

14. Same as problem 12, except that 2 cannot operate machine 1.

15. Same as problem 12, except that machine 3 is broken and cannot be assigned to anyone.

16. A company has determined that the performance of its sales representatives is dependent on the territory to which they are assigned. The following table contains the estimate of the numbers of monthly sales that would result if each sales representative were assigned to each territory. Who should be assigned to each territory to maximize sales?

Territory

|   | 1 | 2 | 3 | 4 | 5 |
|---|-----|-----|-----|-----|-----|
| 1 | 120 | 95 | 210 | 150 | 75 |
| 2 | 140 | 110 | 190 | 180 | 100 |
| 3 | 150 | 180 | 180 | 140 | 120 |
| 4 | 180 | 170 | 170 | 150 | 105 |
| 5 | 130 | 115 | 150 | 160 | 110 |

Sales Representative (rows 1–5)

17. The State Highway Department has received the following bids for three freeway construction projects:

a) *Ajax Construction*
   Sespi Freeway Phase II—$7,000,000
   Altoona-Ithica Interchange—$2,000,000
b) *Consolidated Contractors*
   Sespi Freeway Phase II—$6,000,000
   Altoona-Ithica Interchange—$1,500,000
   Dayton Curve Modification—$1,000,000
c) *Beta Construction*
   Altoona-Ithica Interchange—$1,700,000
   Sespi Freeway Phase II—$6,200,000
   Dayton Curve Modification—$1,100,000

It is the policy not to give any contractor more than one contract at a time. Which contractor should get which project if the goal is to minimize cost?

18. How much money would the state save if it changed its policy in problem 17 to one in which all contracts were given to the lowest bidder? There is now no limit to the number of contracts that can be received by a construction company.

19. How much money would the state save if it changed the policy in problem

17 to one in which each contractor could have a maximum of two contracts at one time? Note: This is slightly tricky, but it can be formulated and solved as an assignment problem.

20. Fair Weather Airlines keeps one spare 747 engine in its parts depots in Los Angeles, Hong Kong, and Paris. If an engine is needed to service an aircraft in any other city, a spare engine is flown from one of the parts depots. Today there is a need for one 747 engine in New York, one in Singapore, and one in Bombay. The extra fuel costs associated with flying these extra engines are as follows:

| To | From | Cost $ |
|---|---|---|
| New York | Los Angeles | 450 |
| | Hong Kong | 750 |
| | Paris | 500 |
| Bombay | Los Angeles | 600 |
| | Hong Kong | 400 |
| | Paris | 550 |
| Singapore | Los Angeles | 500 |
| | Hong Kong | 200 |
| | Paris | 600 |

Between which cities should the spare engines be flown if the airline wants to minimize total costs?

21. The swimming team coach is making assignments for the medley and must pick four swimmers from the five who are available. The best times for each swimmer on each of the four legs of the medley are as follows:

Legs

|  | 1 | 2 | 3 | 4 |
|---|---|---|---|---|
| 1 | 47 | 45 | 40 | 37 |
| 2 | 51 | 46 | 39 | 38 |
| 3 | 49 | 45 | 41 | 38 |
| 4 | 50 | 47 | 42 | 39 |
| 5 | 47 | 46 | 41 | 40 |

Swimmer (rows 1–5)

Which swimmer should be assigned to which leg of the race?

22. Lomita Specialty Machinery, Fixtures, and Tools has an order for six of its laser broaching machines. All parts are in stock except for valve floaters, index pins, finial harps, and knurls. Each part is produced on a machine that is specially designed to produce only that part. Four employees are available to run these machines. Alan, the lead machinist, earns $12 per hour. If he worked one full hour on each of the machines, he would produce 10 valve floaters, 100 index pins, 20 finial harps, or 50 knurls. Bob, the machinist, earns $9 per hour and could produce 7 valve floaters, 90 index pins, 15 finial harps, or 46 knurls per hour. Carl, the apprentice, earns $4 per hour and could produce 70 index pins, 5 finial harps, or 30 knurls per hour. He has not been trained to produce valve floaters. Don, the owner's wife's nephew, earns $7 per hour and is only allowed to touch two machines. He can produce 60 index pins or 25 knurls per hour.

Each laser broaching machine uses 2 valve floaters, 50 index pins, 4 finial harps, and 10 knurls. This is a rush job, so each of the four people will work on one machine until they have finished all of the parts that they are producing. None of the employees will switch machines with any other employee.

a) Who should produce which part if the company wants to minimize the total time spent producing parts?

b) How much total time is spent on part production?

23. Same situation as problem 22.

a) Who should produce which part if the company wants to minimize the total cost of producing parts?

b) How much money will be spent on part production?

24. The Eastern sales region must assign three sales managers to three sales offices. The objective is to find the assignments that maximize the total yearly sales of all three offices. Naturally, only one person can be assigned to each sales office. The expected yearly sales (in millions of dollars) if each individual is assigned to each office are as follows:

| Person | Sales Office Location | | |
|--------|--------|--------|---------|
|        | Albany | Boston | Chicago |
| Smith  | 20     | 23     | 17      |
| Turner | 15     | 16     | 14      |
| Unger  | 17     | 19     | 16      |

a) Which person should be assigned to which office?

b) What are the expected total yearly sales from these assignments?

25. A nameless manager has suggested that the new corporate cost reduction program would benefit if the sales managers were assigned in a way that

minimized total moving cost. Given that the total cost (in thousands of dollars) of moving each sales manager to each office is:

| Person | Sales Office Location | | |
|--------|-------|--------|---------|
|        | Albany | Boston | Chicago |
| Smith  | 65     | 50     | 40      |
| Turner | 80     | 65     | 70      |
| Unger  | 90     | 70     | 80      |

a)  Which person should be assigned to which office?
b)  What are the expected total yearly sales from these assignments?

26. Three people are available for assignment to two machines. Only one person can be assigned to each machine. When assigned to a machine, each person is paid on a piece-rate basis of 1¢ per item produced. These items are sold for 11¢ each. If people are not assigned to a machine, they are paid their base hourly rate. Other data for this problem are as follows:

| Person | Production Rate on Each Machine (Items/Hour) | | Base Hourly Rate ($/Hr) |
|--------|------|------|------|
|        | M1   | M2   |      |
| Adams  | 800  | 700  | 7.00 |
| Baker  | 850  | 800  | 8.00 |
| Cabot  | 900  | 850  | 8.25 |

a)  Which assignments maximize total daily profit (per eight-hour day)?
b)  How many items are produced per day?
c)  How much profit results?

---

CASE STUDY **Transcoastal Airlines**

Transcoastal Airlines, a smaller-than-average airline, has just received approval for six new daily-scheduled flights. Three flights leave New York for San Francisco, and three flights go in the opposite direction. All flights take five hours, and there is a three hour time difference between the two cities. The flight schedule is as follows (with local times used in all cases):

(CONT.)

<u>CASE STUDY</u> **Transcoastal Airlines**   *(CONT.)*

| Flight Number | Leave | | Arrive | |
|---|---|---|---|---|
| | City | Time | City | Time |
| 1 | SF | 8am | NY | 4pm |
| 2 | SF | 11am | NY | 7pm |
| 3 | SF | 5pm | NY | 1am |
| 11 | NY | 9am | SF | 11am |
| 12 | NY | 1pm | SF | 3pm |
| 13 | NY | 6pm | SF | 8pm |

Six full crews will be hired to fly this schedule. The six crews will be paired, with each pair assigned to two flights. Each pair of crews will alternate days flying each flight in each direction. The only restriction on the assignments is that crews must have at least two hours between flights. Transcoastal wants to minimize the total layover time of all crews. Layover time is the total amount of time that elapses from landing on one flight until takeoff on the next flight. Layover time occurs only when a crew is away from their home-base city (the airline does not provide hotel rooms, meals, etc. when a crew is at home). Two decisions must be made:

1. Which pair of flights should be assigned to each crew?

2. In which city should each crew be based?

Transcoastal's president, a great believer in simple solutions, has suggested basing all crews in San Francisco, with one pair of crews flying flights 1 and 11 (17 hours of layover in New York resulting from a 4pm arrival and a departure at 9am the next day), another pair flying flights 2 and 12 (18 hour layover), and the third pair flying flights 3 and 13 (17 hour layover). The total daily layover with this solution equals 52 hours.

A typical two-day schedule for these six San Francisco-based crews (numbered 1 through 6) is as follows:

| Crew Number | Home Base | Day 1 | | Day 2 | |
|---|---|---|---|---|---|
| | | Flight Number | Layover Hours | Flight Number | Layover Hours |
| 1 | SF | 1 | 17 | 11 | 0 |
| 2 | SF | 2 | 18 | 12 | 0 |
| 3 | SF | 3 | 17 | 13 | 0 |
| 4 | SF | 11 | 0 | 1 | 17 |
| 5 | SF | 12 | 0 | 2 | 18 |
| 6 | SF | 13 | 0 | 3 | 17 |

*(CONT.)*

## CASE STUDY **Transcoastal Airlines**   *(CONT.)*

The above schedule is repeated every two days. (Side Issue: It may appear that nobody ever gets a day off, but they do. In a real problem of this type, more than six crews would rotate assignments to fly these flights. The average daily layover would be the same in either case, however.) Transcoastal's vice president believes that either using a different home base for some of the crews or having some crews return on different flights might result in a solution with less layover time. You, as the vice president's staff analyst, have been asked to find this better solution.

# 7
## PERT

# *Project Scheduling*

PERT (Program Evaluation and Review Technique) and CPM (Critical Path Method) are two similar techniques that are used to help manage the schedules of complex projects. Some books draw distinct differences between these two techniques, but we do not. We use the term *PERT*, but you will find that the program can solve most of the problems in books that use the term *CPM*. In its simplest form, PERT provides the following:

1. An estimate of the total amount of time it will take to complete the project.
2. An estimate of the time at which each activity in the project will be completed.
3. An estimate of the earliest time that each activity in the project can begin.
4. A list of the amount of delay that can be incurred in each activity and still not delay the overall project.

Project scheduling is a topic that suffers from a lack of standardized terminology. Students often are confused by the wide variety of terms that are used to describe the same thing. Some of the more frequently encountered terms are given below. The one used in this book is always listed first. Your best bet is to consider these terms to be identical in meaning, unless your book or your instructor introduces a new definition.

*Activities* are referred to in other books as *jobs, arcs,* or *links*.

*Slack* is sometimes called *float*.

The *optimistic* time estimate is also called the *shortest feasible* or *fastest possible* time estimate.

The *modal* time estimate is also called the *most likely* or *most probable*.

The *pessimistic* time estimate is also called the *longest* or *slowest possible*.

PERT has been used with success in construction projects of all types, in the maintenance of complex equipment, the management of R&D projects, and so forth. Frequently, it is a requirement that PERT (or some similar technique) be used to manage government contracts.

## 7.1  Program Description

The program computes the earliest and latest start and finish times for each activity (job) in a project that contains up to 99 activities. Slack for each activity, the critical path, and the expected project completion time are also output.

Time estimates can be entered as either a single estimate or as three estimates (optimistic, modal, and pessimistic). The program output will also include the variance of the expected project completion time if three time estimates were input. The program can also calculate total project costs when activity costs are known (that is, PERT-COST) for single-time-estimate projects.

## 7.2  Problem Preparation

Prior to entering data, the problem must be prepared as follows:

1. Each activity in the project must be given an activity number.
2. These activity numbers must be consecutive integers beginning with the number 1.
3. No activity may have a predecessor with an activity number greater than its own activity number.
4. All project data must be put into a table that is sequenced by activity number (activity 1 is first, activity 2 is second, and so on).
5. The data for each activity should include its activity number, its time estimate (or estimates), its cost, and the activity numbers of its immediate predecessors.

## 7.3  Data Input Overview

The first data value entered to describe the problem structure is the total number of activities in the project. This is followed by a 1 (if you have one time estimate for each activity) or a 3 (if you have three time estimates for each activity). This is the end of problem-structure input for problems with three time estimates. If the problem uses only one time estimate, then the last item input indicates (Y or N) whether activity costs will be included with the problem data. The problem data for each activity are then entered in numerical order (activity 1 is first, activity 2 is second, and so on). For each of these activities, you should enter the time required to complete the activity (if you have three time estimates, enter the optimistic first, the modal next, and the pessimistic last), the activity cost (if costs are known), the total number of immediate predecessors, and the activity numbers of each of the immediate predecessors. All time and cost values must be greater than or equal to zero.

## 7.4 Data Input Details

If you have only one time estimate for each activity, the problem structure input is as follows:

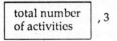

This is followed by input of the problem data:

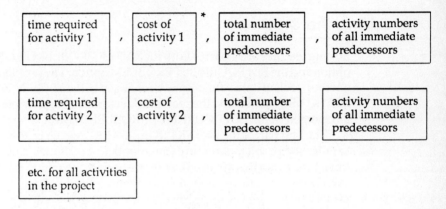

If you have three time estimates for each activity (optimistic, modal, and pessimistic), then the problem structure input is as follows:

```
total number   , 3
of activities
```

This is followed by input of the problem data:

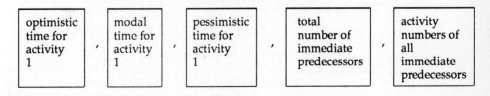

---

*If activity costs are known.

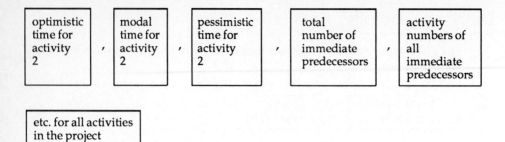

| optimistic time for activity 2 | modal time for activity 2 | pessimistic time for activity 2 | total number of immediate predecessors | activity numbers of all immediate predecessors |

etc. for all activities in the project

## 7.5 Editing the Data

Editing features are a part of both the ENTER PROBLEM FROM KEYBOARD option and the EDIT CURRENT PROBLEM option. The problem structure (but not the problem data values) may be changed in the ENTER PROBLEM FROM KEYBOARD option, and the problem data (but not the problem structure) may be changed in the EDIT CURRENT PROBLEM option.

The first part of the ENTER PROBLEM FROM KEYBOARD option is used to enter the problem structure (the number of activities and whether one or three time estimates are used). After these data are entered, the program will ask if you want to re-enter the problem structure. Type "Y" if any of the problem structure values are incorrect. The program will then repeat all of the problem structure prompts to allow the correct data to be entered.

The EDIT CURRENT PROBLEM option is used to change any of the activity time or cost values. Prompts on the screen will guide you through this. The first prompt will ask you to enter the number of the activity that is to be edited. After the activity number is entered, the program will output the current time and cost values. All these values (changed or unchanged) must be re-entered in response to prompts on the screen. When all editing is complete, enter the number "0" in response to the prompt asking which activity is to be edited. The screen prompt will ask you if you want to save the data. Type "Y" if the data are to be saved on a diskette, or type "N" if not. The program will then return to the PROGRAM OPTIONS menu.

## 7.6 Program Output

The results are output in two parts. The activity number is output first in both parts. Always check the activity numbers, because these are not always listed in numerical order.

The first part of the results also includes the following:

*Expected time*. If you used one time estimate, this value will be identical to it. However, if you used three time estimates, this value will be computed from the values of the optimistic time estimate, the modal time estimate, and the pessimistic time estimate.

*Slack*. This is the maximum amount of time that any single activity can be delayed and not delay the overall project completion time. If delays occur in two or more activities, then you must either analyze the effect on the project by hand, or rerun the problem with the new data.

*Critical path*. This column contains a "YES" for all activities that are on the critical path, and a "NO" for those that are not.

The second part of the results includes the following:

*Activity number*. As described above.

*Earliest start*. This is the earliest possible time that each activity can begin. All predecessors must be completed before this activity can start.

*Earliest finish*. This is the earliest possible completion time of each activity.

*Latest start*. This is the latest time that each activity can begin and not delay the overall project completion time. If the earliest start and latest start times are the same, then the activity is on the critical path

*Latest finish*. This is the latest time that each activity can be completed and not delay the overall project completion time. As with start times, the activity is on the critical path if the earliest finish and latest finish times are the same.

If only one time estimate was entered for each activity, then the last item output is the earliest possible completion time of the overall project. If three time estimates were used for each activity, then the last two items to be output are the EXPECTED COMPLETION TIME, and the CRITICAL VARIANCE (the variance of the expected completion time). If activity costs are used, then the last output will be the projected cost along the critical path, the total project cost, and the project cost profile. The *project cost profile* lists the earliest and latest cost of each time period in the project. These are the total costs that will be incurred if money is spent at a uniform rate over each activity and each activity is completed at its earliest or latest finish time, respectively.

## 7.7 Example Problem P1

For the following project:

1. Find the earliest completion time and the critical path.
2. For how much time can activity 1 be delayed and not delay the project?
3. For how much time can activity 3 be delayed and not delay the project?

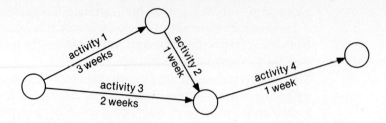

### 7.7.1 Problem Preparation

The activities are already numbered, so the only required preparation is to put the data into a project table:

| Activity | Time | Predecessors |
|----------|------|--------------|
| 1 | 3 | None |
| 2 | 1 | 1 |
| 3 | 2 | None |
| 4 | 1 | 2, 3 |

### 7.7.2 Data Input

The following data values must be input to solve this problem:

**FIGURE 7.1**    Input of problem structure for example problem P1

```
                    -=*=-   SET UP PROBLEM STRUCTURE   -=*=-


    HOW MANY ACTIVITIES
    ENTER NUMBER IN RANGE ( 1  -  99 ) & press ↵    4

    ONE(1) OR THREE(3) TIME ESTIMATES
    Enter a Character ( 1  or  3 ) & press ↵    1

    INPUT ACTIVITY COSTS (Y/N)
    Enter a Character ( Y  or  N ) & press ↵    N


    DO YOU WANT TO RE-ENTER PROBLEM STRUCTURE? (Y/N)
    Enter a Character ( Y  or  N ) & press ↵    N
```

                4, 1, N
                3, 0
                1, 1, 1
                2, 0
                1, 2, 2, 3

Figure 7.1 shows how the problem structure should be input. Figure 7.2 shows how the screen looks after the last data value has been input in response to prompts from the computer.

### 7.7.3 Computer Output

Figure 7.3 contains the output from a run of this problem. The first part of the RESULTS section shows that activity 3 has two weeks of slack, and that all other activities have 0 slack. The critical path consists of activities 1, 2, and 4.

The second part of the RESULTS section shows that activity 3 can begin as early as time 0 or as late as week 2. Similarly, the earliest possible completion of activity 3 is in two weeks, and four weeks is the latest time that activity 3 can be completed and not delay the overall project.

The full project will be completed in five weeks. Therefore, answers to the questions in the example problem are as follows:

1. The earliest completion time is five weeks. Critical path includes activities 1, 2, and 4.

2. Any delay in activity 1 will delay the overall project.

3. Activity 3 can be delayed two weeks and not delay the overall project.

**FIGURE 7.2**  Screen display after entering last data value for example problem P1

```
                  -=*=-  INPUT  DATA  FOR  ACTIVITY  # 4   -=*=-
COMPLETION TIME:   1



PREDECESSOR ACTIVITY NUMBERS

  1=?2
  2=?3


WANT TO RE-ENTER PREDECESSOR ACTIVITY NUMBERS
Enter a Character ( Y  or  N ) & press ↵    N
```

**FIGURE 7.3**   Output from a run of example problem P1

```
                    -=*=-   INFORMATION ENTERED   -=*=-

NUMBER OF ACTIVITIES              :          4

NUMBER OF TIME ESTIMATES          :          1


     ACTIVITY         COMPLETION
      NUMBER            TIME            PREDECESSORS

         1             3.000              NONE

         2             1.000               1

         3             2.000              NONE

         4             1.000               2
                                          3




                    -=*=-   RESULTS   -=*=-


     ACTIVITY         EXPECTED                          CRITICAL
      NUMBER            TIME            SLACK              PATH

         1             3.000           0.000              YES
         2             1.000           0.000              YES
         3             2.000           2.000              NO
         4             1.000           0.000              YES


                 -=*=- ACTIVITY TIME SUMMARY -=*=-

     ACTIVITY                            START            FINISH

         1           EARLIEST           0.000            3.000
                     LATEST             0.000            3.000

         2           EARLIEST           3.000            4.000
                     LATEST             3.000            4.000

         3           EARLIEST           0.000            2.000
                     LATEST             2.000            4.000

         4           EARLIEST           4.000            5.000
                     LATEST             4.000            5.000

EXPECTED COMPLETION TIME          :          5.000


        ----------   E N D   O F   A N A L Y S I S   ----------
```

# 7.8 Example Problem P2

Given the following project description:

| Activity | Time (Days) | | | Immediate Predecessors |
|---|---|---|---|---|
| | Optimistic | Modal | Pessimistic | |
| 1 | 1.5 | 2 | 2.5 | none |
| 2 | 2 | 2.5 | 6 | 1 |
| 3 | 1 | 2 | 3 | none |
| 4 | 1.5 | 2 | 2.5 | 3 |
| 5 | 1 | 1 | 1 | 2,4 |
| 6 | 1 | 2 | 3 | 5 |
| 7 | 3 | 3.5 | 7 | 2,4 |
| 8 | 3 | 4 | 5 | 7 |
| 9 | 2 | 2 | 2 | 7,8 |

Determine:

1. The expected completion time.
2. The critical path.

## 7.8.1 Problem Preparation

No further preparation is needed, because the project description includes the activity numbers, the time estimates, and the immediate predecessors for each activity.

## 7.8.2 Data Input

The following data values must be input to solve this problem:

```
9, 3
1.5, 2, 2.5, 0
2, 2.5, 6, 1, 1
1, 2, 3, 0
1.5, 2, 2.5, 1, 3
1, 1, 1, 2, 2, 4
1, 2, 3, 1, 5
3, 3.5, 7, 2, 2, 4
3, 4, 5, 1, 7
2, 2, 2, 2, 7, 8
```

### 7.8.3 Computer Output

Figure 7.4 contains the output from a run of this problem. The first part of the RESULTS section shows the expected time of each activity. For example, activity 1 has an expected time of 2 days, activity 2 has an expected time of 3 days, and so on.

Activities 3 and 4 have one day slack, and activities 5 and 6 have seven days' slack. All other activities have 0 slack and are on the critical path.

The second part of the RESULTS section shows the earliest and latest start and finish times for every activity. These times are computed using the expected times.

The earliest that activity 4 is expected to start is two days after the project has begun, and the earliest that it is expected to finish is four days after the project has begun.

The latest that activity 4 can begin and not delay the overall project expected completion time is three days after the project has begun. Similarly, completion of activity 4 as late as five days after the project has begun will not delay the overall project schedule.

It is expected that this project will be completed in 15 days. The variance of this project completion time is 1.028 days.

**FIGURE 7.4**   Output from a run of example problem P2

```
                    -=*=-  INFORMATION ENTERED   -=*=-


NUMBER OF ACTIVITIES                 :        9

NUMBER OF TIME ESTIMATES             :        3


  ACTIVITY        OPTIMISTIC        MODAL          PESSIMISTIC
   NUMBER            TIME           TIME              TIME          PREDECESSORS

     1              1.500          2.000            2.500              NONE

     2              2.000          2.500            6.000               1

     3              1.000          2.000            3.000              NONE

     4              1.500          2.000            2.500               3

     5              1.000          1.000            1.000               2
                                                                       4

     6              1.000          2.000            3.000               5

     7              3.000          3.500            7.000               2
                                                                       4
```

(CONT.)

**FIGURE 7.4**  *(CONT.)*

| | | | | |
|---|---|---|---|---|
| 8 | 3.000 | 4.000 | 5.000 | 7 |
| 9 | 2.000 | 2.000 | 2.000 | 7 |
| | | | | 8 |

```
                    -=*=-  RESULTS  -=*=-


    ACTIVITY              EXPECTED                        CRITICAL
     NUMBER                 TIME              SLACK         PATH
        1                  2.000             0.000          YES
        2                  3.000             0.000          YES
        3                  2.000             1.000          NO
        4                  2.000             1.000          NO
        5                  1.000             7.000          NO
        6                  2.000             7.000          NO
        7                  4.000             0.000          YES
        8                  4.000             0.000          YES
        9                  2.000             0.000          YES


           -=*=-  ACTIVITY TIME SUMMARY  -=*=-

    ACTIVITY                              START          FINISH

        1        EARLIEST                 0.000           2.000
                 LATEST                   0.000           2.000

        2        EARLIEST                 2.000           5.000
                 LATEST                   2.000           5.000

        3        EARLIEST                 0.000           2.000
                 LATEST                   1.000           3.000

        4        EARLIEST                 2.000           4.000
                 LATEST                   3.000           5.000

        5        EARLIEST                 5.000           6.000
                 LATEST                  12.000          13.000

        6        EARLIEST                 6.000           8.000
                 LATEST                  13.000          15.000

        7        EARLIEST                 5.000           9.000
                 LATEST                   5.000           9.000

        8        EARLIEST                 9.000          13.000
                 LATEST                   9.000          13.000

        9        EARLIEST                13.000          15.000
                 LATEST                  13.000          15.000

EXPECTED COMPLETION TIME           :        15.000

CRITICAL VARIANCE                  :         1.028

     ----------  E N D   O F   A N A L Y S I S  ----------
```

# 7.9 Project Scheduling Problems

1. Determine the critical path and time for the following problem:

| Job | Immediate Predecessors | Estimated Time to Complete (Hrs) |
|-----|------------------------|----------------------------------|
| A | - | 5 |
| B | - | 6 |
| C | A | 2 |
| D | C | 4 |
| E | A | 1 |
| F | B | 8 |

2. The time actually needed to complete job A in problem 1 was 10 instead of the 5 that was estimated. The estimated times were correct for all other jobs.

   a) Use data contained on the printout from your solution to problem 1 to determine the actual project completion time.

   b) Rerun problem 1 with the new data for job A, and compare the results with your answer to part a. Are they the same?

3. Determine the critical path and time for the following problem:

| Job | Immediate Predecessors | Estimated Time to Complete (Hrs) |
|-----|------------------------|----------------------------------|
| A | - | 7 |
| B | - | 3 |
| C | B | 6 |
| D | A,C | 4 |
| E | D | 9 |
| F | C | 5 |
| G | E,F | 7 |

4. The time actually needed to complete job A in problem 3 was 9 instead of the 7 that was estimated. The estimated times were correct for all other jobs.

   a) Use the data contained in the printout from your solution to problem 3 to determine the actual project completion time.

   b) Rerun problem 3 with the new data for job A, and compare the results with your answer to part a. Are they the same?

5. Draw the PERT network for the following problem:

| Job | Immediate Predecessors | Estimated Time to Complete (Days) | Estimated Cost ($) |
|---|---|---|---|
| A | - | 20 | 1000 |
| B | - | 24 | 3500 |
| C | A | 16 | 2200 |
| D | A,B | 28 | 4000 |
| E | B | 10 | 1700 |

6. What is the project completion time, the total cost incurred by the tenth day if all jobs are completed on time, and the critical path for problem 5?

7. The time actually needed to complete each job in the problem 5 project was exactly the same as the original estimate. Unfortunately, however, job C could not begin immediately after job A was completed. Material delivery delays resulted in job C beginning after 35 days had elapsed.

a) Use the data contained in the printout from your solution to problem 6 to determine the actual project completion time.

b) Rerun problem 6 with the new data for job C, and compare the results with your answer to part a. Are they the same?

8. Draw the PERT network for the following problem:

| Job | Immediate Predecessors | Estimated Time to Complete (Hrs) | Estimated Cost ($) |
|---|---|---|---|
| 1 | - | 10 | 250 |
| 2 | - | 6 | 120 |
| 3 | - | 5 | 50 |
| 4 | 1,2 | 7 | 370 |
| 5 | 3,4 | 2 | 200 |

9. What is the project completion time, total cost, and the critical path for problem 8?

10. The project described in problem 8 had real trouble with job 3. First, the job could not start until two hours after jobs 1 and 2 began. Second, once it began, it took 15 hours to complete instead of the five hours that had been estimated.

a) Use the data contained in the printout from your solution to problem 9 to determine the actual project completion time.

b) Check this result by rerunning problem 9 with the new data for job 3.

11. Given the following PERT network:

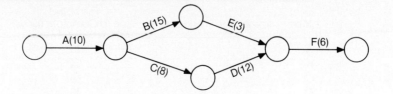

a) What is the earliest project completion time?
b) Find the slack time for each job.
c) Which jobs are on the critical path?
d) Construct the job table that describes this network.

12. Given the following PERT network:

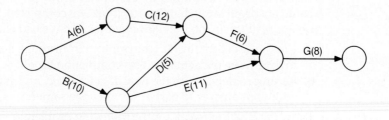

a) What is the earliest project completion time?
b) Find the slack time for each job.
c) Which jobs are on the critical path?
d) Construct the job table that describes this network.

13. Given the following PERT network:

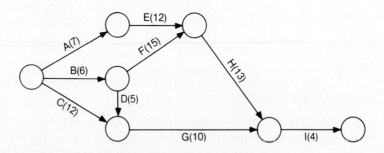

a) What is the earliest project completion time?
b) Find the slack time for each job.
c) Which jobs are on the critical path?
d) Construct the job table that describes the network.

14. The following information is used by a tract housing developer:

| Job Number | Job Description | Jobs That Must Be Completed before This Job Can Begin | Days Required to Complete Job |
|---|---|---|---|
| 1 | Pour Foundation | None | 5 |
| 2 | Build Walls | 1 | 7 |
| 3 | Build Roof | 2 | 5 |
| 4 | Install Plumbing | 2 | 3 |
| 5 | Install Wiring | 2 | 4 |
| 6 | Plaster Walls | 3,4,5 | 4 |
| 7 | Paint Walls | 6 | 2 |
| 8 | Install Lighting Fixtures | 7 | 1 |

a) How long does it take to build a house?

b) If the delivery of roofing materials was delayed three days, by how many days would the completion of the house be delayed?

c) If the installation of plumbing lines takes four days instead of three, and nothing else changed, by how many days would the completion of the house be delayed?

15. The chairperson responsible for running an annual professional development seminar wants to avoid the last minute rush that always seems to occur. The summary report is as follows:

The first step is to convince people to serve on the committee, which usually takes three weeks to accomplish. When the committee is formed, the seminar theme and major session topics must be selected, which also takes three weeks. When the theme and topics are selected, three different activities can begin: (1) Finding a keynote speaker (which usually takes five weeks), (2) finding a place to hold the meeting (which takes three weeks), and (3) finding speakers for each of the sessions (which takes six weeks).

When all the speakers (both keynote and session) are determined, arrangements can be made for audio-visual equipment. This takes one week. The brochure can be designed when all speakers are determined and a place has been found to hold the meeting. Brochure design, checking, and final approval requires six weeks. Once approved, the brochure can be printed and mailed. This takes two weeks. The seminar will take place five weeks after the brochures are mailed. The publicity chairman wants at least 12 weeks between the time the location of the meeting is set and the date of the meeting. This long lead time is needed to get announcements into newsletters and newspapers.

a) How long before the meeting should the chairman begin getting people to serve on the committee?

b) One year it took eight weeks to find a keynote speaker. If the chairman wants to avoid the problems caused by such a delay, how many weeks earlier should it begin? (This is the number of weeks earlier than the answer given to part a).

16. Consider the following network:

|  |  | Time (Days) | | |
| --- | --- | --- | --- | --- |
| Activity | Immediate Predecessors | Optimistic | Modal | Pessimistic |
| A | – | 2 | 6 | 10 |
| B | – | 1 | 4 | 7 |
| C | A | 4 | 8 | 14 |
| D | B | 2 | 6 | 8 |
| E | C,D | 5 | 5 | 5 |

Determine:

a) Critical time and path.

b) Critical path variance.

17. Given the following network diagram and activity times,

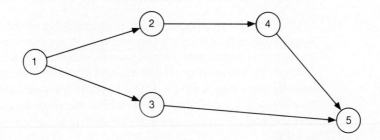

|  | Time (Days) | | |
| --- | --- | --- | --- |
| Activity | Optimistic | Modal | Pessimistic |
| 1-2 | 2 | 3 | 7 |
| 1-3 | 1 | 5 | 9 |
| 2-4 | 8 | 12 | 17 |
| 3-5 | 6 | 7 | 8 |
| 4-5 | 4 | 4 | 4 |

a) What is the expected project completion time?

b) What is the variance?

c) What is the latest start time for activity 3-5 that will not delay the project?

18. Longton Motors is a small, custom race-car manufacturer. It combines standard and custom components to produce a care that meets the buyer's specifications. The typical job has the following schedule data:

| Activity Number | Activity | Time (Days) | Immediate Predecessors |
|---|---|---|---|
| 1 | Engine Delivery | 14 | none |
| 2 | Engine Modification | 6 | 1 |
| 3 | Make Frame and Body | 10 | none |
| 4 | Assemble Car | 2 | 2,3 |
| 5 | Test and Tuning | 4* | 4 |

*Test & tuning requires a minimum of four days, and it typically gets done in that time, but problems occasionally arise that cause this to take up to 12 days.

How long does it take to build a typical car?

19. Longton Motors has orders for two cars. The engine crew works as a team on both engine modification and test and tuning. It can work on only one of these activities at a time. Similarly, the body crew works as a team on either making frames and bodies or on assembly. The work is scheduled as follows:

*Engine Crew*

Car 1 Engine modification

Car 2 Engine modification

Car 1 Test and tuning

Car 2 Test and tuning

*Body Crew*

Car 1 Make frame, and body

Car 2 Make frame, and body

Car 1 Assemble

Car 2 Assemble

The other data given in the previous problem also apply to this problem. How long will it take to complete both cars?

## CASE STUDY **The Research Testing Corporation**

The Research Testing Corporation (RTC) is a $100 million a year corporation located in Boston, Mass. RTC specializes in testing complex chemical compounds and has recently been awarded a contract to study the durability of ten different enamel protective coatings. Each coating will be evaluated with a simulated weather test, a nonabrasive wear test, and an abrasive wear test. All three tests can be run in parallel with different samples of each coating.

The simulated weather test uses 60 days of alternating high pressure water sprays (for two days) and high intensity lights (for 10 days). This cycle is repeated five times on a 24 hour basis. The weather simulator can hold all ten samples. However, it is currently being used and will not be available until August 15. The nonabrasive wear test uses a machine that continuously rolls a hard rubber roller back and forth on a sample of each coating for 25 days. The roller is under a constant 500 lb. load for 20 days and a 2000 lb. load for 5 days. They have only one of these machines, and it can test only five samples at a time. It is also currently being used and will be available on August 20.

The abrasive wear test uses a buffing machine with a fine grit buffing compound. The reflectivity of each sample is checked every five hours during the fifteen days required for this test. This machine is currently available, and can test two samples at a time. It requires 5 days to apply the coatings to the samples, and cure them prior to testing. All of the tests can begin when the samples are ready.

RTC has divided the new contract into the following major tasks:

- Conduct coating tests.
- Write a test report which requires 10 days after the last test is completed.
- Survey organizations who use this type of coating. This survey requires nine weeks.
- Prepare a final report which can not begin until both the test report and the survey are completed. The final report takes two weeks to complete.

a) Today is July 23. What is the earliest completion date for the final report?

b) The chief testing engineer believes that a full eight week nonabrasive test will give more accurate results than the current 50 day test. If this suggestion is implemented, on what date will the final report be completed?

# 8

## NETW

# *Network Models*

Network problems are described by a set of nodes connected by links (or arcs, as they are called in many texts). The various types of network problems are distinguished by different interpretations of the nodes and links. Three types of network models are covered here: *minimum spanning tree, maximum flow,* and *shortest route*

The minimum spanning tree model finds a set of links to connect all nodes in a network so that the sum of the lengths of the selected links is as small as possible. A typical problem involves minimizing the total length of telephone wire required to connect a group of cities so that someone in any one of the cities can call someone in any other city. Note that there is no need to have all cities connected directly to each other, since customers do not care how their call is routed.

The maximum network flow model finds the maximum volume that can flow from any specified node to any other specified node in a network. The maximum flow that can be handled by each link must be known. A typical problem involves the flow of some fluid through a network where each of the links are pipes. As with all management science models, maximum network flow problems are not restricted to this one type of problem. Another type of problem involves the flow of products through the various stages of a production process.

The shortest route model finds the shortest route from any one node to any other node in a network. A typical problem involves finding the shortest time or shortest distance route to move a vehicle (taxi, fire truck, and so on) from one location to another over the streets of a city.

The minimum spanning tree problem is frequently confused with the shortest route problem. One distinction between these two is that a minimum spanning tree problem is almost always a design or construction problem, and a shortest route problem is almost always an operations problem. The links already exist in a shortest route problem, and you are trying to find the shortest route over the existing links (roads, airline routes, wires, and so on) to go from one node to another node. The minimum spanning tree problem involves connecting (or building) the links that connect all nodes with the shortest network.

Another difference between these two models involves the number of nodes that must be included in the solution. The minimum spanning tree problem requires that all nodes be included. The shortest route problem, however, requires only that two nodes (the start node and the destination node) are included. If any other nodes are included in the solution, it is only because including them results in the shortest route between the start node and the destination node.

# 8.1 Program Description

The program solves each of the three models for networks with up to 25 nodes and 25 links. Interpretation of the network, input details, and output details are similar for all three models.

In minimum spanning tree problems, the link lengths represent distances between nodes. The distance between any two nodes must be the same in each direction (symmetric). The program outputs the total length of the minimum spanning tree and identifies all links that are included.

In maximum flow problems, each link length is used to represent the maximum flow rate between two nodes. All flow rates must be one-way flows (asymmetric), so if two-way flow is possible between two modes, this link must be entered as two one-way flows. The program determines the maximum flow rate between any two specified nodes (called the *source* node and the *sink* node). The flow through each link in the network is also part of the program output.

In shortest route problems, each link length is used to represent either the distance or the travel time between two nodes. Problems with either symmetric or asymmetric links can be solved with this model. The program finds the shortest route between any two specified nodes (called the *starting* node and the *destination* node). Output includes the total length of the shortest route and a description of the complete route from the starting node to the destination node.

# 8.2 Problem Preparation

Each node must be identified by a unique integer beginning with the number 1. No gaps are allowed in these node identification numbers. (If you have a network of three nodes, they must be numbered 1, 2, and 3. The program would not run correctly if you numbered them 1, 3, and 7.)

All links must also be identified by integers. Link identification numbers must also begin with "1" and must not contain any gaps. You may select any link to be number 1, any of the remaining links to be number 2, and so on.

Node number 1 must be the source or starting node in maximum flow and shortest route problems. Similarly, in maximum flow and shortest route problems, the sink or destination node must be the highest numbered node in the network. There are no such requirements in minimum spanning tree problems.

## 8.3  Data Input Overview

The program first asks which of the three network models is to be solved. If the shortest route model is selected, the next input indicates whether the network links are symmetric or asymmetric. A network is symmetric when the distance between every pair of nodes is identical in each direction. A network is asymmetric if at least one link is restricted to one-way traffic or if at least one pair of nodes has different distances for travel in each direction. The shortest route model is the only one that allows either type of network. All minimum spanning tree networks must be symmetric, and all maximum flow networks must be asymmetric.

The remaining data describe the length of each link. For each link (in numerical order), input the identification number of the node at one end (called the *start* node), the identification number of the node at the other end (called the *end* node), and the length of the link.

If the network is symmetric, it makes no difference which node identification number is input first. Only one pair of node numbers and one length are input for each link. However, if the network is asymmetric, then *every* entry into the computer must be a one-way link. For each of these entries, the direction of movement (flow or travel) is from the first (start) node to the second (end) node. If a link in the original problem actually allows two-way movement, it must be entered into the computer as if it were two one-way links.

## 8.4  Data Input Details

When entering problem data from the keyboard, the first input indicates the model that is to be solved:

> the number of
> the desired model:
> minimum spanning tree (1)
> maximum flow (2)
> shortest route (3)

If model 3 (shortest route) is selected, this is followed by:

> S if all links
> are symmetric or
> A if all links
> are asymmetric

For all models, the next input is as follows:

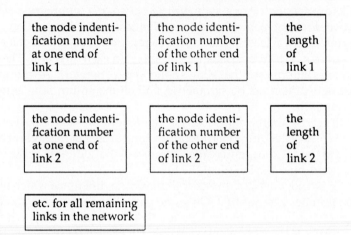

| number of nodes in the network | , | number of links in the network |

The remaining data values describe each of the links:

| the node indentification number at one end of link 1 | the node identification number of the other end of link 1 | the length of link 1 |

| the node indentification number at one end of link 2 | the node identification number of the other end of link 2 | the length of link 2 |

| etc. for all remaining links in the network |

## 8.5 Editing the Data

Editing features are a part of both the ENTER PROBLEM FROM KEYBOARD option and the EDIT CURRENT PROBLEM option. The problem structure (but not the problem data values) may be changed in the ENTER PROBLEM FROM KEYBOARD option and the problem data (but not the problem structure) may be changed in the EDIT CURRENT PROBLEM option.

The first part of the ENTER PROBLEM FROM KEYBOARD option is used to enter the problem structure. This includes an indication of whether links are symmetric or asymmetric (for the shortest route model only), the number of nodes, and the number of links. After these data are entered, the program will ask if you want to re-enter the problem structure. Type "Y" if any of the problem structure values are incorrect. The program will then repeat all of the problem structure prompts to allow the correct data to be entered.

The EDIT CURRENT PROBLEM option is used to change any of the link lengths. Prompts on the screen will guide you through this. The program will first display all the problem data in tabular form at the top of the screen. A message at the bottom of the screen will ask you to enter the number of the link to edit. After pressing the appropriate number, the cursor will move to the left of the value that is to be changed. Type the correct value and press the ENTER key. The cursor will again be at the bottom of the screen. Continue this process until no further values need editing. The program will ask if you want to save these data values. Type "Y" if the edited data are to be saved on a diskette, or type "N" if not. The program will then return to the PROGRAM OPTIONS menu.

# 8.6 Program Output

Each of the three models uses a different output format, so each will be discussed separately.

### 8.6.1 Minimum Spanning Tree

The main portion of the program output names the links that collectively make up the minimum spanning tree. For each of these links, the program outputs the identification number of the node at one end (START NODE), the identification number of the node at the other end (END NODE), and the length of the link (LINK LENGTH). The last item output is the sum of the lengths of all the links that are part of the minimum spanning tree (TOTAL LENGTH).

Some problems may have multiple optimal solutions. When this occurs, a different spanning tree will have the same length as the one that is output. This program does not indicate if multiple optimal solutions exist.

### 8.6.2 Maximum Flow

The program first outputs a table of all flow paths through the network. These flow paths are all from the input node (the lowest numbered START NODE) to the output node (the highest numbered END NODE). The total flow over each path (FLOW) and the node identification numbers of all nodes on each path are also output.

Next the program outputs the flow over each link that is part of the optimal solution. The direction of flow is always from the first node listed (START NODE) to the second node listed (END NODE). The value of the flow over each of these links is given in the last column (FLOW).

Last the program outputs the maximum total flow from the input node through the complete network to the output node. Some problems may have multiple optimal solutions. When this occurs, a different set of flow paths will have the same maximum total flow. This program does not indicate if multiple optimal solutions exist.

### 8.6.3 Shortest Route

#### Information Entered

First, the program will output a table that contains the following for each link:

*Link number.* The link identification number.

*Start node.* The node that is used to enter a link in an asymmetric network.

*End node.* The node that is used to exit a link in an asymmetric network.

*Link length.* The one-way distance from the start node to the end node.

*Reverse length.* The one-way distance from the end node to the start node. If there is no one-way link from the end node to the start node, the program will print a "—". If we were being mathematically fussy about this, it should really be infinity.

#### Results

The program results describe the complete path from the starting node to the destination node. Each link in this path is described by printing the identification number of the node at the beginning of the link (START NODE), the identification number of the node at the end of the link (END NODE), and the length of the link (DISTANCE). The last item output is the total length of the selected path (TOTAL DISTANCE).

Some problems may have multiple optimal solutions. When this occurs, different paths will also have the same distance from start to end. This program does not indicate if multiple optimal solutions exist.

## 8.7 Example Problem ST1

Find the minimum spanning tree for the following network:

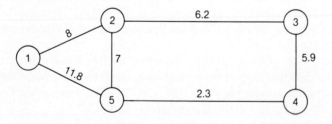

### 8.7.1 Problem Preparation

The nodes are already correctly numbered (1 through 5), so the only required preparation is to assign numbers to the six links. The result of this is as follows:

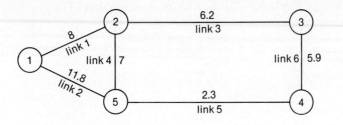

## 8.7.2 Data Input

The following data values must be input to solve this problem:

        5, 6
        1, 2, 8
        1, 5, 11.8
        2, 3, 6.2
        5, 2, 7
        4, 5, 2.3
        3, 4, 5.9

Figure 8.1 shows how the problem structure should be input. Figure 8.2 shows how the screen looks after the last data value has been entered into the input table.

**FIGURE 8.1**    Input of problem structure for example problem ST1

```
          -=*=-   SET UP MINIMUM SPANNING TREE PROBLEM STRUCTURE   -=*=-


ENTER NUMBER OF NODES IN NETWORK
ENTER NUMBER IN RANGE ( 1  -  25 ) & press ↵    5

ENTER NUMBER OF LINKS IN NETWORK
ENTER NUMBER IN RANGE ( 1  -  25 ) & press ↵    6


DO YOU WANT TO RE-ENTER PROBLEM STRUCTURE? (Y/N)
Enter a Character ( Y  or  N ) & press ↵    N
```

**FIGURE 8.2**   Computer screen after input of all data for example problem ST1

```
                    -=*=-  INPUT  DATA  -=*=-


     LINK            START            END            LINK
     NUMBER          NODE             NODE           LENGTH

       1               1               2              8.000
       2               1               5             11.800
       3               2               3              6.200
       4               5               2              7.000
       5               4               5              2.300
       6               3               4         5.9

===================================================================
FOR EACH LINK: ENTER STARTING & ENDING NODE NUMBERS AND DISTANCE BETWEEN NODES
               STARTING & ENDING NODE NUMBERS CAN NOT BE EDITED
               press ↵ TO COMPLETE EACH INFORMATION ITEM
```

## 8.7.3 Computer Output

Figure 8.3 contains the output from a run of this problem. The results show that the total length of the minimum spanning tree is 22.4. The links that are part of the solution include those that connect nodes 1 and 2, 2 and 3, 3 and 4, and 4 and 5.

**FIGURE 8.3**   Output from a run of example problem ST1

```
                    -=*=-  INFORMATION ENTERED  -=*=-


                        MINIMUM SPANNING TREE

     NUMBER OF NODES              :  5
     NUMBER OF LINKS              :  6

     LINK            START            END            LINK
     NUMBER          NODE             NODE           LENGTH

       1               1               2              8.000
       2               1               5             11.800
       3               2               3              6.200
       4               5               2              7.000
       5               4               5              2.300
       6               3               4              5.900
```

(CONT.)

**FIGURE 8.3**   *(CONT.)*

```
            -=*=-   MINIMUM SPANNING TREE RESULTS   -=*=-


        START                END                    LINK
        NODE                 NODE                   LENGTH

          1                   2                    8.000
          2                   3                    6.200
          3                   4                    5.900
          4                   5                    2.300

        TOTAL LENGTH:    22.4


        ----------   E N D   O F   A N A L Y S I S   ----------
```

# 8.8  Example Problem MF1

Find the maximum flow from node 1 to node 3:

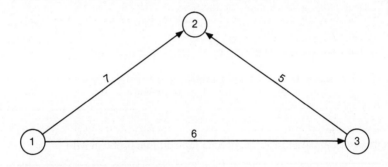

## 8.8.1 Problem Preparation

The nodes are already correctly numbered (1 through 3) and the maximum possible flow between each pair of nodes is shown on the link that connects them. The only required preparation is to assign link numbers to each of the three links. The result is as follows:

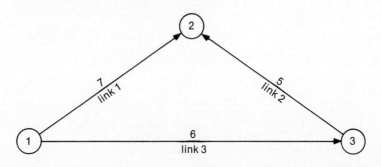

## 8.8.2 Data Input

The following data values must be input to solve this problem:

        3, 3
        1, 2, 7
        3, 2, 5
        1, 3, 6

Figure 8.4 shows how the problem structure should be input. Figure 8.5 shows how the screen looks after the last data value has been entered into the input table.

FIGURE 8.4    Input of problem structure for example problem MF1

```
              -=*=-   SET UP MAXIMUM FLOW PROBLEM STRUCTURE   -=*=-

ENTER NUMBER OF NODES IN NETWORK
ENTER NUMBER IN RANGE ( 1  -  25 ) & press ↵    3

ENTER NUMBER OF LINKS IN NETWORK
ENTER NUMBER IN RANGE ( 1  -  25 ) & press ↵    3


DO YOU WANT TO RE-ENTER PROBLEM STRUCTURE?  (Y/N)
Enter a Character ( Y  or  N ) & press ↵    N
```

FIGURE 8.5    Computer screen after input of all data for example problem MF1

```
                    -=*=-   INPUT  DATA   -=*=-


     LINK            START             END
    NUMBER           NODE              NODE              FLOW

      1               1                 2                7.000
      2               3                 2                5.000
      3               1                 3         6

================================================================
FOR EACH LINK: ENTER STARTING & ENDING NODE NUMBERS AND FLOW BETWEEN NODES
           STARTING & ENDING NODE NUMBERS CAN NOT BE EDITED
              press ↵ TO COMPLETE EACH INFORMATION ITEM
```

### 8.8.3 Computer Output

Figure 8.6 contains the output from a run of this problem. This simple problem has flow only over the link connecting nodes 1 and 3. The maximum possible flow is 6.

## 8.9  Example Problem MF2

Find the maximum flow from node A to node C:

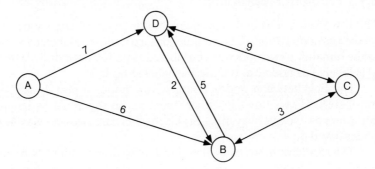

**FIGURE 8.6**   Output from a run of example problem MF1

```
                        -=*=-   INFORMATION ENTERED   -=*=-


                                 MAXIMUM FLOW

      NUMBER OF NODES                    :   3
      NUMBER OF LINKS                    :   3

        LINK           START             END
       NUMBER          NODE              NODE                  FLOW

         1              1                 2                    7.000
         2              3                 2                    5.000
         3              1                 3                    6.000


                    -=*=-   MAXIMUM FLOW RESULTS   -=*=-

OPTIMAL FLOW FROM:

NODE 1 TO NODE  3

FLOW        NODES THAT DEFINE EACH PATH

 6         1    3
                    START                 END
                    NODE                  NODE                 FLOW

                     1                     3                  6.000
```

(CONT.)

**FIGURE 8.6**   *(CONT.)*

```
            MAXIMUM TOTAL NETWORK FLOW:    6


            ----------   E N D   O F   A N A L Y S I S   ----------
```

## 8.9.1 Problem Preparation

There are four nodes in this problem. Node A is the source node, so it must be
labeled as node 1. Node C is the sink node, so it must be labeled as node 4. Either
of the remaining two nodes can be labeled as node 2 or node 3. Arbitrarily, node
D is labeled as node 2 and node B is labeled node 3.

    The link between nodes D and C (or nodes 2 and 4, as they are now
numbered) allows flows in either direction, so this must be entered into the
computer as two one-way links. Similarly, there are two one-way links between
nodes 3 and 4.

    The resultant network (where L refers to link number, N refers to a node
number, and F refers to the maximum flow over a link) looks like the following:

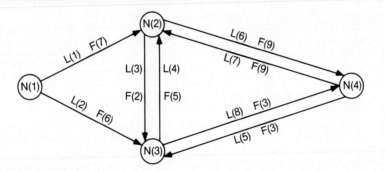

## 8.9.2 Data Input

The following data values must be input to solve this problem:

      4, 8
      1, 2, 7
      1, 3, 6
      2, 3, 2
      3, 2, 5
      4, 3, 3
      2, 4, 9
      4, 2, 9
      3, 4, 3

## 8.9.3 Computer Output

Figure 8.7 contains the output from a run of this problem. The first part of the RESULTS section shows that there are three flow paths through this network. Seven units flow from node 1 through node 2 to node 4, two units flow from node 1 through nodes 3 and 2 to node 4, and three units flow from node 1 through node 3 to node 4.

The second part of the RESULTS section shows the total flow through each link that connects each pair of nodes. Seven units flow from node 1 to node 2, five units flow from 1 to 3, nine units flow from 2 to 4, two units flow from 3 to 2, and

**FIGURE 8.7**   Output from a run of example problem MF2

```
                     -=*=-   INFORMATION ENTERED   -=*=-


                              MAXIMUM FLOW

        NUMBER OF NODES                    :   4
        NUMBER OF LINKS                    :   8

         LINK              START            END
        NUMBER             NODE             NODE                FLOW

           1                 1               2                7.000
           2                 1               3                6.000
           3                 2               3                2.000
           4                 3               2                5.000
           5                 4               3                3.000
           6                 2               4                9.000
           7                 4               2                9.000
           8                 3               4                3.000


                     -=*=-   MAXIMUM FLOW RESULTS   -=*=-

OPTIMAL FLOW FROM:

NODE 1 TO NODE   4

FLOW        NODES THAT DEFINE EACH PATH

 7          1    2    4
 2          1    3    2    4
 3          1    3    4
                 START            END
                 NODE             NODE                FLOW

                  1                2                7.000
                  1                3                5.000
                  2                4                9.000
                  3                2                2.000
                  3                4                3.000

        MAXIMUM TOTAL NETWORK FLOW:      12


        ----------   E N D   O F   A N A L Y S I S   ----------
```

three units flow from 3 to 4.

A total of 12 units flow from the input at node 1 to the output at node 4.

# 8.10 Example Problem SR1:

Find the shortest route from node 1 to node 5:

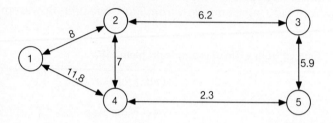

## 8.10.1 Problem Preparation

The nodes are properly numbered, so the only required preparation is to number the links:

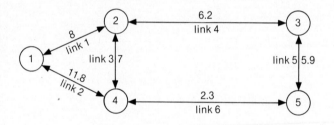

## 8.10.2 Data Input

The following data values must be input to solve this problem:

        S, 5, 6
        1, 2, 8
        1, 4, 11.8
        2, 4, 7
        2, 3, 6.2
        3, 5, 5.9
        5, 4, 2.3

Figure 8.8 shows how the problem structure should be input. Figure 8.9 shows how the screen looks after the last data value has been entered into the input table. Values for REVERSE LENGTH are automatically placed into the table by the program.

**FIGURE 8.8**    Input of problem structure for example problem SR1

```
              -=*=-  SET UP SHORTEST ROUTE PROBLEM STRUCTURE   -=*=-


SYMMETRIC (S) OR ASYMMETRIC (A) NODES
Enter a Character ( S  or  A ) & press ↵      S

ENTER NUMBER OF NODES IN NETWORK
ENTER NUMBER IN RANGE ( 1  -  25 ) & press ↵     5

ENTER NUMBER OF LINKS IN NETWORK
ENTER NUMBER IN RANGE ( 1  -  25 ) & press ↵     6


DO YOU WANT TO RE-ENTER PROBLEM STRUCTURE? (Y/N)
Enter a Character ( Y  or  N ) & press ↵    N
```

**FIGURE 8.9**    Computer screen after input of all data for example problem SR1

```
              -=*=-   INPUT  DATA  -=*=-


    LINK          START          END           LINK        REVERSE
   NUMBER          NODE          NODE          LENGTH        LENGTH

      1             1             2            8.000         8.000
      2             1             4           11.800        11.800
      3             2             4            7.000         7.000
      4             2             3            6.200         6.200
      5             3             5            5.900         5.900
      6             5             4      2.3




FOR EACH LINK:  ENTER STARTING & ENDING NODE NUMBERS AND DISTANCE BETWEEN NODES
                STARTING & ENDING NODE NUMBERS CAN NOT BE EDITED
                press ↵ TO COMPLETE EACH INFORMATION ITEM
```

## 8.10.3 Computer Output

Figure 8.10 contains the output from a run of this problem. The RESULTS section of the output shows that the shortest route goes from node 1 to node 4 and then to node 5. The total distance is 14.1

**FIGURE 8.10**   Output from a run of example problem SR1

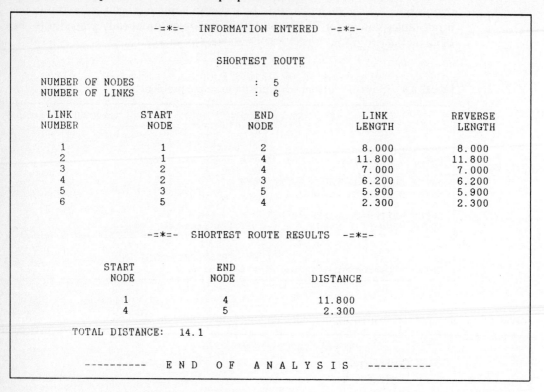

```
                        -=*=-   INFORMATION ENTERED   -=*=-


                            SHORTEST ROUTE

   NUMBER OF NODES                    :  5
   NUMBER OF LINKS                    :  6

     LINK             START            END            LINK            REVERSE
    NUMBER            NODE             NODE           LENGTH           LENGTH

       1                1               2              8.000            8.000
       2                1               4             11.800           11.800
       3                2               4              7.000            7.000
       4                2               3              6.200            6.200
       5                3               5              5.900            5.900
       6                5               4              2.300            2.300


             -=*=-   SHORTEST ROUTE RESULTS   -=*=-


            START            END
            NODE             NODE             DISTANCE

             1                4               11.800
             4                5                2.300

       TOTAL DISTANCE:   14.1


       ----------   E N D   O F   A N A L Y S I S   ----------
```

# 8.11  Example Problem SR2

Find the shortest route from node A to node C:

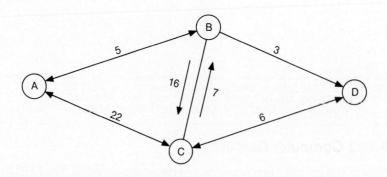

### 8.11.1 Problem Preparation

Two adjustments are required for this problem. First the nodes must be assigned node numbers, where node A must be given node number 1 (because it is the starting node), and node C must be given node number 4 (because it is the destination node). Node B is given node number 2 and node D is given node number 3. Next all the links must be redrawn as one-way links.

The result of these adjustments (where L refers to a link number, N refers to a node number, and D is the distance between two nodes) is as follows:

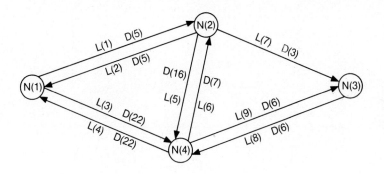

### 8.11.2 Data Input

The following data values must be input to solve this problem:

A, 4, 9
1, 2, 5
2, 1, 5
1, 4, 22
4, 1, 22
2, 4, 16
4, 2, 7
2, 3, 3
3, 4, 6
4, 3, 6

### 8.11.3 Computer Output

Figure 8.11 contains the output from a run of this problem. The RESULTS section of the output shows that the shortest route goes from node 1 to node 2, then to node 3, and finally to node 4. The total distance is 14.

**FIGURE 8.11**    Output from a run of example problem SR2

```
          -=*=-   INFORMATION ENTERED  -=*=-


                  SHORTEST ROUTE

   NUMBER OF NODES              :  4
   NUMBER OF LINKS              :  9

     LINK          START          END         LINK        REVERSE
    NUMBER         NODE           NODE        LENGTH       LENGTH

      1              1             2           5.000        5.000
      2              2             1           5.000        5.000
      3              1             4          22.000       22.000
      4              4             1          22.000       22.000
      5              2             4          16.000        7.000
      6              4             2           7.000       16.000
      7              2             3           3.000          -
      8              3             4           6.000        6.000


     LINK          START          END         LINK        REVERSE
    NUMBER         NODE           NODE        LENGTH       LENGTH

      9              4             3           6.000        6.000


        -=*=-   SHORTEST ROUTE RESULTS  -=*=-


        START          END
        NODE           NODE        DISTANCE

         1              2           5.000
         2              3           3.000
         3              4           6.000

   TOTAL DISTANCE:   14

   ----------   E N D   O F   A N A L Y S I S   ----------
```

# 8.12  Network Problems

## 8.12.1 Minimum Spanning Tree Problems

1. Find the minimum spanning tree for the following network:

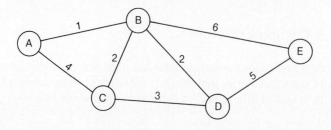

2. Find the minimum spanning tree for the following network:

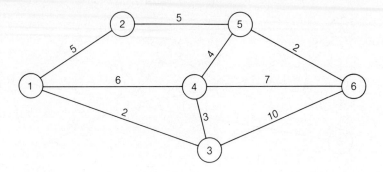

3. Find the minimum spanning tree for the following network:

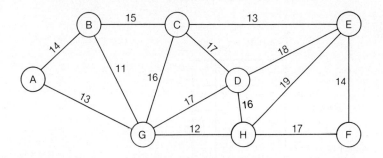

4. Find the minimum spanning tree for the following network:

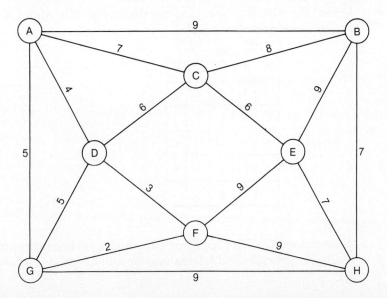

5. Find the minimum spanning tree for the following network:

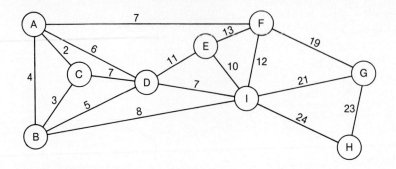

6. Find the minimum spanning tree that connects cities A through D if all table entries are distances in miles.

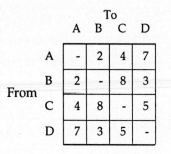

|      | To |     |     |     |
|------|----|-----|-----|-----|
|      | A  | B   | C   | D   |
| **A** | -  | 2   | 4   | 7   |
| **B** | 2  | -   | 8   | 3   |
| **C** | 4  | 8   | -   | 5   |
| **D** | 7  | 3   | 5   | -   |

From

7. Find the minimum spanning tree that connects locations A to E if all table entries are distances in miles:

|      | To |     |     |     |     |
|------|----|-----|-----|-----|-----|
|      | A  | B   | C   | D   | E   |
| **A** | -  | 3   | 5   | 4   | -   |
| **B** | 3  | -   | 7   | 2   | 1   |
| **C** | 5  | 7   | -   | -   | 6   |
| **D** | 4  | 2   | -   | -   | 5   |
| **E** | -  | 1   | 6   | 5   | -   |

From

8. Intermountain Telephone Company intends to install lines to connect Gold City, Copperville, and Adams Junction to its telephone exchange in Durango.

Survey crews have determined that the lowest cost route between each pair of cities is as follows:

Between Durango and:
   Gold City—$570,000
   Copperville—$230,000
   Adams Junction—$340,000
Between Gold City and:
   Copperville—$890,000
   Adams Junction—$150,000
Between Copperville and Adams Junction—$90,000

a) Which routes should be used to connect all cities at the minimum cost?
b) What is the minimum cost?

9. A cable T.V. company has received approval to begin service in the city. It needs three transmitters (at locations, B, C, and D) to ensure high-quality service to all subscribers. The cost (in millions of dollars) of connecting each of the transmitters to its main station at location A are shown in the following figure:

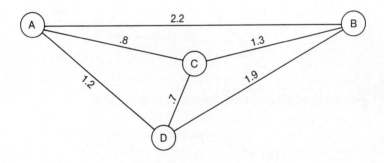

What is the minimum cost of a network that allows station A to transmit a signal to transmitters at B, C, and D?

10. A small oil company's business has grown to the point where it is no longer economical to use trucks to deliver gasoline from the refinery at Danning to each of the four other cities. The costs (in millions of dollars) of building a pipeline between each pair of cities is given in the table.

|  | To: | | | | |
| From: | Apton | Berryville | Connors | Danning | Eggar |
| Apton | - | 2.3 | 7.2 | 1.6 | 5.5 |
| Berryville | 2.3 | - | 6.7 | 3.1 | 5.4 |
| Connors | 7.2 | 6.7 | - | 7.5 | 10.3 |
| Danning | 1.6 | 3.1 | 7.5 | - | 6.2 |
| Eggar | 5.5 | 5.4 | 10.3 | 6.2 | - |

Which lines should be built to minimize the total cost of constructing a pipe network that will allow the company to pump gasoline from Danning to any other city?

### 8.12.2 Maximum Flow Problems

11. Find the maximum flow from A to E:

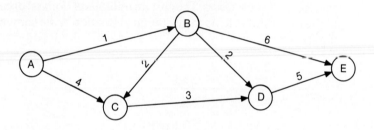

12. Find maximum flow from node 1 to node 6:

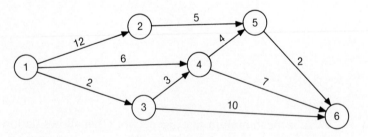

13. Use the same network given in problem 12 to find the maximum flow from node 3 to node 6.

14. Find the maximum possible flow through the network from A to D, if all table entries are the maximum possible flow (in gallons per minute) between each pair of nodes:

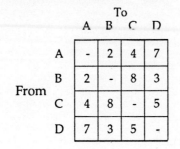

To

|      |   | A | B | C | D |
|------|---|---|---|---|---|
|      | A | - | 2 | 4 | 7 |
| From | B | 2 | - | 8 | 3 |
|      | C | 4 | 8 | - | 5 |
|      | D | 7 | 3 | 5 | - |

15. Find the maximum possible flow from A to E through the network, if all table entries are the maximum possible flow (in cubic feet per minute) between each pair of nodes:

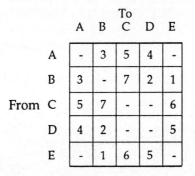

To

|      |   | A | B | C | D | E |
|------|---|---|---|---|---|---|
|      | A | - | 3 | 5 | 4 | - |
|      | B | 3 | - | 7 | 2 | 1 |
| From | C | 5 | 7 | - | - | 6 |
|      | D | 4 | 2 | - | - | 5 |
|      | E | - | 1 | 6 | 5 | - |

16. Find the maximum flow from A to D if all table entries are in gallons per minute. (Note that the maximum possible flow between each pair of nodes is not symmetric.)

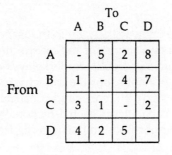

To

|      |   | A | B | C | D |
|------|---|---|---|---|---|
|      | A | - | 5 | 2 | 8 |
| From | B | 1 | - | 4 | 7 |
|      | C | 3 | 1 | - | 2 |
|      | D | 4 | 2 | 5 | - |

17. Find the maximum flow from location $X_1$ to location $X_4$. Note that the link between $X_2$ and $X_3$ is the only one that allows two-way flow.

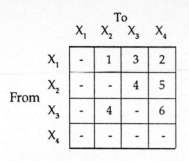

18. The phone company has just completed a new microwave telephone network between Los Angeles and New York. There is one link between Los Angeles and Denver (with a capacity of 2000 simultaneous calls), one between Los Angeles and Phoenix (100 call capacity), one between Phoenix and St. Louis (700 call capacity), one between Denver and New York (2300 call capacity), one between St. Louis and New York (800 call capacity), and one between Denver and St. Louis (900 call capacity). What is the maximum number of simultaneous calls that can be handled between Los Angeles and New York?

19. The following network is a simplified version of the San Francisco freeway system:

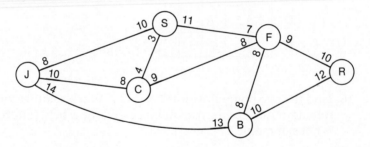

Each number represents the freeway capacity in thousands of vehicles per hour. The numbers at each end represent the maximum flow out of the node. Thus the freeway from San Jose (J) to Berkeley/Oakland (B) has a capacity of 14,000 vehicles per hour, but the capacity from B to J is only 13,000 vehicles per hour. Design differences and construction projects will generally result in different capacities in each direction. What is the capacity of this freeway system for northbound traffic going from San Jose (J) to San Rafael (R)?

20. The effective capacity of the freeway to handle through traffic has been reduced because a baseball game has just ended at Candlestick Park (C). The capacity from C to San Francisco (F) is now 4 instead of 9, the capacity from C to Skyline Drive (S) is 2 instead of 4, and the capacity from C to J is 6 instead

of 8. What is the northbound (J) to (R) through-traffic capacity of the freeway during this period of congestion?

## 8.12.3 Shortest Route Problems

21. Find the shortest route from A to E:

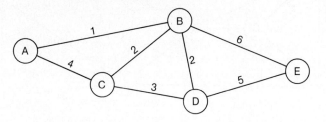

22. Find the shortest route from node 1 to node 6:

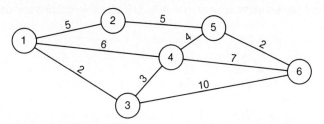

23. Use the same network given in problem 22 to find the shortest route from node 2 to node 3.

24. What is the shortest route from A to E in the following network?

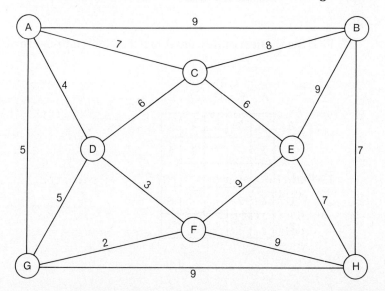

25. What is the shortest route from D to F in the following network?

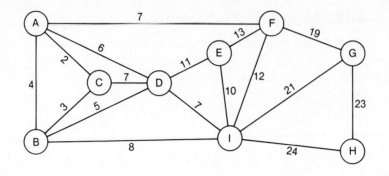

26. Find the shortest route from A to D if all table entries are distances in miles:

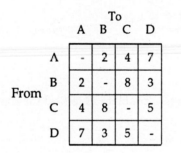

To

|  | | A | B | C | D |
|---|---|---|---|---|---|
| | A | - | 2 | 4 | 7 |
| From | B | 2 | - | 8 | 3 |
| | C | 4 | 8 | - | 5 |
| | D | 7 | 3 | 5 | - |

27. Find the shortest route from A to E if all table entries are distances in miles:

To

|  | | A | B | C | D | E |
|---|---|---|---|---|---|---|
| | A | - | 3 | 5 | 4 | - |
| | B | 3 | - | 7 | 2 | 1 |
| From | C | 5 | 7 | - | - | 6 |
| | D | 4 | 2 | - | - | 5 |
| | E | - | 1 | 6 | 5 | - |

28. Find the shortest route from A to D if all table entries are distances in miles:

|  |  | To |  |  |
|---|---|---|---|---|
|  | A | B | C | D |
| A | - | 5 | 2 | 8 |
| From B | 1 | - | 4 | 7 |
| C | 3 | 1 | - | 2 |
| D | 4 | 2 | 5 | - |

29. The Ajax Corporation has performed an extensive study of its computer needs for the next four years. It knows that computers become cheaper every year, but it also knows that obtaining a new computer involves conversion costs that are sometimes substantial. The analysts have presented the following data to management:

| Year in Which Computer is Available | Computer | Conversion Cost | Yearly Cost |
|---|---|---|---|
|  | Current |  | 1,000,000 |
| Now | A | 250,000 | 810,000 |
| Next Year | B | 200,000 | 650,000 |
| 2 Years | C | 250,000 | 500,000 |
| 3 Years | D | 300,000 | 400,000 |

What sequence of computers should the company acquire if it wishes to minimize total computer-related expenditures over the next four years?

30. Short-Haul Truck Lines ships items to cities throughout California. Its minimum package rates between cities are as follows:

|  | Pomona | San Diego |
|---|---|---|
| Long Beach | 3.10 | 4.90 |
| Palm Springs | 1.90 | 2.10 |
| Colton | 1.20 | 5.90 |

It owns six trucks that are run on a fixed route between each pair of cities. Thus one truck always runs between Long Beach and Pomona, another truck makes all of its runs between Colton and San Diego, and so on. If any package is not shipped directly to its destination, there is a 25¢ handling charge each time the package must be transferred to another truck. What is the lowest cost routing between Colton and San Diego?

---

## CASE STUDY Midwest Stamping Corporation

Midwest Stamping Corp. must replace a 15 ton punch press that is used to produce deep-draw flange brackets. Three alternatives are available: a $50,000 press that can produce 150,000 flange brackets per year, a $65,000 press that can produce 250,000 flange brackets per year, and an $80,000 press that can produce 400,000 flange brackets per year. Installation (including shipping, rewiring, etc.) of any new press in any year costs $7,000. Space limitations prevent Midwest from obtaining more than one press at a time.

Each press will be leased at a yearly cost equal to 25% of the press purchase price. All operating costs (production of flange brackets, maintenance, etc.) equal an additional 10% of the press purchase price per year. The $7,000 installation cost will not be financed. None of the prices, costs, or rates are expected to change over the next four years.

Midwest's sales department has developed the following flange bracket sales forecast for the next four years: 100,000 next year, 200,000 in the second year, 350,000 in the third year, and 550,000 in the fourth year. If the installed press does not have the capacity to meet these sales levels, Midwest will buy flange brackets from another supplier for 10¢ each.

Midwest's president wants to determine which press to get in which year to minimize the total cost of meeting the forecasted sales levels. Presses may be obtained and installed at the beginning of any year, and presses installed in one year may be removed in later years if such a move minimizes total costs over the four-year planning horizon.

a) Formulate the problem.

b) Which presses should be obtained when?

c) What is the optimal total four-year cost of meeting the forecasted sales levels?

# 9
## DECS

# *Decision Analysis Models*

Decision analysis models are used to help select the best alternative in a complex decision situation. A decision analysis problem is characterized by the need to select one alternative from a list of two or more alternatives. Decision analysis problems are difficult because the payoffs from each alternative are affected by uncontrollable future events called states of nature. The decision maker is aware of all states of nature, but does not know which one will actually occur until after the alternative is selected.

Decision analysis problems are divided into decision making under uncertainty and decision making under risk. In a decision making under uncertainty problem, the decision maker knows which alternatives are available, which states of nature can occur, and the payoff that will result from each alternative/state-of-nature pair. No information is known regarding the probability of each state of nature.

Decision making under risk is used in situations in which information *is* available regarding the probability of each state of nature. The following are typical questions addressed in decision making under risk:

1. Which alternative provides the best average long-run payoff (expected value)?
2. What would be the payoff if perfect information were available prior to making the decision (expected payoff with perfect information)?
3. What is the maximum amount of money that should be paid for perfect information (expected value of perfect information)?
4. How does the availability of additional information affect the probabilities of each event (posterior probabilities)?
5. What is the expected payoff if the additional information is used (expected payoff with sample information)?
6. What is the maximum amount of money that should be paid for the additional information (expected value of sample information)?

Decision analysis is a topic that does not have standardized terminology. Some of the more important terms are listed next, with the first term being the one used in this book:

*Alternatives* are also called *actions, acts, alternative actions, alternative courses of action, alternative choices, choices, decision alternatives, options,* and *strategies*.

*Decision analysis* is also called *decision theory*.

*States of nature* are also called *events, future events,* and *possible events.* The computer output and many of the problems in this chapter call these *states*.

Some books use the term "decision making under uncertainty" as a general descriptor of what we have divided into decision making under uncertainty and decision making under risk. Other books use "decision making under risk" as the general topic descriptor. As with all terminology differences, you must be careful to ensure that they do not cause the incorrect interpretation of a problem's results.

# 9.1  Program Description

The program determines the optimal alternative for either decision making under uncertainty or decision making under risk. For decision making under uncertainty problems, the program outputs the optimal alternative and the payoff for each of five different decision criteria (maximax, maximin, equal likelihood, minimax regret, and Hurwicz). The program selects only one alternative using each criterion. Thus the program will not output information about other alternatives that may have a payoff equal to the selected alternative.

For decision making under risk, the program determines the optimal decision from among a set of alternatives based on maximizing or minimizing the expected value of the resultant payoff. Both the expected payoff and the expected value of perfect information are also output. If additional information is available to the decision maker, the program also determines the marginal probabilities, the posterior probabilities, the expected payoff with sample information, and the expected value of sample information. The program will handle up to 15 states of nature, 15 alternatives, and sample information with up to 15 different predictions.

# 9.2  Problem Preparation

The payoff data should be arranged in tables prior to input. All data tables have the states of nature as rows. Thus the payoff table will have states of nature as rows, and alternatives as columns. If additional information is available, a conditional probability table must also be input. It has states of nature as rows and the predictions as columns. Some books use the reverse arrangement for the payoff table, but all books use the same arrangement for the conditional probability table.

## 9.3  Data Input Overview

For all problems, the first items to be input are the number of possible states of nature (rows) and the number of different alternatives (columns). If the probabilities of the states of nature are not known, the initial data values are followed by a "U" to indicate that this is a problem of decision making under uncertainty. If the probabilities of the states of nature are known, the initial data values are followed by an "R" to indicate that this is a problem of decision making under risk. This is followed by a "1" for maximization problems or a "−1" for minimization problems.

Next the payoff table is entered row by row with each payoff entered into one cell of a spreadsheet-like table. The first of these values is the payoff that would result if the first alternative was selected and the first state of nature actually occurred. The next value is the payoff that would result if the second alternative was selected and the first state of nature actually occurred. The remaining payoffs are entered in the same sequence.

For decision making under uncertainty problems, the payoff values are followed by the input of the Hurwicz coefficient (called the coefficient of optimism in some books). It is used to compute the balance between the most optimistic criterion (maximax) and the most pessimistic criterion (maximin). A Hurwicz coefficient of one gives the same results as the maximax criterion, and a Hurwicz coefficient of zero gives the same results as the maximin criterion.

For decision making under risk problems, the payoff values are followed by the probabilities of each state of nature (the prior probabilities). The last set of data for a decision making under risk problem describes the additional information that is available from market research, a consultant, or some other source. If no additional information is to be used in the problem, then type an "N." No further data need be input. If there is additional information, however, then this set of data must be input as a conditional probability table. First type a "Y" and follow this by the number of different predictions that can be made. The remainder of the input consists of the conditional probability table arranged as follows.

The rows must correspond to the states of nature that were input as rows in the payoff table. Each column represents one of the possible predictions that might be made regarding these states of nature. This is the standard format of rows being used for actual results and columns being used for predictions. Each entry in the table is the probability that each prediction was made given that the state of nature actually occurred. The sum of the probabilities in each row must be one.

## 9.4 Data Input Details

For *decision making under uncertainty* problems, the problem structure input includes the following:

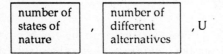

For *decision making under risk* problems, the problem structure input includes the following:

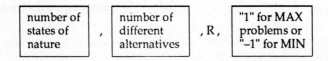

For both decision making under risk and decision making under uncertainty problems, the payoffs are entered into the cells of an on-screen table as follows:

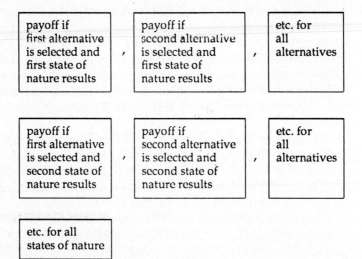

For decision making under uncertainty problems, the one remaining input data value is:

| value of Hurwicz coefficient |
|---|

For decision making under risk problems, the next data values are entered into the cells of another on-screen table:

```
┌─────────────────┐
│ prior probability│
│ of first         │
│ state of nature  │
└─────────────────┘

┌─────────────────┐
│ prior probability│
│ of second        │
│ state of nature  │
└─────────────────┘

┌─────────────────┐
│ etc.            │
└─────────────────┘
```

If the problem has no conditional table, the last item to be input is as follows:

N

If the problem does have a conditional table, the next items to be input are as follows:

Y,
```
┌─────────────────┐
│ The number of   │
│ different possible│
│ predictions     │
└─────────────────┘
```

This is followed by entering the conditional probabilities into the cells of a third on-screen table:

```
┌─────────────────┐   ┌─────────────────┐   ┌─────────────┐
│ probability of  │   │ probability of  │   │ etc. for    │
│ the first       │   │ the second      │   │ all         │
│ prediction      │ , │ prediction      │ , │ predictions │
│ given that the  │   │ given that the  │   │             │
│ first state of  │   │ first state of  │   │             │
│ nature occurred │   │ nature occurred │   │             │
└─────────────────┘   └─────────────────┘   └─────────────┘

┌─────────────────┐
│ etc. for all    │
│ states of nature│
└─────────────────┘
```

## 9.5 Editing the Data

Editing features are a part of both the ENTER PROBLEM FROM KEYBOARD option and the EDIT CURRENT PROBLEM option. The problem structure (but not the problem data values) may be changed in the ENTER PROBLEM FROM KEYBOARD option and the problem data (but not the problem structure) may be changed in the EDIT CURRENT PROBLEM option.

The first part of the ENTER PROBLEM FROM KEYBOARD option is used to enter the problem structure. This includes the number of states of nature, the number of different alternatives, the type of problem (uncertainty or risk), and (for the risk problems only) whether the problem is max or min. After these data are entered, the program will ask if you want to re-enter the problem structure. Type "Y" if any of the problem structure values are incorrect. The program will then repeat all the problem structure prompts to allow the correct data to be entered.

The EDIT CURRENT PROBLEM option may be used to change any of the payoff values. In addition, the Hurwicz coefficient may be changed in uncertainty problems. In decision making under risk problems, the prior probabilities and the conditional probability values may be changed.

The change procedure is similar for all of these. The new value of the item to be changed is entered into a cell of the same on-screen table that was used for the original data entry. When all editing is done, the full set of data may be saved on a data diskette. After this, the program will return to the PROGRAM OPTIONS menu.

## 9.6 Program Output

Each set of output values is described after the heading that appears on the printout. The acronym that is in most common use for each of these items is given in parentheses.

*Expected value of each alternative.* These are the expected values of the payoffs that would result if each of the alternatives were selected (EMV or expected monetary value).

*Optimal alternative.* The number of the alternative with the highest expected value is printed here. (Optimal EMV is often given as EMV*.)

Some problems may have multiple optimal solutions. When this occurs, a different alternative will have the same expected payoff. This program gives no indications of multiple optimal solutions, but you can check the EXPECTED VALUE OF EACH ALTERNATIVE to see if any exist.

*Expected payoff with perfect info.* This is the expected payoff that would result if we knew in advance which state of nature would occur (EPPI or expected payoff with perfect information).

*EOL for optimal alternative.* The expected opportunity loss is the difference between EPPI and EMV* (EOL* = EPPI – EMV*).

*Expected value of perfect info.* The expected value of perfect information is most commonly referred to as EVPI. In general, EVPI = EOL*.

*Marginal probabilities.* These are the marginal probabilities—the probabilities that each of the predictions will be made. Note that these values are output in a column, but they refer to the predictions that were input as column headings in the conditional probability table.

*Revised probabilities.* These are the revised probabilities that each state of nature will occur given that each prediction was made. Note that the rows in this matrix refer to the predictions, and the columns refer to the states of nature.

*Expected payoff with added info.* This is often referred to as the expected payoff with sample information (EPSI). It is the expected payoff that results if the predictions are used to aid in making the decision.

*Expected value of added info.* This is often referred to as the expected value of sample information (EVSI). It is the difference between EPSI and EMV* (EVSI = EPSI – EMV*).

*Sensitivity analysis of payoff values.* This provides lower and upper limits for the payoff values over which the current solution is optimal.

## 9.7 Example Problem DA1

A construction company must decide whether to build apartments, build condominiums, or invest its cash in bonds. The decision is complicated by a rent control initiative that is on the ballot in the next election. If rent control passes, the apartment project will net only $100,000, and the condominium project will net $300,000. If the rent control initiative fails, however, the apartment project will net $500,000 and the condominium project will net only $100,000. If they decide to invest in the bonds, they will net $200,000 whether rent control passes or not. It is estimated that the rent control initiative has a .6 probability of passing.

The company can hire Political Forecasters, Inc., to conduct a voter survey. In past elections, when initiatives actually did pass, they had predicted passage 90% of the time. When initiatives failed, they had predicted failure 80% of the time.

1. Should the construction company hire Political Forecasters, Inc., to conduct a voter survey?

2. What is the maximum that it should pay for this survey?

### 9.7.1 Problem Preparation

This problem has two states of nature (the initiative will pass or fail) and three alternatives (apartments, bonds, or condominiums). The payoff table is (all values in thousands of dollars) as follows:

|  |  | Alternatives | | |
|  |  | Apartments | Bonds | Condominiums |
| --- | --- | --- | --- | --- |
| Rent Control Initiative | Passes | 100 | 200 | 300 |
| | Fails | 500 | 200 | 100 |

The prior probability of the first state of nature (initiative passes) is .6, and the prior probability of the second state of nature (initiative fails) is .4.

This problem has a conditional table with two different predictions (pass or fail). The table looks like the following:

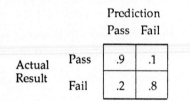

|  |  | Prediction | |
|  |  | Pass | Fail |
| --- | --- | --- | --- |
| Actual Result | Pass | .9 | .1 |
| | Fail | .2 | .8 |

### 9.7.2 Data Input

The following data values must be input to solve this problem:

```
2, 3, R, 1
100, 200, 300
500, 200, 100
.6, .4
Y, 2
.9, .1
.2, .8
```

Figure 9.1 shows how the problem structure should be input. Figure 9.2 shows how the screen looks after the last payoff value has been entered into the on-screen table. Similarly, Figure 9.3 shows the computer screen after entering all prior probabilities, and Figure 9.4 shows the computer screen after entering all the conditional probabilities.

**FIGURE 9.1**   Input of problem structure for example problem DA1

```
                         -=*=-   INPUT  PROBLEM  STRUCTURE   -=*=-

     ENTER NUMBER OF STATES
     ENTER NUMBER IN RANGE ( 1  -  15 ) & press ⏎   2

     ENTER NUMBER OF ALTERNATIVES
     ENTER NUMBER IN RANGE ( 1  -  15 ) & press ⏎   3

     DECISION MAKING UNDER RISK (R) - OR UNCERTAINTY (U)
     Enter a Character ( R  or  U ) & press ⏎    R

     IS THE PROBLEM TYPE MAXIMIZATION (1)  OR  MINIMIZATION (-1)
     Enter a Character ( 1  or  -1 ) & press ⏎    1

     DO YOU WANT TO RE-ENTER PROBLEM STRUCTURE? (Y/N)
     Enter a Character ( Y  or  N ) & press ⏎    N
```

**FIGURE 9.2**   Computer screen after input of all payoff values for example problem DA1

```
                                          ENTER PAYOFF VALUES

          STATES        1          2            3
             1       100.000    200.000      300.000
             2       500.000    200.000 ▌    100.000
```

**FIGURE 9.3**   Computer screen after input of prior probabilities for example problem DA1

```
                                       ENTER PRIOR PROBABILITIES

          STATES   1
             1      0.6000
             2     ▌0.4000
```

**FIGURE 9.4**   Computer screen after input of conditional probabilities for example problem DA1

```
                                        ENTER CONDITIONAL TABLE

          STATES   1        2
             1      0.9000 0.1000
             2      0.2000 ▌0.8000
```

### 9.7.3 Computer Output

Figure 9.5 contains the output from a run of this problem. The EXPECTED VALUE OF EACH ALTERNATIVE shows that alternative 1 (build apartments) has an expected value of $260,000, alternative 2 (buy bonds) has an expected value of $200,000, and alternative 3 (build condominiums) has an expected value of $220,000. Thus, without any further information, they should build apartments.

The output also shows that the expected payoff would be $380,000 if the builder knew the rent control initiative results in advance. Thus the expected value of perfect information is $120,000.

If Political Forecasters, Inc., is hired, they can be expected to predict rent control passage 62% and rent control failure 38% of the time (the marginal probabilities). When passage is predicted, they will be right 87.1% and wrong 12.9% of the time. When failure is predicted, they will be right 84.21% and wrong 15.79% of the time.

Using the services of Political Forecasters, Inc., results in an expected payoff of $336,000. Thus the maximum that the construction company should pay for the survey is $76,000 ($336,000–$260,000). Therefore, the answers to the original questions are as follows:

1. Yes

2. $76,000

**FIGURE 9.5**  Output from a run of example problem DA1

```
                    -=*=-   INFORMATION ENTERED   -=*=-


     NUMBER OF STATES                :   2

     NUMBER OF ALTERNATIVES          :   3

     NUMBER OF PREDICTIONS           :   2

     PROBLEM TYPE                     :   MAXIMIZATION



                          PAYOFF TABLE

   STATES           PAYOFF FROM EACH ALTERNATIVE

                    1           2           3

     1           100.00      200.00      300.00
     2           500.00      200.00      100.00

   STATES   PRIOR PROBABILITIES

     1       0.6000
     2       0.4000
```

(CONT.)

**FIGURE 9.5**  *(CONT.)*

```
                              CONDITIONAL TABLE
      STATES          CONDITIONAL PROBABILITIES
                    1      2

       1     0.9000 0.1000
       2     0.2000 0.8000


                       DECISION MAKING UNDER RISK

                        -=*=-  RESULTS  -=*=-


        EXPECTED VALUE OF EACH ALTERNATIVE

          260.00      200.00      220.00

        OPTIMAL ALTERNATIVE              :        A1

        EXPECTED PAYOFF WITH PERFECT INFO :     380.00

        EOL FOR OPTIMAL ALTERNATIVE      :       120.00

        EXPECTED VALUE OF PERFECT INFO   :       120.00


     PRED    MARGINAL PROBABILITIES

       1     0.6200
       2     0.3800


     PRED    REVISED PROBABILITIES

       1     0.8710 0.1290
       2     0.1579 0.8421


        EXPECTED PAYOFF WITH ADDED INFO  :      336.00

        EXPECTED VALUE OF ADDED INFO     :       76.00


                          SENSITIVITY ANALYSIS

                           PAYOFF  VALUES

            LOWER              CURRENT              UPPER

            33.33              100.00            NO LIMIT
           400.00              500.00            NO LIMIT

          NO LIMIT             200.00              300.00
          NO LIMIT             200.00              350.00

          NO LIMIT             300.00              366.67
          NO LIMIT             100.00              200.00


         ----------  E N D   O F   A N A L Y S I S  ----------
```

## 9.8 Example Problem DA2

The rent control issue in example problem DA1 has become quite controversial. Nobody (including Political Forecasters, Inc.) will predict the probability of the initiative's passage or failure. The construction company still must make a decision on the project prior to the election. What should it do?

### 9.8.1 Problem Preparation

This problem has two states of nature (the initiative will pass or fail) and three alternatives (apartments, bonds, or condominiums). The payoff table is (all values in thousands of dollars) as follows:

|  |  | Alternatives | | |
|---|---|---|---|---|
|  |  | Apartments | Bonds | Condominiums |
| Rent Control Initiative | Passes | 100 | 200 | 300 |
|  | Fails | 500 | 200 | 100 |

Unlike example problem DA1, this problem has neither prior probabilities nor a conditional table and must be solved using the decision making under uncertainty option. We will assume pessimism and use a Hurwicz coefficient of .3.

### 9.8.2 Data Input

The following data values must be input to solve this problem:

```
2, 3, U
100, 200, 300
500, 200, 100
.3
```

### 9.8.3 Computer Output

Figure 9.6 contains the output from a run of this problem. The RESULTS show that alternative 1 (apartments) provides the optimum payoff under all criteria except one. If the maximin criterion is used, alternative 2 (bonds) should be selected.

The PAYOFF column contains the result of applying each criterion to the payoff matrix. The maximax payoff of 500 is the largest payoff value in the payoff matrix. The maximin payoff of 200 is the largest of the minimum payoffs in each column (100, 200, and 100). The likelihood payoff of 300 is the expected value if all states had an equal probability of occurring. The minimax regret payoff of 200 is the maximum regret that can occur if alternative 1 is selected. It is the largest difference between the selected alternative payoff (100) and the best other payoff (300) for each state. The Hurwicz rule payoff results from .3 times 500 plus .7 times 100.

**FIGURE 9.6**   Output from a run of example problem DA2

```
                    -=*=-  INFORMATION ENTERED  -=*=-


        NUMBER OF STATES                 :  2

        NUMBER OF ALTERNATIVES           :  3

        HURWICZ COEFFICIENT              :  .3


                              PAYOFF TABLE

        STATES          PAYOFF FROM EACH ALTERNATIVE

                    1            2            3

          1       100.00       200.00       300.00
          2       500.00       200.00       100.00


                  DECISION MAKING UNDER UNCERTAINTY

                    -=*=-   RESULTS   -=*=-


          CRITERION                  ALTERNATIVE           PAYOFF

          1.  MAXIMAX                    A1                500.00

          2.  MAXIMIN                    A2                200.00

          3.  LIKELIHOOD                 A1                300.00

          4.  MINIMAX REGRET             A1                200.00

          5.  HURWICZ RULE               A1                220.00


            ----------  E N D   O F   A N A L Y S I S   ----------
```

## 9.9 Decision Analysis Problems

1. Given the following profit payoff table:

Alternatives

|        |    | A1   | A2  | A3   | A4   |
|--------|----|------|-----|------|------|
|        | S1 | 100  | -50 | 0    | 300  |
| States | S2 | 25   | 0   | 200  | -200 |
|        | S3 | -150 | 100 | -100 | 0    |

a) What is the optimal alternative if the maximax decision criterion is used?
b) What is the payoff under this criterion?
c) What is the optimal alternative if the maximin decision criterion is used?
d) What is the payoff under this criterion?
e) What is the optimal alternative if the equal likelihood decision criterion is used?
f) What is the payoff under this criterion?
g) What is the optimal alternative if the minimax regret decision criterion is used?
h) What is the payoff under this criterion?
i) What is the optimal alternative if the Hurwicz decision criterion is used (with a Hurwicz coefficient = .4)?
j) What is the payoff under this criterion?

2. Given the following cost table:

Alternatives

|        |    | A1  | A2  | A3  |
|--------|----|-----|-----|-----|
|        | S1 | 100 | 0   | 300 |
| States | S2 | 200 | 400 | 100 |
|        | S3 | 50  | 100 | 200 |
|        | S4 | 0   | 200 | 300 |

a) What is the optimal alternative if the maximax decision criterion is used?
b) What is the payoff under this criterion?
c) What is the optimal alternative if the maximin decision criterion is used?

d) What is the payoff under this criterion?
e) What is the optimal alternative if the equal likelihood decision criterion is used?
f) What is the payoff under this criterion?
g) What is the optimal alternative if the minimax regret decision criterion is used?
h) What is the payoff under this criterion?
i) What is the optimal alternative if the Hurwicz decision criterion is used (with a Hurwicz coefficient = .7)?
j) What is the payoff under this criterion?

3. Given the following profit table:

Alternatives

|         |     | A1   | A2   | A3   |
|---------|-----|------|------|------|
|         | S1  | 1000 | 900  | –600 |
| States  | S2  | 200  | 400  | 100  |
|         | S3  | 0    | –200 | 800  |

a) What is the optimal alternative if the maximax decision criterion is used?
b) What is the payoff under this criterion?
c) What is the optimal alternative if the maximin decision criterion is used?
d) What is the payoff under this criterion?
e) What is the optimal alternative if the equal likelihood decision criterion is used?
f) What is the payoff under this criterion?
g) What is the optimal alternative if the minimax regret decision criterion is used?
h) What is the payoff under this criterion?
i) What is the optimal alternative if the Hurwicz decision criterion is used (with a Hurwicz coefficient = .2)?
j) What is the payoff under this criterion?

4. The buyer at the Household Appliance Emporium must decide on the size of its air conditioner order. The order must be sent in prior to the beginning of the summer selling season. If a large number of air conditioners are ordered and the summer is hot, net will be $10,000. However, if the summer is warm this order will net only $8000. Similarly, if the summer is cool the profit will be only $5000.

If the buyer decides to order only a medium number of air conditioners, the profits will be $6000 in a hot summer, $8000 in a warm summer, and $7000 in a cool summer. If the buyer decides to order only a small number of air conditioners, the profits will be $5000 in a hot summer, $5500 in a warm summer, and $6000 in a cool summer. The buyer has no way of determining whether the summer will be hot, warm, or cool.

a) What is the optimal alternative if the maximax decision criterion is used?
b) What is the payoff under this criterion?
c) What is the optimal alternative if the maximin decision criterion is used?
d) What is the payoff under this criterion?
e) What is the optimal alternative if the equal likelihood decision criterion is used?
f) What is the payoff under this criterion?
g) What is the optimal alternative if the minimax regret decision criterion is used?
h) What is the payoff under this criterion?
i) What is the optimal alternative if the Hurwicz decision criterion is used (with a Hurwicz coefficient = .5)?
j) What is the payoff under this criterion?

5. The physical facilities manager at Labon Corporation must make a decision regarding repairs to the roof of the main plant. Three options are available.

The manager can do a spray tar job, but it must be redone every few years. The spray job will cost $200,000 over the next 20 years if there is good weather, but bad weather will increase the need to respray and raise the cost to $300,000.

A second option is to wait until leaks occur and patch only the leaks. If good weather results, this option will cost only $100,000, but bad weather will result in damage and repair costs of $500,000.

The third option is to do a full reroofing job. It will cost $250,000 and last 20 years (whether weather is good or bad).

a) What is the optimal alternative if the maximax decision criterion is used?
b) What is the payoff under this criterion?
c) What is the optimal alternative if the maximin decision criterion is used?
d) What is the payoff under this criterion?
e) What is the optimal alternative if the equal likelihood decision criterion is used?
f) What is the payoff under this criterion?

    g) What is the optimal alternative if the minimax regret decision criterion is used?

    h) What is the payoff under this criterion?

    i) What is the optimal alternative if the Hurwicz decision criterion is used (with a Hurwicz coefficient = .9)?

    j) What is the payoff under this criterion?

6. Given the following payoff table:

|  |  | Alternatives | | | | Probability |
|---|---|---|---|---|---|---|
|  |  | A1 | A2 | A3 | A4 |  |
| States | S1 | 100 | –50 | 0 | 300 | .2 |
|  | S2 | 25 | 0 | 200 | –200 | .5 |
|  | S3 | –150 | 100 | -100 | 0 | .3 |

    a) Which alternative maximizes expected value?

    b) What is the expected payoff?

    c) What is the maximum you are willing to pay for perfect information?

7. Students at a local university have set up a newspaper stand. They buy papers for 15¢ and sell them for 25¢. Papers not sold at the end of the day have no value. When demand exceeds supply, students may buy additional papers for 30¢. Because of their interest in maintaining the stand, students always meet demand. Papers are bought in multiples of 100 up to a maximum of 400.

    a) $P(100) = 0.2$, $P(200) = 0.3$, $P(300) = 0.4$, and $P(400) = 0.1$. Determine the optimal stocking policy based on maximizing expected value.

    b) What is the expected value of this operation on perfect information?

8. Determine the minimum cost strategy for the following cost table:

|  |  | Alternatives | | | Probability |
|---|---|---|---|---|---|
|  |  | A1 | A2 | A3 |  |
| States | S1 | 100 | 0 | 300 | .2 |
|  | S2 | 200 | 400 | 100 | .1 |
|  | S3 | 50 | 100 | 200 | .6 |
|  | S4 | 0 | 200 | 300 | .1 |

9. For the following payoff table:

|  | | A1 | A2 | A3 | P |
|---|---|---|---|---|---|
| | S1 | 1000 | 900 | −600 | .2 |
| States | S2 | 200 | 400 | 100 | .3 |
| | S3 | 0 | −200 | 800 | .5 |

a) Determine the alternative that maximizes the expected payoff.
b) Determine the expected payoff with perfect information.
c) Determine the maximum one should pay for perfect information.

10. For the following payoff table determine the value of X for which you are indifferent between the two alternatives.

|  | | Alternatives | | Probability |
|---|---|---|---|---|
| | | A1 | A2 | |
| | S1 | X | 100 | .4 |
| States | S2 | 200 | 300 | .6 |

11. Todd Enterprises produces a perishable chemical product at a cost of $10 per pound. The product sells for $20 per pound. For planning purposes, the company is considering possible demands of 100, 200, or 300 units. If the demand is greater than production, the firm, in an attempt to maintain a good service image, will satisfy the excess demand with a special production run at a cost of $45 per pound. The product, however, always sells at the $20 per pound price.

a) Set up the payoff table for this problem if $P(100) = 0.4$, $P(200) = 0.3$, and $P(300) = 0.3$.

b) How many units should they produce? What is the expected profit?

12. Velasco Corporation is considering the introduction of a new gasoline additive product. Historically, products of this type have recorded a 70% chance of being well received by the motoring public. The following payoff table is relevant:

| State | Velasco's Alternatives ($000) | |
|---|---|---|
| | Introduce | Hold up |
| Well Received | 500 | −100 |
| Poorly Received | −200 | 100 |

a) Select the optimal alternative.

Velasco has the opportunity to purchase a market survey for $45,000. The past performance of the marketing firm is outlined below.

| State | Prediction Well Received | Poorly Received |
|-------|--------------------------|-----------------|
| Well Received | .9 | .1 |
| Poorly Received | .3 | .7 |

b) Should Velasco purchase the survey?
c) What price should Velasco pay?

13. The Dendix Corporation is considering the acquisition of one of two firms: Sav-Less and Poor Year. The financial results of this decision (in millions of dollars) will be influenced by the state of the economy over the next year, and are shown in the following table:.

| State of Economy | Alternatives Buy Sav-Less | Buy Poor Year |
|------------------|---------------------------|---------------|
| Improve | 0 | 100* |
| Decline | 25 | –50 |

*All payoffs are in millions of dollars

The probability that the economy will improve is .4. What is the optimal action?

14. For the above problem, Dendix is considering the use of an economic forecasting service. The service charges $100,000 for one of their special forecasts. The service has the following record:

| State of Economy | Prediction Economy Improves | Economy Declines |
|------------------|-----------------------------|------------------|
| Improve | .8 | .2 |
| Decline | .3 | .7 |

What is the maximum Dendix should pay for this service?

15. For the above problem, what is the impact of Dendix's decision if the first row in the conditional table is changed to .9 and .1, respectively?

## CASE STUDY **Motorking Corporation**

Motorking, a market leader in the production of specialized engine oil additives, is considering the introduction of its new "gas extender" product. Motorking's manufacturing facility can produce up to 50,000 cases of the new product per year at a variable cost of $5 per case. Set-up cost for a production run is $100,000. If orders exceed 50,000 cases, they will be subcontracted to a local refining company which will produce them at a variable cost of $9 per case. Marketing and overhead cost $12 per case whether the product is manufactured by Motorking or by the vendor.

Motorking's production manager is considering three production levels for the new product: 50,000 cases, 70,000 cases, and 100,000 cases. The level of sales for the new product will depend on the state of the economy. Sales estimates prepared by the marketing manager indicate that if the economy is strong then Motorking will sell 100,000 cases, if the economy is moderate then 70,000 cases will be sold, and if the economy is weak only 50,000 cases will be sold. The marketing department forecast shows a 45 percent chance of a strong market and a 20 percent chance of a weak market.

The new product is priced at $40 per case. All unsold cases are purchased by a liquidator at a 55 percent discount. Before deciding on a level of production, the production manager wishes to evaluate the possibility of hiring a local market research firm to conduct a survey. The manager has received a proposal from Decision Systems Inc. (DSI). DSI proposes to conduct the survey for $20,000. In the past, DSI has demonstrated the following performance:

- Correctly predicted a strong economy 10 out of 15 times (three times they predicted a moderate economy and two times a weak economy).

- Correctly predicted a moderate economy 7 out of 10 times (two times they predicted a strong economy and one time a weak economy).

- Correctly predicted a weak economy 5 out of 6 times (one time they predicted a moderate economy).

The production manager wishes to know:

a) The optimal total number of cases to be produced.
b) The number of cases to be obtained from the vendor.
c) If Motorking should purchase the forecasting service.
d) What is the maximum Motorking should pay DSI for the service?
e) What is the maximum they should pay for perfect information?

# 10

## DTRE

# Decision Tree Model

Decision trees provide a convenient way to analyze complex decision problems that require a sequence of alternatives to be selected before obtaining the final payoff. The typical problem has a series of choices with random events interspersed between the choices. The random event results are not known to the decision maker prior to selecting any alternative.

Decision tree problems are usually more complex than those discussed in the decision analysis chapter, and are often a sequence of decision analysis problems. The output from a decision tree analysis is a plan that tells the decision maker which alternative to select at every decision point in the problem.

## 10.1 Program Description

This program is in two parts. The first part (called Bayesian analysis) uses prior probabilities and conditional probabilities to compute the marginal probabilities and posterior probabilities given that each of the possible predictions has taken place. It can analyze up to 10 states of nature and 10 predictions of these states of nature. These revised probabilities can then be used as input to the second part of the program.

The second part of the program (called decision tree analysis) determines the optimal alternative for every decision node in a decision tree. The program may be run to maximize (profits, etc.) or minimize (costs, etc.). The program also computes the expected payoff at each node if the optimal alternatives are selected each time you go through the decision tree. The program can handle decision trees with up to 100 nodes. A maximum of 10 branches can exit from each node.

## 10.2 Problem Preparation

No special preparation is needed for the Bayesian analysis part of the program except to make sure that the conditional probability table (sometimes called a prediction likelihood table) has the states of nature as rows and the predictions as columns. *Some books reverse this and have the states of nature as columns.*

The descriptions of data entry procedures in this chapter assume that the decision tree is drawn with the start node at the far left. All paths through the decision tree go to the right and eventually reach a terminal node.

Identification numbers must be assigned to each node in the decision tree. Each node identification number must be an integer. The first node must be given the number "0" and all other nodes must be numbered one unit larger than the previously numbered node. No gaps are allowed in the node numbers. Thus a tree with four nodes must have the nodes numbered 0, 1, 2, and 3. Every node must have an identification number that is larger than the identification number of any node to its left.

Each alternative (branches that go to the right of decision nodes) must also be given an identification number. The lowest numbered alternative must be number "1," and no gaps may appear in the remaining alternative numbers. There are no precedence rules regarding alternative numbers.

## 10.3 Data Input Overview

The first item to be input indicates whether Bayesian analysis is desired. If it is, the number of states of nature and the number of predictions are input. These are followed by the conditional probability table. This table contains values of the probabilities that a specific prediction will be made given that a specific state of nature has occurred. The last items to be input are the prior probabilities (the long-run probabilities that the states of nature will occur). The program will not retain the Bayesian analysis results, so any data that are to be used for input to the decision tree must be copied from the screen. Any number of sets of data may be processed in the Bayesian analysis portion of the program before either proceeding to decision tree analysis or returning to the PROGRAM OPTIONS menu.

The first item to be entered in decision tree analysis is the number of nodes in the tree. All decision tree node data must be entered in numerical order. Thus the data for node "0" is always entered first, the data for node "1" is next, and so on. Decision trees can have three types of nodes (decision nodes, chance nodes, and terminal nodes), and each is entered into the computer differently. The first data value identifies the type of node. Decision nodes are type 1, chance nodes are type 2, and terminal nodes are type 3.

For a *decision node*, the second item to be input is the number of branches to its right. For each branch, you input its identification number and the identification number of the node that is at its end.

For a *chance node*, the second item to be input is the number of branches to its right. For each branch, you input the probability of selecting it and the identification number of the node at its end.

For a *terminal node*, the second item to be input is the payoff that occurs when it is reached. If there is no payoff associated with a terminal node, the payoff must be entered as zero.

## 10.4  Data Input Details

The first Decision Tree Model Options menu:

```
1 = BAYESIAN ANALYSIS
2 = DECISION TREE ANALYSIS
3 = RETURN TO PROGRAM MENU
```

is used to select Bayesian analysis (by typing "1") or to go directly to decision tree analysis (by typing "2"). If Bayesian analysis is selected, this must be followed by the size of the conditional probability table:

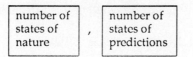

| number of states of nature | , | number of states of predictions |
|---|---|---|

Next, each conditional probability value is input into one cell of a spreadsheet-like table:

| probability of the first prediction given that the first state of nature occurred | , | probability of the second prediction given that the first state of nature occurred | , | etc. for all predictions |
|---|---|---|---|---|

| etc. for all states of nature |
|---|

Last, each prior probability is input into one cell of a spreadsheet-like table:

| prior probability for the first state of nature |
|---|

| prior probability for the second state of nature |
|---|

| etc. for all states of nature |
|---|

The results of the Bayesian analysis will be output immediately. The program will ask if you want to print these results. The program does not save these results. This will be followed by a display of the Decision Tree Model Options menu:

```
1 = BAYESIAN ANALYSIS
2 = DECISION TREE ANALYSIS
3 = RETURN TO PROGRAM MENU
```

Selecting option 1 repeats the Bayesian analysis, selecting option 3 returns to the PROGRAM OPTIONS menu, and selecting option 2 continues on to the decision tree analysis part of the program. This is discussed next.

First enter the problem type (1 for max and –1 for min), then enter the number of nodes in the tree. The next set of data describes the node at the far left of the decision tree (node "0"). The next set of data describes node number "1." All the remaining sets of data describe the nodes in numerical order. The format for each set of data depends on whether it is a decision node, a chance node, or a terminal node.

The data format for all decision nodes is as follows:

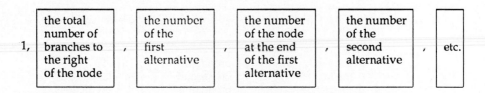

The data format for all chance nodes is as follows:

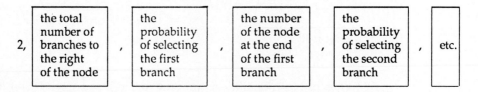

The data format for all terminal nodes is as follows:

3, | The payoff for the node |

# 10.5  Editing the Data

The EDIT CURRENT PROBLEM option can be used to change any of the probabilities or any of the payoffs in the decision tree analysis part of the program (decision nodes cannot be edited). The program will guide you through a series of easy-to-use menus and prompts to make the changes. As with all the CMMS programs, the new set of data may be saved on a diskette after editing is complete.

## 10.6  Program Output

The Bayesian analysis output is in two parts. The first part contains the marginal probabilities (the long-run probabilities that each of the predictions will be made).

The second part contains all of the revised (or posterior) probabilities. These are the probabilities that each state of nature will occur given that each prediction was made. Each row of output describes one prediction, and all output is sequenced in numerical order. Each column describes one state of nature, and these are also in numerical order. The rows are numbered, but the columns are not.

The decision tree analysis output is also in two parts. The first part contains a table of nodes, expected payoffs, and selected alternatives. Each row of this table contains a node number, the expected payoff at this node, and (if it is a decision node) the alternative that should be selected if this node is reached when going through the decision tree. The second part of the output contains the expected system payoff. This is the expected payoff that results from a large number of passes through the tree.

Some problems may have multiple optimal solutions. When this occurs, a different set of selected alternatives will provide the same payoff. The program does not indicate if multiple optimal solutions exist, but entering the expected payoff values into a diagram of the decision tree can be done to quickly check if there are any other optimal solutions.

## 10.7  Example Problem DT1

An investor is deciding among a number of alternatives:

1. Buy a stock that has a .4 probability of increasing in value by $5000, and a .6 probability of decreasing in value by $1000.

2. Put the money in a savings and loan account that would increase in value by $1500.

3. Keep the money in a checking account that will neither earn nor lose money.

Which of these three alternatives should be selected?

## 10.7.1 Problem Preparation

First we must draw the decision tree. Next we must assign sequence numbers to all alternatives and to all nodes in the tree. The result is as follows:

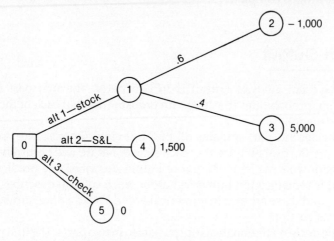

## 10.7.2 Data Input

The following data values must be input to solve this problem:

    2, 1, 6
    1, 3, 1, 1, 2, 4, 3, 5
    2, 2, .6, 2, .4, 3
    3, -1000
    3, 5000
    3, 1500
    3, 0

The program will guide you through a series of easy-to-use menus and prompts to enter the data. The first set of data is, as with all the programs, the problem structure. The remaining data are the problem data. The data values shown above are interpreted as follows:

### Problem Structure

| Data Values | Interpretation |
| --- | --- |
| 2 | Selects DECISION TREE ANALYSIS from the OPTIONS MENU |
| 1 | Indicates that this is a MAX problem |
| 6 | Number of nodes in the network |

**Problem Data**

| Data Values | Interpretation |
|---|---|
| 1, 3 | Node 0 is a decision node with 3 branches to its right. |
| 1, 1 | Alternative 1 has node 1 at its end |
| 2, 4 | Alternative 2 has node 4 at its end |
| 3, 5 | Alternative 3 has node 5 at its end |
| 2, 2 | Node 1 is a chance node with 2 branches to its right |
| 0.6, 2 | There is a 0.6 probability of taking the branch with node 2 at its end |
| 0.4, 3 | There is a 0.4 probability of taking the branch with node 3 at its end |
| 3, –1000 | Node 2 is a terminal node with a payoff of –1000 |
| 3, 5000 | Node 4 is a terminal node with a payoff of 5000 |
| 3, 1500 | Node 5 is a terminal node with a payoff of 1500 |
| 3, 0 | Node 6 is a terminal node with a payoff of 0 |

## 10.7.3 Computer Output

Figure 10.1 contains the output from a run of this problem. The RESULTS show that alternative 2 should be selected to obtain an expected payoff of $1500.

**FIGURE 10.1**   Output from a run of example problem DT1

```
            -=*=-   INFORMATION ENTERED   -=*=-


                    MAXIMIZATION


            -=*=-  DECISION NODES  -=*=-

                            ALTERNATIVE            ENDING
   NODE         BRANCHES       NUMBER               NODE
    0              3              1                   1
                                 2                   4
                                 3                   5
                                                  (CONT.)
```

**FIGURE 10.1**   *(CONT.)*

```
              -=*=-   CHANCE NODES   -=*=-

                                                  ENDING
   NODE            BRANCHES         PROBABILITY    NODE
    1                 2               0.6000         2
                                      0.4000         3



              -=*=-   TERMINAL NODES   -=*=-

   NODE            PAYOFF

    2            -1,000.00
    3             5,000.00
    4             1,500.00
    5                 0.00


              -=*=-   RESULTS   -=*=-

              MAXIMIZATION PROBLEM

                  EXPECTED          SELECTED
   NODE            PAYOFF           ALTERNATIVE

    0             1,500.00             2
    1             1,400.00
    2            -1,000.00
    3             5,000.00
    4             1,500.00
    5                 0.00

              EXPECTED PAYOFF =   1500


   ----------  E N D   O F   A N A L Y S I S  ----------
```

## 10.8  Example Problem DT2

Another investor is considering a stock that has a 0.1 probability of a $500,000 return, a 0.2 probability of a $100,000 return, and a 0.7 probability of a $10,000 loss.

This investor is also considering the purchase of some real estate. If purchased, there is a 0.4 chance of an up market with a $200,000 return. If the real estate market is down (a 0.6 probability), the investor can either sell at a loss of $20,000 or fix up the property at a cost of $30,000.

If the property is fixed up, there is a 0.25 probability of an up market with a profit (not including fix-up costs) of $210,000. There is also a 0.75 probability of a down market

If the market is down after fixing up the property, the investor can sell to the first buyer that arrives for a profit of $20,000. The investor can also hold out for a better price and not sell to the first buyer that arrives. If the investor selects this alternative, there is an even chance that a profit of $40,000 or a loss of $5000 will be realized. None of these latter profits or losses include the fix-up costs.

### 10.8.1 Problem Preparation

This problem includes a payoff (the fix-up costs) that is not at a terminal node. In such a case, you must add this payoff to all terminal nodes that are to its right. Thus the $210,000 return becomes a $180,000 payoff after the $30,000 fix-up costs are subtracted. Similarly, the $20,000 return, the $40,000 return, and the $5000 loss become, respectively, a $10,000 loss, a $10,000 return, and a $35,000 loss.

The resultant tree (with alternative numbers and node numbers assigned) is shown in Figure 10.2.

### 10.8.2 Data Input

The following data values must be input to solve this problem:

        2, 1, 16
        1, 2, 1, 1, 2, 5
        2, 3, .1, 2, .2, 3, .7, 4
        3, 500000
        3, 100000
        3, −10000
        2, 2, .4, 6, .6, 7
        3, 200000
        1, 2, 3, 8, 4, 9
        3, −20000
        2, 2, .25, 10, .75, 11
        3, 180000
        1, 2, 5, 12, 6, 13
        3, −10000
        2, 2, .5, 14, .5, 15
        3, 10000
        3, −35000

### 10.8.3 Computer Output

Figure 10.3 contains the output from a run of this problem. The results show that alternatives 2, 4, and 5 should be selected. A more complete way of describing this result is as follows:

Always select alternative 2, and sell for a $200,000 return if the market is

**FIGURE 10.2**   Decision tree for example problem DT1

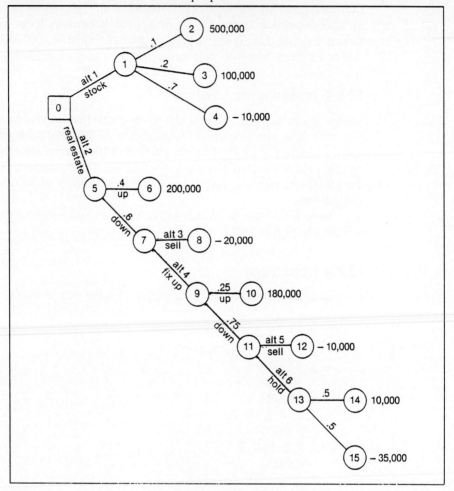

**FIGURE 10.3**   Output from a run of example problem DT2

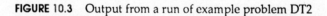

```
          -=*=-   INFORMATION ENTERED   -=*=-

                   MAXIMIZATION

          -=*=-   DECISION NODES   -=*=-
```

(CONT.)

**FIGURE** 10.3   *(CONT.)*

| NODE | BRANCHES | ALTERNATIVE NUMBER | ENDING NODE |
|------|----------|--------------------|-------------|
| 0    | 2        | 1                  | 1           |
|      |          | 2                  | 5           |
| 7    | 2        | 3                  | 8           |
|      |          | 4                  | 9           |
| 11   | 2        | 5                  | 12          |
|      |          | 6                  | 13          |

-=*=-   CHANCE NODES   -=*=-

| NODE | BRANCHES | PROBABILITY | ENDING NODE |
|------|----------|-------------|-------------|
| 1    | 3        | 0.1000      | 2           |
|      |          | 0.2000      | 3           |
|      |          | 0.7000      | 4           |
| 5    | 2        | 0.4000      | 6           |
|      |          | 0.6000      | 7           |
| 9    | 2        | 0.2500      | 10          |
|      |          | 0.7500      | 11          |
| 13   | 2        | 0.5000      | 14          |
|      |          | 0.5000      | 15          |

-=*=-   TERMINAL NODES   -=*=-

| NODE | PAYOFF      |
|------|-------------|
| 2    | 500,000.00  |
| 3    | 100,000.00  |
| 4    | -10,000.00  |
| 6    | 200,000.00  |
| 8    | -20,000.00  |
| 10   | 180,000.00  |
| 12   | -10,000.00  |
| 14   | 10,000.00   |
| 15   | -35,000.00  |

-=*=-   RESULTS   -=*=-

MAXIMIZATION PROBLEM

| NODE | EXPECTED PAYOFF | SELECTED ALTERNATIVE |
|------|-----------------|----------------------|
| 0    | 102,500.00      | 2                    |

(CONT.)

**FIGURE 10.3** *(CONT.)*

```
                    EXPECTED              SELECTED
   NODE             PAYOFF                ALTERNATIVE

    1              63,000.00
    2             500,000.00
    3             100,000.00
    4             -10,000.00
    5             102,500.00
    6             200,000.00
    7              37,500.00                 4
    8             -20,000.00
    9              37,500.00
   10             180,000.00
   11             -10,000.00                 5
   12             -10,000.00
   13             -12,500.00
   14              10,000.00
   15             -35,000.00

                  EXPECTED PAYOFF =   102500
   ----------     E N D   O F   A N A L Y S I S     ----------
```

up, but select alternative 4 if the market is down. After fixing up the property, sell for a $180,000 return if the market is up, but select alternative 5 (and sell for a $10,000 loss) if the market is down.

The result of this sequence of selections over a large number of identical investments would be an expected return of $102,500.

## 10.9 Example Problem DT3

The following conditional probability table specifies the probability that each prediction was made given that each state of nature actually occurred. This means, for example, that $P'(a \mid A) = .5$.

Prediction

|  |  | a | b | c |
|---|---|---|---|---|
| Actual States of Nature | A | .5 | .3 | .2 |
|  | B | .2 | .5 | .3 |
|  | C | .1 | .3 | .6 |

The prior probabilities of each of the states of nature are:

$P(A) = .2$

$P(B) = .5$

$P(C) = .3$

1. What is the probability that prediction a will be made?
2. What is the probability that prediction c will be made?
3. Given that prediction a is made, what is the probability that state of nature C will occur?

4. Given that prediction b is made, what is the probability that state of nature A will occur?

## 10.9.1 Problem Preparation

This problem is already arranged in the proper format for data input. The only thing to note is that the states of nature and the predictions will be given numbers in the output as follows:

| Original Problem | Computer Output |
|---|---|
| State of Nature | State |
| A | 1 |
| B | 2 |
| C | 3 |

| Original Problem | Computer Output |
|---|---|
| Prediction | Prediction |
| a | 1 |
| b | 2 |
| c | 3 |

## 10.9.2 Data Input

The following data values must be input to solve this problem:

        1, 3, 3
        .5, .3, .2
        .2, .5, .3
        .1, .3, .6
        .2, .5, .3

Figure 10.4 shows how the computer screen looks after input of the conditional probabilities. Figure 10.5 shows how the computer screen looks after input of the prior probabilities.

**FIGURE 10.4**   Computer screen after all conditional probabilities for example problem DT3

```
                                            ENTER CONDITIONAL TABLE

         STATES   1        2       3
            1     0.5000  0.3000  0.2000
            2     0.2000  0.5000  0.3000
            3     0.1000  0.3000  0.6000
```

**FIGURE 10.5**   Computer screen after input of prior probabilities for example problem DT3

```
                                            ENTER PRIOR PROBABILITIES

         STATES   1
            1     0.2000
            2     0.5000
            3     0.3000
```

### 10.9.3 Computer Output

Figure 10.6 contains the output from a run of this problem. The results show the following:

1. There is a .23 probability that prediction "a" will be made. It is given in the output as the marginal probability for prediction 1.
2. There is a .37 probability that prediction "c" will be made.
3. There is a 0.1304 probability that state of nature C (column 3 of the revised probability table) will occur, given that prediction "a" (row 1 of the same table) is made.
4. There is a 0.15 probability that state of nature A will occur, given that prediction "b" is made.

## 10.10 Decision Tree Problems

1. Given the following conditional probability table and prior state probabilities:

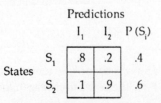

Predictions

| | | $I_1$ | $I_2$ | $P(S_i)$ |
|---|---|---|---|---|
| | $S_1$ | .8 | .2 | .4 |
| States | | | | |
| | $S_2$ | .1 | .9 | .6 |

Determine the revised conditional probabilities.

**FIGURE 10.6**   Output from a run of example problem DT3

```
Pred.   Marginal Probabilities
  1     0.2300
  2     0.4000
  3     0.3700

                                            Bayesian Analysis
                                                Results




Pred.   Revised Probabilities
  1     0.4348 0.4348 0.1304
  2     0.1500 0.6250 0.2250
  3     0.1081 0.4054 0.4865
```

2. Given the following conditional probability table and prior state probabilities:

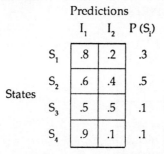

Determine the revised conditional probability.

3. In Southeast Africa it rains 30% of the time. A farmer has purchased a barometer that predicts rain 90% of the time when it actually rains and sunshine 80% of the time when the sun actually shines. Determine the following:

a) The probability of rain given a prediction of rain.
b) The probability of sunshine given a prediction of sunshine.

4. North-South and East-West Airlines both provide direct service from Moscow to New York. Records show that 60% of all passengers fly on North-South (the least expensive of the two passenger lines). Historical data indicate that a passenger has an 80% chance of arriving on time via North-South and a 90% chance via East-West.

a) What is the probability of a random passenger arriving on time?
b) Given that a particular passenger arrived on time, what is the probability that the passenger was on North-South?

5. Compute revised probabilities for the following data: $P(A) = .2$, $P(B) = .3$, $P(C) = .1$, and $P(D) = .4$.

Predictions

|  | a | b | c | d |
|---|---|---|---|---|
| A | .8 | .1 | 0 | .1 |
| B | .2 | .6 | .1 | .1 |
| C | .1 | .3 | .5 | .1 |
| D | 0 | .1 | 0 | .9 |

States (rows A, B, C, D)

6. Given $P(a \mid A) = .8$, $P(b \mid B) = .9$, and $P(A) = .3$, find the following:

a) $P(A \mid a)$
b) $P(B \mid b)$

7. Compute the revised probabilities for the following data: $P(A) = .1$, $P(B) = .2$, $P(C) = .1$, $P(D) = .4$, and $P(E) = .2$.

Predictions

|  | A | B | C | D | E |
|---|---|---|---|---|---|
| A | .6 | 0 | 0 | .2 | .2 |
| B | 0 | .5 | .3 | .2 | 0 |
| C | .1 | .1 | .7 | 0 | .1 |
| D | .2 | 0 | .1 | .7 | 0 |
| E | .1 | .1 | .1 | .1 | 6 |

States (rows A, B, C, D, E)

8. The Win-Place-Show Horserace Forecasting Service provides prediction for local races. In an upcoming match race, the current assigned probabilities are:

$$P(\text{Seatoad})_{\text{win}} = .6$$
$$P(\text{Landtoad})_{\text{win}} = .4$$

The forecasting service has the following historical record:

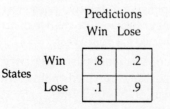

Predictions

|  | Win | Lose |
|---|---|---|
| Win | .8 | .2 |
| Lose | .1 | .9 |

States (rows Win, Lose)

If the service predicts that Landtoad will win, compute the revised probabilities.

9. Ace Manufacturing produces a mechanical product with a 20% failure rate. Ace Management is considering the installation of a new test device that is designed to identify a defective product prior to shipment. The accuracy of the new device is given below:

Test Device Results

|  |  | Operational | Defective |
|---|---|---|---|
| State | Operational | .8 | .2 |
|  | Defective | .1 | .9 |

Compute the revised probabilities for producing operational and defective productions using these data.

10. The Baloney Meat Packing Company uses an independent inspection company to grade and stamp its meat. Baloney stocks three grades of meat in the following proportions: Prime (30%), Choice (30%), and Grade A (40%). The following conditional table applies:

Stamped Grade

|  |  | Prime | Choice | Grade A |
|---|---|---|---|---|
| Actual Grade | Prime | .9 | .1 | 0 |
|  | Choice | .1 | .8 | .1 |
|  | Grade A | .1 | .2 | .7 |

a) Determine the probability that a piece of meat stamped Prime is Prime.
b) Determine the probability that a piece of meat stamped Choice is Grade A.

11. Doeing Aircraft Company is considering building an assembly plant in the deep South. Two alternatives are under serious consideration: A large plant costing $10,000,000 and a smaller facility costing $4,000,000. The following payoff table relates the potential market climate to income over the life of each plant:

Plant Size

|  |  | Small Plant | Large Plant | Market Probability |
|---|---|---|---|---|
| Market | Moderate | $6m | $9m | .6 |
|  | Strong | $10m | $20m | .4 |

In addition, management has the option of initially building the smaller plant and, if the market is strong, constructing an additional facility at a cost of $7 million. Use a decision tree to solve for the optimal decision based on maximizing expected value.

12. Solve the following decision tree based on maximizing expected value:

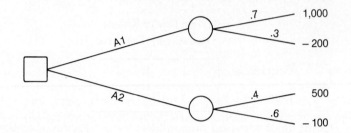

13. Solve the following decision tree based on maximizing expected value.

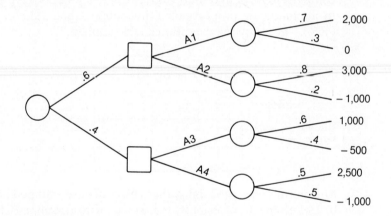

14. Given the following payoff table:

|      | A1   | A2  | A3  |
|------|------|-----|-----|
| S1   | 100  | 0   | -50 |
| S2   | 50   | 200 | 0   |
| S3   | -200 | 50  | 150 |

a) Set up the corresponding decision tree if $P(S1) = .4$, $P(S2) = .3$, and $P(S3) = .3$

b) Determine the optimal action to maximize the payoff.

15. A company is considering submitting a bid to the government for producing a perpetual motion machine. The company's marketing department has developed the following bidding data:

| Bid | Probability of Winning |
|-----------|------|
| 1,000,000 | .8 |
| 3,000,000 | .5 |

The company has two methods of producing the machine. The first involves a well-tested process with production costs estimated at $600,000 per machine. The second involves an experimental process which results in a 60% probability of producing a machine for $450,000 and a 40% probability that the cost will be $1,200,000.

a) How much should the company bid?

b) If it gets the contract, should it use the experimental process or the well-tested process?

c) What is the expected payoff?

16. Construct a decision tree for the following data and select the optimal action.

| Node | Type | | Ending Node |
|------|----------|--------------|------|
| | | *Alternatives* | |
| 0 | Decision | 1 | 1 |
| | | 2 | 2 |
| | | *Probability* | |
| 1 | Chance | .4 | 3 |
| | | .6 | 4 |
| | | *Payoff* | |
| 2 | Terminal | −1000 | - |
| 3 | Terminal | 1500 | - |
| 4 | Terminal | 500 | - |

a) Which alternative should be selected?

b) What is the expected payoff?

17. Solve problem #12 in Chapter 9 with a decision tree.

18. The Dendix Corporation is considering the acquisition of one of two firms: Sav-Less and Poor Year. The financial results of this decision will be influenced by the state of the economy over the next year.

| | Actions ($ Million) | |
| State of Economy | Buy Sav-Less | Buy Poor Year |
| --- | --- | --- |
| Improve | 0 | 100 |
| Decline | 25 | –50 |

The probability that the economy will improve is .4. Use a decision tree to identify the optimal action

19. For the above problem, Dendix is considering the use of an economic forecasting service. The service charges $100,000 for one of their special forecasts. The service has the following record:

| | Prediction | |
| State of Economy | Economy Improves | Economy Declines |
| --- | --- | --- |
| Improve | 0.8 | 0.2 |
| Decline | 0.3 | 0.7 |

Use a decision tree to determine if Dendix should buy the service. What is

the maximum Dendix should pay for this service?

20. For the above problem, what is the impact on Dendix's decision if the first row in the conditional table is changed to 0.9 and 0.1, respectively?

---

CASE STUDY **Abell Computers**

The owner of Abell Computers has decided to explore the possibility of developing and selling a new personal computer graphics package. Abell's software development group estimates that it will cost $750,000 to develop the new package.

If successful, the new package will increase two-year profits by $2.5 million (all of Abell's product decisions are based upon a two-year time horizon). They estimate that there is a 70 percent chance that the new package will be successful. If the package is a failure, however, two-year profits will increase by only $100,000. Neither of these two-year profit projections include the $750,000 development cost.

Abell is considering the use of an outside market appraisal before

(CONT.)

CASE STUDY **Abell Computers**   *(CONT.)*

going ahead with the development of this package. Two firms have offered to do the forecast. Dudley Forecasting, one of the largest market research firms in the West, has proposed a comprehensive survey costing $250,000. Dudley's track record is impressive. On similar forecasts in the past, they had predicted success in 90 percent of the cases when the project was actually successful. Also, they had predicted failure in 85 percent of the cases when the project actually failed.

The other firm, Jones & Jones, has proposed a more modest effort costing only $125,000. Their past performance is less impressive than Dudley's, but is still competitive. On past successful project, they had predicted success 70 percent of the time. On failures, they had predicted failure 65 percent of the time.

a) Should Abell hire on of the market research firms? If so, which one?

b) Should Abell develop the new package?

c) What is the optimal total two-year profit?

d) What will the expected two-year profit be if they hire Dudley?

e) What will the expected two-year profit be if they hire Jones & Jones?

f) What is the maximum amount that Abell would be willing to pay Dudley for a forecast?

# 11
## MRKV

# *Markov Models*

The Markov model (called Markov chains in some books) can be applied to a variety of problems, but is usually described by using a marketing application with a fixed number of brands for sale. Customers make only one purchase during each time period, and they buy only one brand each time they make a purchase. The current market share held by each brand is known. The brand loyalty and brand switching behavior for all future purchases is also known.

Typical questions addressed in this Markov problem include the following:

1. How many customers will buy each brand in the next purchase period?

2. How many customers will buy each brand in any specified future period?

3. In the long run (after a very large number of purchase periods have passed), how many customers will buy each brand in each purchase period?

The term *state* refers to each of the actions that can be taken by a customer. A customer must be in one and only one state during each period of a Markov problem. Customers may stay in the same state (purchase the same brand) or switch to a different state (purchase a different brand) in each of the subsequent periods. The probabilities of switching from state to state are called *transition probabilities*.

The states in problems similar to the above example are called *recurrent*. Another important form of Markov model includes *absorbing* states. In such a problem, there will be one or more states that cannot be left once they are entered. For example, if one analyzed the progress of students through the courses in a university, every student would eventually either graduate or leave without graduating. Once any student reached either of these two states, he or she would no longer take any courses. Thus these would be absorbing states. If a problem has absorbing states, everyone must eventually end up in one of these states. If a problem has one or more absorbing states, the nonabsorbing states are called *transient* states.

# 11.1 Program Description

This program analyzes either recurrent state or absorbing state Markov problems. If the problem has no absorbing states, the program can be used to predict long-run (or steady state) market share from the transition probability matrix. It can also use the transition probability matrix and the current market share to predict the market share in either any specified future period or all periods from the current period to any specified future period. This program also computes mean first passage times, first passage time variances, and expected recurrence times.

For Markov chains with absorbing states, the program determines the mean number of periods that one will remain in each transient state prior to absorption, the mean time to absorption given that one begins in any transient state, and the probability of being absorbed into each of the absorbing states.

The program can handle problems with up to 12 different states. Any number of these can be absorbing states.

# 11.2 Problem Preparation

The only special preparation required for this program occurs when there are absorbing states in the problem. In such a case, the transition probability matrix must be arranged so the absorbing state data form an identity matrix (a matrix with all zeros and ones, where the ones are all on the diagonal that goes from the upper left corner to the lower right corner) in the upper left corner.

When you rearrange your matrix, make sure that the final form of the matrix has each state in the same row and column. (The state in row 1 must also be in column 1, the state in row 2 must also be in column 2, and so on.)

# 11.3 Data Input Overview

The first item input is the number of rows (states, products, and so on) that are in the problem. The next item is the number of absorbing states. The transition probability matrix values are then entered into the computer from left to right for every row.

No further input is required if the problem has at least one absorbing state. If the problem has no absorbing states, the next input indicates whether market share analysis is to be done by the program. If market share analysis is desired, you must also input the current market share and the number of periods that will elapse between the current period and the future period.

# 11.4 Data Input Details

The first data values (the problem structure) are as follows:

| total number of states | , | number of absorbing states |
|---|---|---|

If there are absorbing states, then the next set of data is as follows:

1, | zeros for all remaining columns |

If there is another absorbing state:

0,1, | zeros for all remaining columns |

Each of the remaining absorbing states is entered with the "1" located one column to the right of the "1" in the previous entry.

Next, data for each of the recurrent (or transient) states are entered.

| transition probability for column 1 | transition probability for column 2 | etc. for all columns |
|---|---|---|

No further input is needed when the problem contains absorbing states. If the problem contains only recurrent states, you will be asked if you want a Market Share Analysis. Type a "Y" if you want market share analysis or an "N" if you do not.

If you want market share analysis, then the following additional data must be input:

| number of periods in the future |

This is followed by the current market share values:

| current market share for column 1 |

| current market share for column 2 |

| etc. for all columns |

## 11.5 Editing the Data

Any of the transition probability matrix values may be changed by selecting the editing option from the program menu. The number of periods in the market share analysis and the initial market share probabilities may also be changed. On-screen prompts will guide you through the editing process.

When all editing is done, the full set of data may be saved on a data diskette before returning to the PROGRAM OPTIONS menu.

## 11.6 Program Output

If the problem has no absorbing states, the following items are output:

*Steady state probabilities.* The probabilities that the system will be in each of the states after an infinite number of periods. In the brand purchase example, this would be the long run market share for each of the brands. (Also called "long run," "long term," "equilibrium," or "limiting" market share.)

*Mean first passage times.* The mean number of periods that will elapse before a customer of one brand will switch to another specified brand for the first time.

*First passage time variances.* The variances for each of the first passage times.

*Expected recurrence times.* The mean number of periods that will elapse before a customer of one brand again purchases that same brand.

*Market share analysis.* If you selected market share analysis, the first item output in a table of market share for all products from period 1 to period N + 1 (where N is the number of periods you selected for the market share analysis). All problems begin at period 1, so if you want the market share 3 periods from now, the computer will output the market share at the beginning of periods 1 through 4. The last item output is the *transition matrix* after period N. This is the result obtained by taking the original transition probability matrix and raising it to the Nth power.

If the problem has any absorbing states, then a different output format is used:

*Time to absorption by state.* The numbers in this matrix (called the fundamental matrix in many texts) show the mean number of periods that one will remain in each of the transient states prior to being absorbed. Each row of data was generated under the assumption that one began in that row.

*Time to absorption.* This portion of the output contains the mean number of periods that one will take to be absorbed given that one began in each of the transient states. Each value is equal to the sum of the values in the corresponding row of the fundamental matrix.

*Conditional probabilities*. These are the probabilities that one will end up in each of the absorbing states (the columns in this part of the output) given that one begins in each of the transient states (the rows in this part of the output).

# 11.7  Example Problem MAR1

A manufacturer owns an electric forge that is either in good operating condition, in need of minor repairs and operating at reduced capacity, or shut down for repairs. The following matrix contains the transition probabilities for the various states.

|  | Operating | Needs Repair | Shut Down |
|---|---|---|---|
| Operating | .7 | .2 | .1 |
| Needs Repair | .3 | .6 | .1 |
| Shut Down | .2 | .3 | .5 |

1. Determine the steady-state probability for each state.
2. If the forge is currently shut down for repairs, how many periods will typically elapse before it is in good operating condition?
3. If the forge is currently shut down, how many periods will typically elapse before it will be shut down again?
4. If the forge is currently operating, what is the probability that it will be operating three periods from now?

## 11.7.1  Problem Preparation

This problem is already prepared in matrix form, so the data can be entered directly into the computer.

## 11.7.2  Data Input

The following data values must be input to solve this problem:

3, 0
.7, .2, .1
.3, .6, .1
.2, .3, .5
Y
3
1, 0, 0

Figure 11.1 shows how the problem structure should be input. Figure 11.2 shows how the screen appears when the last of the transition probabilities has been entered. The current market share values are entered similarly.

**FIGURE 11.1**   Input of problem structure for example problem MAR1

```
                              -=*=-   DATA   INPUT   -=*=-



        ENTER THE TOTAL NUMBER OF STATES
        ENTER NUMBER IN RANGE ( 2   -   12 ) & press ↵    3


        ENTER NUMBER OF ABSORBING STATES
        ENTER NUMBER IN RANGE ( 0   -   2 ) & press ↵     0



        DO YOU WANT TO RE-ENTER PROBLEM STRUCTURE? (Y/N)
        Enter a Character ( Y   or   N ) .& press ↵    N
```

**FIGURE 11.2**   Computer screen after input of all transition probabilities for example problem MAR1

```
                         -=*=-   DATA   INPUT   -=*=-
   STATES    1      2      3

       1    0.700  0.200  0.100
       2    0.300  0.600  0.100
       3    0.200  0.300  0






     ENTER VALUE FOR DATA POINT  -OR-  AN 'E' TO EDIT  -OR-  A 'Q' TO ABORT ENTRY

   ENTER PROBABILITY FOR   STATE IN ROW 3 COLUMN 3
   ENTER NUMBER IN RANGE ( 0   -   1  ) & press ↵ ?.5
```

## 11.7.3 Computer Output

Figure 11.3 contains the output from a run of this problem. The answers to example problem MAR1 are read from the output as follows:

1. The steady-state probability for each state is the first item output in the RESULTS section: The answers are (to 2 decimal places): operating, .47; needs repair, .36; and shut down, .17.

2. If the forge is currently shut down (state 3), it will typically take 4.18 periods before it is in good operating condition (state 1). This was obtained from the MEAN FIRST PASSAGE TIMES part of the output.

3. If the forge is currently shut down (state 3), it will typically take 6 periods before it is shut down again. This was obtained from column 3 of the EXPECTED RECURRENCE TIMES.

4. If the forge is currently operating, there is a .514 probability that it will be operating three periods from now. This was obtained from column 1 of the MARKET SHARE AT BEGINNING OF PERIOD 4.

**FIGURE 11.3** Output from a run of example problem MAR1

```
                    -=*=-   INFORMATION ENTERED   -=*=-

        TOTAL NUMBER OF STATES            :        3

        NUMBER OF ABSORBING STATES        :        0



                          TRANSITION TABLE

    STATES    1     2     3

       1     0.700 0.200 0.100
       2     0.300 0.600 0.100
       3     0.200 0.300 0.500




                    MARKET SHARE PROBABILITIES

                    SHARE

       1            1.000
       2            0
       3            0




                MARKET SHARE ANALYZED FOR  3   PERIODS

                    -=*=-   RESULTS   -=*=-

                    STEADY STATE PROBABILITIES

        0.472 0.361 0.167
```

(CONT.)

**FIGURE 11.3**   *(CONT.)*

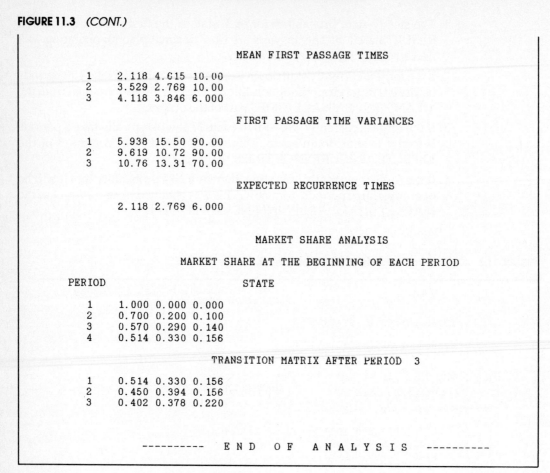

```
                        MEAN FIRST PASSAGE TIMES

        1    2.118 4.615 10.00
        2    3.529 2.769 10.00
        3    4.118 3.846 6.000


                        FIRST PASSAGE TIME VARIANCES

        1    5.938 15.50 90.00
        2    9.619 10.72 90.00
        3    10.76 13.31 70.00

                        EXPECTED RECURRENCE TIMES

             2.118 2.769 6.000


                        MARKET SHARE ANALYSIS

                MARKET SHARE AT THE BEGINNING OF EACH PERIOD

     PERIOD                      STATE

        1    1.000 0.000 0.000
        2    0.700 0.200 0.100
        3    0.570 0.290 0.140
        4    0.514 0.330 0.156

                        TRANSITION MATRIX AFTER PERIOD  3

        1    0.514 0.330 0.156
        2    0.450 0.394 0.156
        3    0.402 0.378 0.220


        ----------  E N D   O F   A N A L Y S I S  ----------
```

# 11.8  Example Problem MAR2

Mr. Hugh Highpower is in the process of considering his chances for promotion. His ultimate objective is to become president; however, there is the possibility that too aggressive behavior on his part will result in his termination. There are four positions that H. H. can hold in the company:

- Janitor
- Department head
- Vice president
- President

The probabilities of moving from any one position to any other position are as follows:

|     | F   | J   | D   | VP  | P   |
| --- | --- | --- | --- | --- | --- |
| F   | 1   | 0   | 0   | 0   | 0   |
| J   | 0   | .3  | .4  | .1  | .2  |
| D   | .1  | .2  | .3  | .3  | .1  |
| VP  | .2  | .3  | 0   | .3  | .2  |
| P   | 0   | 0   | 0   | 0   | 1   |

The table shows that if he gets fired, Mr. Highpower cannot hold any other job in the company. The table also shows that the job of president is permanent and will be held until retirement.

1. Assuming H. H. is currently a department head, what is the probability he will become president in the long run?
2. How many years does he have to wait to become president or to be terminated?

## 11.8.1 Problem Preparation

The only preparation needed for this problem is to move the two absorbing states (F and P) to form an identity matrix in the upper left corner of the transition probability matrix. The result is as follows:

|     | P   | F   | J   | D   | VP  |
| --- | --- | --- | --- | --- | --- |
| P   | 1   | 0   | 0   | 0   | 0   |
| F   | 0   | 1   | 0   | 0   | 0   |
| J   | .2  | 0   | .3  | .4  | .1  |
| D   | .1  | .1  | .2  | .3  | .3  |
| VP  | .2  | .2  | .3  | 0   | .3  |

## 11.8.2 Data Input

The following data values must be input to solve this problem:

```
5, 2
1, 0, 0, 0, 0
0, 1, 0, 0, 0
```

.2, 0, .3, .4, .1
.1, .1, .2, .3, .3
.2, .2, .3, 0, .3

## 11.8.3 Computer Output

Figure 11.4 contains the output from a run of this problem. The answers to example problem MAR2 are read from the output as follows:

1. The conditional table contains the probabilities of being absorbed into each of the absorbing states. Thus there is a 60 percent chance of becoming president from H. H.'s current position as department head (state 4).

2. The time to absorption shows the mean number of periods that H. H. will remain in the transient states prior to absorption. Thus from the department head position, it will typically take four periods to be absorbed (that is, made president or fired).

**FIGURE 11.4** Output from a run of example problem MAR2

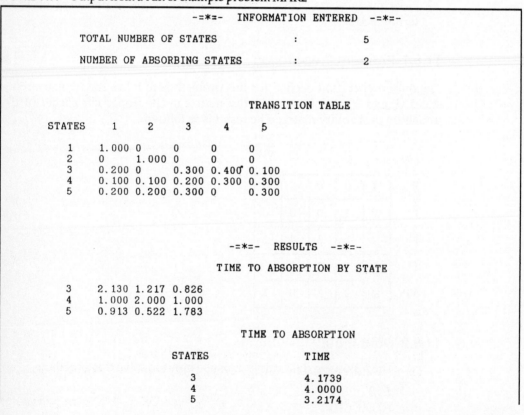

```
                    -=*=-  INFORMATION ENTERED  -=*=-

     TOTAL NUMBER OF STATES              :        5

     NUMBER OF ABSORBING STATES          :        2



                         TRANSITION TABLE

     STATES    1     2     3     4     5

       1     1.000 0     0     0     0
       2     0     1.000 0     0     0
       3     0.200 0     0.300 0.400 0.100
       4     0.100 0.100 0.200 0.300 0.300
       5     0.200 0.200 0.300 0     0.300




                    -=*=-   RESULTS   -=*=-

                 TIME TO ABSORPTION BY STATE

       3     2.130 1.217 0.826
       4     1.000 2.000 1.000
       5     0.913 0.522 1.783

                    TIME TO ABSORPTION

              STATES              TIME

                 3                4.1739
                 4                4.0000
                 5                3.2174
```

(CONT.)

**FIGURE 11.4**   *(CONT.)*

```
                        CONDITIONAL PROBABILITIES BY STATE

        3     0.713 0.287
        4     0.600 0.400
        5     0.591 0.409


              ----------   E N D   O F   A N A L Y S I S   ----------
```

# 11.9 Markov Problems

1. Given the following transition matrix, determine the steady state probabilities:

|      | S1 | S2 | S3 |
|------|----|----|----|
| S1   | .5 | .3 | .2 |
| S2   | .3 | .6 | .1 |
| S3   | .1 | .2 | .7 |

2. Given the following transition matrix where product two (P2) currently has 100% of the market:

|      | P1 | P2 | P3 |
|------|----|----|----|
| P1   | .3 | .6 | .1 |
| P2   | .7 | 0  | .3 |
| P3   | .2 | .3 | .5 |

a) What is each product's market share after two periods have elapsed?
b) What is each product's long-run market share?
c) How many periods will typically elapse before a product 1 customer buys product 3?
d) How many periods will typically elapse before a current product 2 customer returns to buy product 2 after buying other products?

3. Given the following transition matrix where all four products currently share the market equally:

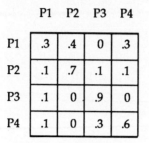

|      | P1 | P2 | P3 | P4 |
|------|----|----|----|----|
| P1   | .3 | .4 | 0  | .3 |
| P2   | .1 | .7 | .1 | .1 |
| P3   | .1 | 0  | .9 | 0  |
| P4   | .1 | 0  | .3 | .6 |

a) What is each product's market share after two periods have elapsed?

b) What is each product's long-run market share?

c) How many periods will typically elapse before a product 1 customer buys product 3?

d) How many periods will typically elapse before a current product 2 customer returns to buy product 2 after buying other products?

4. Suppose 70% of all output from an assembly line are good products that can be shipped to customers. Furthermore, 10% are bad and must be scrapped. The remaining 20% have some correctable defect. These latter items are run through the same line again. Items going through the second time have the same probabilities of being good, scrap, or requiring rework.

a) How many times is the average item run through the line before it is either good or scrap?

b) What is the percentage of good parts output by the line?

5. Given the following absorbing state matrix, determine:

a) The average time to absorption.

b) The probability of being absorbed in each state.

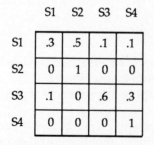

|      | S1 | S2 | S3 | S4 |
|------|----|----|----|----|
| S1   | .3 | .5 | .1 | .1 |
| S2   | 0  | 1  | 0  | 0  |
| S3   | .1 | 0  | .6 | .3 |
| S4   | 0  | 0  | 0  | 1  |

6. A market research firm has compiled the following brand loyalty data on soft drink buyers:

|  | | Next Week's Purchase | | |
|---|---|---|---|---|
|  | | Hiho | Quench | Refresh |
|  | Hiho | .7 | .2 | .1 |
| Last Purchase | Quench | .1 | .9 | 0 |
|  | Refresh | .7 | .2 | .1 |

a) What is the long-run market share for each soft drink?
b) If the current market share for the three products is:

| Product | Market Share |
|---|---|
| Hiho | .25 |
| Quench | .35 |
| Refresh | .40 |

What will each product's market share be in two weeks?

7. Weekly stock prices for the Bovay Company have been observed to rise, remain the same, and fall according to the following transition matrix:

|  | Up | No Change | Down |
|---|---|---|---|
| Up | .4 | .5 | .1 |
| No Change | .3 | .5 | .2 |
| Down | .1 | .6 | .3 |

a) Determine the steady state probabilities.
b) Determine the mean recurrence times.

8. Management at XYZ Corporation has been unhappy with the low reliability of its old computer. It seems to be down more often than up. The following data show the transition probabilities on a one-hour basis:

|  | Operational | Down |
|---|---|---|
| Operational | .8 | .2 |
| Down | .4 | .6 |

a) If the system is currently down, what is the probability of being down one hour from now?

b) If the system is currently operational, what is the probability of being down three hours from now?

c) What are the long-run probabilities that the computer will be operational or down?

9. The Computer Center experts want management to approve the purchase of a new computer that has the following system performance:

|  | Operational | Down |
|---|---|---|
| Operational | .9 | .1 |
| Down | .2 | .8 |

If every hour of down time costs the center $1000, how much more should they be willing to pay per hour for a new computer to replace the computer described in problem 8?

10. The current import car market share in the United States is 30%. The probability that an owner of a U.S.-made care will buy another U.S.-made car is 70%. The probability that an owner of a foreign-made car will buy another foreign-made car is 80%.

a) Determine the market share for foreign- and U.S.-made vehicles after two and five years.

b) Determine the steady state probabilities for foreign- and U.S.-made vehicles.

11. A security guard patrols the first four floors of a high-rise building according to the following transition matrix:

|  | To | | | |
|---|---|---|---|---|
|  | Floor 1 | Floor 2 | Floor 3 | Floor 4 |
| **From** Floor 1 | 0 | .5 | .3 | .2 |
| Floor 2 | .4 | 0 | .4 | .2 |
| Floor 3 | .1 | .3 | 0 | .6 |
| Floor 4 | .2 | .3 | .5 | 0 |

a) Determine the steady state probabilities.

b) Determine the expected recurrence times.

12. Determine the mean time to absorption for the following transition matrix:

|        |    | S1 | S2 | S3 | S4 |
|--------|----|----|----|----|----|
|        | S1 | 1  | 0  | 0  | 0  |
| States | S2 | .3 | .4 | .2 | .1 |
|        | S3 | .1 | .5 | .1 | .3 |
|        | S4 | .1 | .2 | .1 | .6 |

13. A prison inmate's monthly status is governed by the following transition matrix:

|                     | Free | Trustee | Solitary Confinement |
|---------------------|------|---------|----------------------|
| Free                | 1    | 0       | 0                    |
| Trustee             | .3   | .5      | .2                   |
| Solitary Confinement| 0    | .3      | .7                   |

a) Determine the number of periods before becoming free (absorbed).
b) Determine the probability of becoming free.

14. The process of drilling for oil can be described according to the following Markov chain. Two of the states (pay dirt and dry hole) are terminal. Once production is achieved or the hole is dry, drilling operations are discontinued. The two other states (postpone drilling and continue drilling) are transient. The time frame for this process is monthly.

|                   | Pay Dirt | Dry Hole | Postpone | Continue Drilling |
|-------------------|----------|----------|----------|-------------------|
| Pay Dirt          | 1        | 0        | 0        | 0                 |
| Dry Hole          | 0        | 1        | 0        | 0                 |
| Postpone          | .3       | .1       | .2       | .4                |
| Continue Drilling | .2       | .1       | .6       | .1                |

a) Determine the number of months before hitting pay dirt or a dry hole.
b) What is the probability of hitting pay dirt?

CASE STUDY  **Lime Juice Bottling Company**

Sales for the total California soft drink market are $150 million per month and are projected to remain at this level for the next 12 months. The Lime Juice Company is considering a major advertising campaign (at a cost of $500,000 per month) to improve market share over this period. The current market is dominated by Queen Cola (with 25% of the market) and Splash (with 20% of the market). Lime Juice has only 5% of the market and other smaller bottlers collectively have the remaining 50% of the market. Consumer studies have determined the following brand loyalty and brand switching behavior:

|  | Next Month's Purchase | | | |
|---|---|---|---|---|
| Last Purchase | Lime Juice | Splash | Queen Cola | Other |
| Lime Juice | 0.55 | 0.10 | 0.15 | 0.20 |
| Splash | 0.05 | 0.70 | 0.10 | 0.15 |
| Queen Cola | 0.05 | 0.20 | 0.70 | 0.05 |
| Other | 0.05 | 0.05 | 0.05 | 0.85 |

The marketing department believes that, as a result of the new ad campaign, fewer Lime Juice customers will switch to other brands and more of those who switch from the other brands will switch to Lime Juice. Specific estimates of the new brand loyalty and brand switching probabilities are as follows:

|  | Next Month's Purchase | | | |
|---|---|---|---|---|
| Last Purchase | Lime Juice | Splash | Queen Cola | Other |
| Lime Juice | 0.58 | 0.09 | 0.14 | 0.19 |
| Splash | 0.07 | 0.70 | 0.09 | 0.14 |
| Queen Cola | 0.07 | 0.19 | 0.70 | 0.04 |
| Other | 0.07 | 0.04 | 0.04 | 0.85 |

a) What will Lime Juice's market share be after 3 months with and without the ad campaign?

b) What will Lime Juice's long run market share be with and without the ad campaign?

(CONT.)

CASE STUDY  **Lime Juice Bottling Company**   *(CONT.)*

c) What is the net financial benefit (or loss) of the ad campaign in the third month?

d) What is the net financial benefit (or loss) of the ad campaign in the twelfth month?

e) How does the ad campaign affect the number of months that elapse between the time that a Lime Juice customer buys another brand until they again buy Lime Juice?

# 12
## INVN

# *Inventory Models*

The classic inventory problem addresses the question of how frequently one should reorder stock and how many items should be requested to minimize the total costs of ordering and holding inventory. The model used to solve this problem is called the Economic Order Quantity (EOQ) model. The basic form of the EOQ model contains the following assumptions:

1. Demand is deterministic. This means that items are requested by customers and removed from inventory at exactly the same rate every time period.
2. All times that are ordered to restock inventory arrive exactly when expected.
3. Shortages (also called stockouts) are not permitted.
4. Order costs are constant. Each order that is placed to restock costs the company a fixed amount of money. This cost is independent of the size of the order.
5. Holding costs are constant. Thus each item costs the company a fixed amount of money for each time period that the item is held in inventory.
6. The objective of the company is to minimize the total of reorder costs and inventory holding costs.

The inventory program solves this basic problem and the following three extensions:

1. *The situation when shortages are permitted*. The additional assumptions that relate to the shortage situation include:
   a) No orders will be cancelled. All customers will wait until the company receives the items.
   b) Each item that is short (backordered) costs the company a fixed amount of money for each time period that the item is backordered.
2. *The situation when the item is produced by the company instead of being ordered from an outside source*. This model is usually called the optimal production

lot size model. The following assumptions apply when production is permitted:

a) The production rate is constant and is larger than the demand rate.
b) The order cost is still a constant, but should be viewed as the setup cost for a production run.

3. *The situation when demand is stochastic.* The additional assumptions that apply to this type of problem are as follows:

a) Demand is normally distributed with a known mean and standard deviation.
b) The lead time for deliveries is a constant.
c) Shortages are permitted.

The optimal production lot size model can be solved with or without shortages, but it cannot be solved with stochastic demand.

## 12.1 Program Description

This program solves the EOQ model (with or without shortages) and optimal production lot size model (with or without shortages). Output for both of these models includes the order quantity, reorder level, order costs, holding costs, total cost, and maximum inventory levels.

The program can also be used to solve problems where demand is stochastic. Output from the program includes both the optimal order quantity and reorder level. If the shortage cost rate is known, the program computes both the safety stock level, safety stock cost, and total shortage costs. If the shortage cost rate is unknown, then the program requires an estimate of the highest acceptable shortage probability.

## 12.2 Problem Preparation

No special problem preparation is required to use the inventory program except to make sure that time, money, and quantity units are identical throughout the problem. If you use months as the time unit for demand, you must use months as the time unit for holding costs and lead time.

## 12.3 Data Input Overview

The first set of input values are as follows:

*Product demand.* The rate at which products are purchased or used. Input the mean value of product demand if demand is stochastic.

*Order cost.* The total cost of ordering any size lot of the product. Order costs include the costs of personnel who place the order, delivery costs, and so on. If production is permitted, the order cost also includes the production run setup costs.

*Holding cost.* The cost of holding one item in inventory for one time period.

*Lead time.* The time period between placing and delivering an order.

Next indicate whether product demand is constant or stochastic. If demand is constant, indicate whether shortages are permitted. If they are, input the *shortage cost rate.* Next, indicate if production is permitted. If it is, input the *production rate.* The production rate must always be larger than product demand.

If demand is stochastic, first input the *demand over lead time.* Demand is usually at the same rate at all times. If, however, demand slows down or increases during the lead-time period, a different value may be entered here. Next, input the *demand standard deviation.* The remaining data for a stochastic demand problem describe the shortage costs. Shortage cost is the cost per out-of-stock item per time period. It includes cost of good will, and any other costs that management believes are incurred when an item is out of stock. If the shortage cost is known, then it should be input here. If the shortage cost is not known, then input the *critical stockout probability.* This is the stockout level that management considers to be acceptable.

All time, money, and unit measures must be consistent in all input. If months are used as a measure of time for demand, be sure to use months for holding costs and lead time.

## 12.4  Data Input Details

The first data values are as follows:

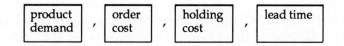

### 12.4.1 Deterministic Demand

If demand is deterministic, enter an "N" in response to the STOCHASTIC DEMAND (Y/N)? prompt. Then, if shortages are not permitted, enter an "N" in response to SHORTAGES PERMITTED (Y/N)?, but if shortages are permitted, enter the following:

Y,   | shortage cost |

If production is not permitted, enter an "N" in response to PRODUCTION PERMITTED (Y/N)?, but if production is permitted, enter the following:

Y,  | production rate |

### 12.4.2 Stochastic Demand

If demand is stochastic, enter a "Y" in response to the STOCHASTIC DE- MAND (Y/N)? prompt, and follow this by:

| demand over lead time |

| demand standard deviation |

If shortage costs are known, the next input is as follows:

Y,  | shortage cost per unit per period |

But if shortage costs are not known, the next input is as follows:

N,  | critical stockout probability |

## 12.5 Editing the Data

The EDIT CURRENT PROBLEM option begins with an on-screen display of a table containing all input values. Enter the number of the item you want to change, and then enter the new value. Continue until all values have been changed, then type "8" to indicate that you want to return to the program menu.

When editing is completed, the revised data may be saved on a data diskette before returning to the PROGRAM OPTIONS menu.

## 12.6 Program Output

The program output includes the following:

*Optimal order quantity.* The number of items that should be ordered or produced each time inventory needs to be replenished. The computer will often output results that cannot be implemented (such as the EOQ value of 7098.212 in the second example problem of this chapter). In real inventory problems, the decision maker would round these to a more appropriate value.

*Reorder level.* The inventory level at which a new order for stock should be placed.

*Maximum inventory.* The maximum number of units that will ever be in inventory. This point will be reached either when a restocking order is received (for the EOQ model) or when production stops (for the optimal production lot size model). This item is output only if your problem has deterministic demand.

*Safety stock.* The amount of extra inventory that is held to keep stockouts to an appropriately low level. This item is output only if your problem has stochastic demand.

*Stockouts per period.* The mean number of stockouts per period. This item is output only for stochastic demand problems where the shortage cost is known.

*Ordering costs.* The total cost of ordering inventory per period.

*Holding costs.* The total cost of holding inventory per period. The cost of holding safety stock is not included.

*Safety stock costs.* The total cost of holding safety stock in inventory per period.

*Shortage costs.* The total cost of stockouts per period.

*Total inventory costs.* The total of ordering, holding, safety stock, and shortage costs per period.

# 12.7 Example Problem INV1

A distributor has an annual demand of 5000 shirts. It costs $20 to place an order with the manufacturer and 20¢ per shirt per year in inventory carry costs.

1. How many shirts should be included in each order to replenish stock?
2. What is the total yearly inventory cost of this policy?

## 12.7.1 Problem Preparation

The first four data items for this problem are as follows:

Product Demand: 5000 shirts/year
Order Cost: $20

Holding Cost: $0.20/shirt/year

Lead Time: No information is given about lead time, so use zero.

No information is given about stochastic demand, so you should assume that it is deterministic. Similarly, you should assume that no shortages and no production are permitted.

### 12.7.2 Data Input

The following data values must be input to solve this problem:

5000, 20, .2, 0
N
N
N

Figure 12.1 shows how these data values should be input in response to prompts from the computer.

### 12.7.3 Computer Output

Figure 12.2 contains the output from a run of this problem. The output shows that 1000 shirts should be included in each order to replenish stock. The total cost of this policy is $200 per year.

# 12.8 Example Problem INV2

The distributor in example problem INV1 has added an internal manufacturing capacity of 10,000 shirts per year (working 250 days per year). It takes one day and costs $500 to set up a production run. The company has also decided

**FIGURE 12.1**   Computer screen after input of data for example problem INVN1

```
                     -=*=-    DATA   INPUT   -=*=-

   ENTER PRODUCT DEMAND & press ←┘                          5000

   ENTER ORDERING COSTS & press ←┘                          20

   ENTER HOLDING COSTS & press ←┘                           .2

   ENTER DELIVERY LEAD TIME & press ←┘                      0


   STOCHASTIC DEMAND
   Enter a Character ( Y  or  N ) & press ←┘    N
```

**FIGURE 12.2**   Output from a run of example problem INVN1

```
                    -=*=-   INFORMATION ENTERED   -=*=-


    PRODUCT DEMAND                  :          5,000.000

    ORDERING COSTS                  :             20.000

    HOLDING COSTS                   :              0.200

    DELIVERY LEAD TIME              :              0.000



                       -=*=-   RESULTS   -=*=-


    OPTIMAL ORDER QUANTITY          :          1,000.000

    REORDER LEVEL                   :              0.000

    MAXIMUM INVENTORY               :          1,000.000

    ORDERING COSTS                  :            100.000

    HOLDING COSTS                   :            100.000

    TOTAL  INVENTORY COSTS          :            200.000



           ----------  E N D   O F   A N A L Y S I S  ----------
```

to permit shortages, and estimates that it will incur a "good will" loss of 50¢ per shirt per week for all unfilled orders. Determine the optimal order quantity and the total yearly inventory cost for this new situation.

## 12.8.1 Problem Preparation

The first four data values are as follows:

> Product Demand: 5000 shirts/year (same as INV1)
> Order Cost: $500 (the setup cost)
> Holding Cost: $0.20/shirt/year (same as INV1)
> Lead Time: 0.004 years (1 day divided by 250 days/year)

The remaining data values are:

> Shortage Cost: $26/shirt/year ($0.50/shirt/week times 52 weeks/year)
> Production Rate: 10,000 shirts/year

## 12.8.2 Data Input

The following must be input to solve this problem:

5000, 500, .2, .004
N
Y, 26
Y, 10000

Figure 12.3 and Figure 12.4 show the input of this problem into the computer.

## 12.8.3 Computer Output

Figure 12.5 contains the output from a run of this problem. The output shows that 7098.212 shirts should be included in each production run. The total cost of this policy is $704.40 per year.

**FIGURE 12.3**   Computer screen after input of first half of data for example problem INVN2

```
                         -=*=-   DATA   INPUT   -=*=-


   ENTER PRODUCT DEMAND & press ↵                                    5000

   ENTER ORDERING COSTS & press ↵                                    500

   ENTER HOLDING COSTS & press ↵                                     .2

   ENTER DELIVERY LEAD TIME & press ↵                               .004



   STOCHASTIC DEMAND
   Enter a Character ( Y  or  N ) & press ↵    N
```

**FIGURE 12.4**   Computer screen after input of second half of data for example problem INVN2

```
                         -=*=-   DATA   INPUT   -=*=-

   SHORTAGES PERMITTED
   Enter a Character ( Y  or  N ) & press ↵     Y

   ENTER SHORTAGE COSTS & press ↵                                   26


   PRODUCTION PERMITTED
   Enter a Character ( Y  or  N ) & press ↵     Y

   ENTER PRODUCTION RATE & press ↵                                  10000
```

**FIGURE 12.5**   Output from a run of example problem INVN2

```
                -=*=-   INFORMATION ENTERED   -=*=-


     PRODUCT DEMAND                 :        5,000.000

     ORDERING COSTS                 :          500.000

     HOLDING COSTS                  :            0.200

     DELIVERY LEAD TIME             :            0.004

     SHORTAGE COSTS                 :           26.000

     PRODUCTION RATE                :       10,000.000



                    -=*=-   RESULTS   -=*=-


     OPTIMAL ORDER QUANTITY         :        7,098.212

     REORDER LEVEL                  :           20.000

     MAXIMUM INVENTORY              :        3,522.014

     ORDERING COSTS                 :          352.201

     HOLDING COSTS                  :          349.513

     SHORTAGE COSTS                 :            2.689

     TOTAL INVENTORY COSTS          :          704.403



          ----------  E N D   O F   A N A L Y S I S   ----------
```

# 12.9  Example Problem INV3

A grocer sells 1000 cans of peaches per week. Demand is stochastic with a standard deviation of 200 cans per week. It costs $20 to place an order and stock the shelves when it arrives. Orders have a one-week lead time. If the grocer runs out of peaches, it estimates lost future business of $5 per can per week. It also estimates that it costs an average of 5¢ per week to keep a can on the shelf.

The grocer wants to know how frequently to order, how many cans to include in the order, and the cost of this ordering policy.

## 12.9.1  Problem Preparation

The first four data values are as follows:

Product Demand: 1000 cans/week

Order Cost: $20

Holding Cost: $0.05/can/week

Lead Time: 1 week

The remaining data values are as follows:

Demand Over Lead Time: 1000 cans

Demand Standard Deviation: 200 cans/week

Shortage Cost: $5/can/week

## 12.9.2 Data Input

The following must be input to solve this problem:

1000, 20, .05, 1
Y, 200
Y, 5

Figure 12.6 and Figure 12.7 show the input of this problem into the computer.

## 12.9.3 Computer Output

Figure 12.8 shows the results for this problem. The grocer should order every 6.26 days if it works a seven-day week. (Determined by dividing EOQ of 894.427 by demand of 1000 and multiplying this result by 7 days per week.) It should request about 894 cans in each order. The cost of this ordering policy will be $70.34 per week.

**FIGURE 12.6**    Computer screen after input of first half of data for example problem INVN3

```
                    -=*=-   DATA   INPUT   -=*=-


ENTER PRODUCT DEMAND & press ↵                              1000

ENTER ORDERING COSTS & press ↵                             20

ENTER HOLDING COSTS & press ↵                               .05

ENTER DELIVERY LEAD TIME & press ↵                          1



STOCHASTIC DEMAND
Enter a Character ( Y  or  N ) & press ↵     Y
```

**FIGURE 12.7**   Computer screen after input of second half of data for example problem INVN3

```
                          -=*=-   DATA  INPUT  -=*=-


     ENTER DEMAND OVER LEAD TIME & press ↵                    1000

     ENTER STANDARD DEVIATION & press ↵                       200


     SHORTAGE COSTS KNOWN
     Enter a Character ( Y  or  N ) & press ↵      Y


     ENTER SHORTAGE COSTS & press ↵                              5
```

**FIGURE 12.8**   Output from a run of example problem INVN3

```
                     -=*=-   INFORMATION ENTERED  -=*=-


     PRODUCT DEMAND                  :        1,000.000

     ORDERING COSTS                  :           20.000

     HOLDING COSTS                   :            0.050

     DELIVERY LEAD TIME              :            1.000

     DEMAND OVER LEAD TIME           :        1,000.000

     STANDARD DEVIATION              :          200.000

     SHORTAGE COSTS                  :            5.000



                       -=*=-   RESULTS  -=*=-


     OPTIMAL ORDER QUANTITY          :          894.427

     REORDER LEVEL                   :        1,465.954

     SAFETY STOCK                    :          465.954

     STOCKOUTS PER PERIOD            :            0.465

     ORDERING COSTS                  :           22.361

     HOLDING COSTS                   :           22.361

     SAFETY STOCK COSTS              :           23.298

     SHORTAGE COSTS                  :            2.323

     TOTAL INVENTORY COSTS           :           70.342

          ----------  E N D   O F   A N A L Y S I S  ----------
```

# 12.10 Inventory Problems

1. Order Cost = $3
   Holding Cost = $5 per unit per year
   Demand = 1000 units per year

   a) What is the value of EOQ?
   b) What is the optimal total yearly cost?

2. Order Cost = $10
   Holding Cost = $5 per unit per year
   Demand = 1000 units per month

   a) What is the value of EOQ?
   b) What is the total yearly cost of the optimal policy?

3. Order Cost = $12
   Cost per unit = $50
   Holding Cost = 2% of unit cost per month
   Demand = 500 units per month

   a) What is the value of EOQ?
   b) What is the optimal total yearly cost?

4. It cost $7 to place an order for any number of units of a product that is used at a uniform rate of 1400 units per year. Each unit in inventory has a holding cost of $10 per year.

   a) What is the optimal order size?
   b) What is the optimal total yearly cost?

5. A discount store sells 200 toasters per month. Each toaster costs the store $6. They estimate that it costs them $15 to have any size order of toasters delivered to the store. They also estimate that this investment in inventory costs them 2% of the inventory cost per month.

   a) How many toasters should they order when their stock gets low?
   b) What is the total yearly cost?

6. Order (setup) Cost = $150
   Carrying Cost = $6 per unit per year
   Demand = 5000 units per year
   Production Rate = 8000 units per year.

   a) What is the optimal production lot size?
   b) What is the total yearly cost?

7. Order (setup) Cost = $30
   Carrying Cost = $96 per item per year
   Demand = 200 items per month
   Production Rate = 500 items per month

       a) How many items should be produced in each run?

       b) What is the total yearly cost of this policy?

8. What is the answer to problem 1 if shortages are allowed and each unit that runs short costs $2 per year?

9. What is the answer to problem 1 if shortages are allowed and each unit that was short costs $2 per month?

10. What is the answer to problem 2 if shortages are allowed and each unit that was short costs $1 per year?

11. If an order takes one week to be delivered in problem 1, at what level of inventory should they reorder?

12. If an order takes three days to be delivered in problem 2, at what level of inventory should they reorder? The company works 250 days per year.

13. A company uses 5000 gear-pin subassemblies per year. These are used in the speed reduction unit assembly line, which runs two shifts per day, all year long. Ordering and delivery of any size lot of the gear-pin subassemblies costs $100. Storage of the gear-pin subassemblies in the plant costs $3 per unit per year. What is the optimum order size for gear-pin subassemblies?

14. A retail chain sells 12,000 "Never Start" car batteries annually. The cost of placing an order to the manufacturer is $100 per order and holding costs are $1 per month. Determine the optimal order quantity and the total costs of the policy.

15. Assuming the retail chain can produce its own version of the "Never Start" at a rate of 2000 per month, determine the optimal order quantity, maximum inventory level, and total costs using the data given in problem 14. Setup costs in this problem are the same ($100) as order costs were in problem 14.

16. Because of a large projected demand, the retail chain in problem 15 has decided to permit back orders. Management has assigned a $2 per month shortage cost. With a monthly production rate of 2000, determine the optimal order quantity, maximum inventory level, and total costs.

17. A housing tract developer has found that houses in the Shady Oaks development have been selling at a steady twenty per month. They have over 200 acres available and want to build houses on a schedule that will maximize profit. Whenever the developer builds, a crew is used to build a fixed number of houses. When these houses are done, the crew is used in other developments being built by the same corporation. The crews can build at a rate of 50 houses per month. Each house costs $100,000 to build, and all building is financed with short-term construction loans. The developer pays an average of 30% per year in taxes and interest on each unsold house. Obtaining the loan, delivering material, and getting the

crew to the construction site costs $20,000 for each batch of houses. How many houses should the crew build at one time?

18. A stapler company has been using its own punch press to produce the handles for one of its staplers. It produces 12,000 of these staplers per year at a steady rate. The punch press has a setup cost of $50, and the cost to produce handles is $0.15 each. The company has an offer from another company to ship 1000 sets of handles on the first of each month for a total cost of $140 per shipment. The punch press can produce handles at a rate of 20,000 per year. All sets of handles that have not been assembled into staplers are assessed an inventory carrying cost at a rate of 3% of handle production or purchase cost per month. If the total yearly cost of using the outside company to supply sets of handles is $1705.20 ($1680 purchase cost plus $25.20 inventory carrying cost), what is the total yearly cost of producing the sets of handles internally?

19. It costs the city a total of $35,000 to train a class of recruits at the police academy. The city has a need for 300 new academy graduates per year, but graduates cannot be put to work in the field until an opening exists in one of the divisions. All graduates who are waiting for an assignment to a division are paid at the rate of $1200 per month. If division openings occur steadily over the year, how many recruits should be trained in each class?

20. A wholesale produce distributor sells 5000 lugs of tomatoes per seven-day week. Each lug costs $2. It requires one day (lead time) and costs $250 to send a truck to pick up and deliver a load of tomatoes to the central warehouse. Once in the warehouse, storage, handling, refrigeration, and spoilage generates costs equal to $0.30 per lug per day.

a) What is the optimal number of lugs to order?
b) What is the minimum reorder level?
c) What is the total cost for this policy?

21. The Save-Less Drug Company sells 500,000 bottles of a cure-all annually. The cost of holding a bottle is $0.10 per year and the cost of ordering is $5 per order. The shortage cost, as assigned by management, is $0.50 per bottle per year. The demand over the one week lead time is 10,000 with a standard deviation of 4000. Determine the optimal order quantity, reorder level, and total cost.

22. A fast food franchise sells 6000 cases of french fries per month. Each case costs $20. Monthly holding cost is estimated as 5% of the price, and the cost to order any number of cases is $10. The demand for the product over the lead time (one week) is normally distributed with a mean of 1440 and standard deviation of 300. Management does not wish to be out of stock more than 5% of the time. Determine the optimal order quantity, reorder level, and total cost.

23. A high technology laser has an annual demand of 480 units. The cost of

placing an order is $1000 and the cost of holding is $2400 per unit per year. Demand tends to be normally distributed with an average demand over lead time of 40 and a standard deviation of 10.

a) Determine the optimal reorder quantity.
b) Determine the order point if a service level of 90% is required.
c) Compute the cost of the optimal policy.

24. Referring to problem 23, if the shortage cost is $5000,

a) Determine the order point.
b) Compute the cost of the optimal policy.
c) Compare the cost results with problem 23.

---

## CASE STUDY  **Primrose Lamps**

Primrose Lamps manufactures quality lamps for both home and office. Primrose's premium lamp wholesales for a price of $250. The company serves only the Houston metropolitan area and demand is constant at 150 lamps per month. Primrose's vice president for operations has recently received a letter from one of their main suppliers regarding future lamp-shade orders. Basically, the supplier's new policy is that the minimum order is 5 cartons (with 10 lamp shades per carton). For orders of 25 cartons or more, the supplier offers a 2 % discount. The base price of each lamp shade will remain at $25.00.

Primrose currently orders 150 shades per month. This order level was recommended by the vice president to lower annual carrying costs (which equal 25% of the purchase or manufacturing cost) and order costs (which equal $100 per order). Primrose's vice president has identified the following four options:

a) Continue ordering 150 lamp shades per month.

b) Order the shades on an EOQ basis.

c) Order shades in lots of 25 cartons or more to take advantage of the 2% discount.

d) Purchase a specialized machine to manufacture the lamp shades themselves. This machine can produce 10 shades per day, 250 days per year. Setup requires five hours at an average labor rate of $20 per hour. All other production costs (labor, material, etc.) total $18.50 per shade.

Which of these options should be selected?

# 13

## QUES

# *Queuing Models*

Queuing models are used to predict the behavior of waiting lines. Every queuing situation involves customers (which may be people, machines, airplanes, computer jobs, and so on) who arrive at the facility and will wait in line until a server (clerk, repairman, airport runway, computer, and so on) is free and can begin processing the customers. The queuing models provide a prediction of:

1. The mean number of customers in the queue.
2. The mean number of customers in the system. (The system includes all customers in the queue plus all customers being served.)
3. The mean wait time in the queue. (How long does the average customer wait in line before service begins?)
4. The mean wait time in the system. (How long does the average customer spend waiting in line and being served?)

A frequently encountered problem in business use of queuing analysis involves the design of a system to achieve a desired performance level at minimum cost. The major issue in such an analysis involves the balance between the cost of providing service and the cost of customer delays.

The terminology used in most books is relatively standardized, so no major differences are likely to be found between your book and this book. The one possible exception to this is that some books use *channel* where we use *server*. The use of *channel* derives from the early development of queuing theory and its application to the design of telephone systems. There are no differences between these terms.

## 13.1 Program Description

This program can be used to analyze any one of the following seven queuing models:

1. Single server.
2. Single server with finite queue length.
3. Single server with finite calling population.
4. Single server with arbitrary service time distribution.
5. Multiple server.
6. Multiple server with finite queue length.
7. Multiple server with finite calling population.

For each of these, the program computes the mean number of customers in the system and in the queue, the mean wait time in the system and the queue, and the percentage of time that the server is idle. In addition, the balking percentage is determined for alternatives 2 and 6.

The multiple server models are restricted to 30 or fewer servers. Unless otherwise specified in the preceding list, each of these seven alternatives finds the steady-state solution for a queuing environment with an infinite calling population whose arrival rate is Poisson. Service times are exponential, and queue lengths are unbounded. All customers wait in a single queue in all models, and the customer at the front of the queue goes to the first available server as soon as the server has finished processing the previous customer. All customers enter the queue (no balking), and no customers leave the queue once it is entered. No priorities are used so all customer service is on a first-come, first-served basis.

An economic analysis option is available for any of the seven alternatives. If this option is selected, the program computes the system operating cost, the customer waiting cost, and the total cost. Multiple server models have an additional option that eases the task of determining the optimal number of servers. If this option is selected, the program will request an upper and lower limit for the number of servers. For every number of servers between these limits, the program will output the mean system wait time, the mean number of customers in the system, and the total cost.

## 13.2 Problem Preparation

No special problem preparation is required for any of these queuing models. As with any queuing problem, always check to make sure that you are using arrival and services *rates* and not arrival or service *times*. Also make sure that the same time units are being used for arrival rate, service rate, service cost rate, and waiting cost rate.

## 13.3 Data Input Overview

The program input for each of the queuing model alternatives is very simple. Even the most complex alternatives require only ten data values. For each alternative, you first input the number of the alternative that has been selected.

This is followed by the customer arrival rate. Next you input the rate that customers can be served by *each* server.

The definition of the customer arrival rate changes slightly when the finite calling population alternatives (number 3 and 7) are used. In all other alternatives, the customer arrival rate is the rate that customers arrive at the *system*. In alternatives 3 and 7, however, the customer arrival rate is the rate at which *each* customer needs to use the system. The time spent waiting for service and being served is not included in this latter computation of customer arrival rate. Thus the system arrival rate is equal to the product of the customer arrival rate and the mean number of customers outside the system.

The next set of input data depends on the alternative that you have selected:

If you selected alternative 1, there is no more data required, but if you selected any other alternative, you must input additional data.

For alternative 2, you input the maximum number of customers that can be in the system. Be careful here. Remember that the number of customers in the system is one more than the number of customers in the queue.

For alternative 3, you input the total number of customers that use the facility (the size of the calling population).

For alternative 4, you input the standard deviation of the service time.

For alternative 5, you input the number of servers that are available to process customers.

For alternative 6, you input the number of servers, and then the maximum number of customers that can be in the system. Since this is a multiple server facility, the maximum number of customers in the queue is equal to the difference between these two inputs (maximum number of customers minus number of servers). If the maximum number of customers in the system is smaller than the number of servers, then the length of the queue will be zero, not a negative number.

For alternative 7, you input the number of servers, and then the number of customers that use the facility (the size of the calling population).

The next set of input data for multiple server models concerns optimal server analysis. If optimal server analysis is desired, input a "Y" and follow it with the lower server limit, the upper server limit, the service cost rate, and the waiting cost rate. No additional input is required in this case. If optimal server analysis is not desired, input an "N" and the program will request the same input (described in the following paragraph) that is requested for single server models.

The last set of input data is used to describe the economic analysis. Input "N" if no economic analysis is desired. Input "Y" if economic analysis is desired, and follow this with the service cost rate (the cost per server per unit time), and the waiting cost rate (the cost per customer in the system per unit time).

## 13.4 Data Input Details

The first set of data for each of the seven alternatives is as follows:

For alternative 1:

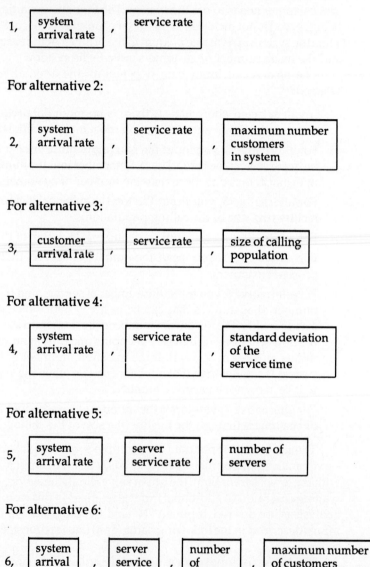

1, | system arrival rate | , | service rate |

For alternative 2:

2, | system arrival rate | , | service rate | , | maximum number customers in system |

For alternative 3:

3, | customer arrival rate | , | service rate | , | size of calling population |

For alternative 4:

4, | system arrival rate | , | service rate | , | standard deviation of the service time |

For alternative 5:

5, | system arrival rate | , | server service rate | , | number of servers |

For alternative 6:

6, | system arrival rate | , | server service rate | , | number of servers | , | maximum number of customers in system |

For alternative 7:

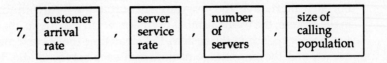

7,  customer arrival rate , server service rate , number of servers , size of calling population

The following set of data must be input for multiple server models (alternatives 5 through 7) in which optimal server analysis is desired:

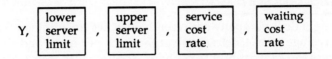

Y,  lower server limit , upper server limit , service cost rate , waiting cost rate

Input "N" for a multiple server model if optimal server analysis is not desired.

The last set of data for all single server models, and all multiple server models that did not request optimal server analysis, is

N

if economic analysis is not desired, or

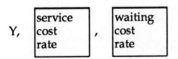

Y,  service cost rate , waiting cost rate

if economic analysis is desired.

## 13.5 Editing the Data

Editing of any data value may be done during original data entry or by selecting the EDIT CURRENT PROBLEM option. The value that will be changed is always blinking in the on-screen table. If you want to change a different value, use the up or down arrow keys to move, then type the new value.

The EDIT CURRENT PROBLEM option cannot be used to change from one queuing model to another. If that is desired, the complete problem must be entered by using the ENTER PROBLEM FROM TERMINAL option.

## 13.6 Program Output

For each alternative, the program will output the mean number of customers in the system, the mean number of customers in the queue, the mean time that a customer spends in the system, the mean time that a customer spends in the queue, and the percentage of time that each server is idle. In addition, for alternatives 2 and 6, the program will output the balking percentage (the percentage of customers that went elsewhere for service).

## 13.7 Example Problem Q1

A freight dock company has recently installed an automatic cargo unloader. An average of 10 trucks arrive at the dock per hour, and the unloader can process trucks at a rate of 12 per hour. The unloader costs $200 per hour to operate, and each truck and driver costs $50 per hour while waiting and being loaded.

Determine the following:

1. The average number of trucks in the system.
2. The average number of trucks in the queue.
3. The average time a truck is in the system.
4. The average time a truck waits before unloading begins.
5. How much money is spent per hour on the unloading and truck waiting costs?

### 13.7.1 Problem Preparation

This is a single server problem with no restrictions, so alternative 1 should be used to solve the problem. The key input data are as follows:

Arrival Rate = 10 trucks/hour

Service Rate = 12 trucks/hour

Service Cost Rate = $200 per hour

Waiting Cost Rate = $50 per hour

### 13.7.2 Data Input

The following data values must be input to solve this problem after selecting model 1:

10, 12, Y, 200, 50

Figure 13.1 shows how the on-screen table looks after these data values are input.

FIGURE 13.1   Computer screen after input of all data for example problem Q1

```
                        QUES - New Problem

    Arrival Rate           10

    Service Rate           12


    Number of Servers       1


    Economic Analysis?      Y          Service Cost Rate    200
                                       Waiting Cost Rate     50
```

## 13.7.3 Computer Output

Figure 13.2 contains the output from a run of this problem. The RESULTS show that, typically, there are 5 trucks in the system and 4.167 trucks waiting in line. The average time a truck spends in the system is 0.5 hour, or 30 minutes. The average time spent waiting before unloading begins is 0.417 hour. The unloader costs $200 per hour and waiting trucks cost $250 per hour.

FIGURE 13.2   Output from a run of example problem Q1

```
                -=*=-  INFORMATION ENTERED  -=*=-


        ALTERNATIVE CHOSEN           :    SINGLE SERVER

        Arrival Rate                 :       10.000
        Service Rate                 :       12.000

        Number of Servers            :          1

        Service Cost Rate            :      200.000
        Waiting Cost Rate            :       50.000


                  -=*=-  RESULTS  -=*=-


        SERVER IDLE (PERCENT)        :       16.667

        EXPECTED NUMBER IN SYSTEM    :        5.000

        EXPECTED NUMBER IN QUEUE     :        4.167
```

(CONT.)

**FIGURE 13.2** *(CONT.)*

```
EXPECTED TIME IN SYSTEM        :          0.500

EXPECTED TIME IN QUEUE         :          0.417

COST OF SERVICE                :        200.000

COST OF WAITING                :        250.000

TOTAL COST                     :        450.000



          ---------- E N D   O F   A N A L Y S I S  ----------
```

# 13.8 Example Problem Q2

A small gas station has one pump that can serve 25 customers per hour. The station is popular because prices are low, and customers arrive at a rate of 20 per hour. There is only room for three cars in the station (one being served and two waiting in line). If another car tried to wait in line, it would block traffic. The result is that there are never more than three cars in the station. Customers who find the station full (two cars in line) leave immediately and go to a competitor.

1. How long does a typical customer wait before being served?
2. How many customers go to a competitor in a typical hour?

## 13.8.1 Problem Preparation

This problem has a single server with a finite queue length, so alternative 2 should be used to solve the problem. The key input data are:

Arrival Rate = 20 cars/hour

Service Rate = 25 cars/hour

Maximum Number of Customers in the System = 3

## 13.8.2 Data Input

The following data values must be input to solve this problem after selecting model 2:

20, 25, 3, N

Figure 13.3 shows how the on-screen table looks after these data values are input.

FIGURE 13.3 Computer screen after input of all data for example problem Q2

```
                        QUES - New Problem


    Arrival Rate            20

    Service Rate            25


    Number of Servers        1

    Maximum in System        3

    Economic Analysis?       N
```

## 13.8.3 Computer Output

Figure 13.4 contains the output from a run of this problem. The RESULTS for example problem Q2 show that a typical customer waits 0.034 hour (or 2 minutes) before being served.

The output does not show the number of customers who go to the competitors per hour, but this result can easily be calculated by multiplying the fraction of customers who do not enter the queue (0.17344) and the number of potential customers who arrive per hour (20). Therefore, about 3.5 customers go to competitors each hour.

**FIGURE 13.4**   Output from a run of example problem Q2

```
              -=*=-   INFORMATION ENTERED   -=*=-


    ALTERNATIVE CHOSEN            :    SINGLE SERVER - FINITE QUEUE

    Arrival Rate                 :        20.000
    Service Rate                 :        25.000

    Number of Servers            :           1
    Maximum in System            :           3



                    -=*=-  RESULTS   -=*=-


    BALKING RATE (PERCENT)       :         17.344

    SERVER IDLE (PERCENT)        :         33.875

    EXPECTED NUMBER IN SYSTEM    :          1.225
```

(CONT.)

**FIGURE 13.4**   *(CONT.)*

```
EXPECTED NUMBER IN QUEUE          :          0.564

EXPECTED TIME IN SYSTEM           :          0.074

EXPECTED TIME IN QUEUE            :          0.034


          ----------  E N D   O F   A N A L Y S I S  ----------
```

# 13.9  Example Problem Q3

A stamping plant has 12 presses that frequently need to be repaired. The records show that, on the average, one of the presses breaks down after two days of operation. These records also show that a repairman takes an average of one day to repair a press.

1. Typically, how many presses are down?
2. Typically, how long is a press out of service?

## 13.9.1  Problem Preparation

This is a single server model with a finite calling population. Alternative 3 should be used to solve the problem.

This type of problem is often formulated incorrectly, because the machines (presses) are the customers and the person (repairman) is the server. The machines "arrive" for service when they break down and need repair. The repairing of a machine is the service in this case.

The data for this problem are:

Arrival Rate = 0.5 press/day
Service Rate = 1 press/day
Size of Calling Population = 12 presses

## 13.9.2  Data Input

The following data values must be input to solve this problem after selecting model 3:

0.5, 1, 12, N

Figure 13.5 shows how these data values should be input in response to prompts from the computer.

**FIGURE 13.5**    Computer screen after input of all data for example problem Q3

| QUES - New Problem | |
|---|---|
| Arrival Rate | .5 |
| Service Rate | 1 |
| | |
| Number of Servers | 1 |
| Population Size | 12 |
| Economic Analysis? | N |

### 13.9.3 Computer Output

Figure 13.6 contains the output from a run of this problem. The RESULTS show that, typically, there will be 10 presses down (10 customers in the system), and each press will be down for 10 days (mean time in the system is 10).

**FIGURE 13.6**    Output from a run of example problem Q3

```
            -=*=-   INFORMATION ENTERED   -=*=-


    ALTERNATIVE CHOSEN           :    SINGLE SERVER - FINITE POPULATION

    Arrival Rate                 :         0.500
    Service Rate                 :         1.000

    Number of Servers            :           1
    Population Size              :          12



                 -=*=-   RESULTS   -=*=-


    SERVER IDLE (PERCENT)        :         0.000

    EXPECTED NUMBER IN SYSTEM    :        10.000

    EXPECTED NUMBER IN QUEUE     :         9.000

    EXPECTED TIME IN SYSTEM      :        10.000

    EXPECTED TIME IN QUEUE       :         9.000


        ----------  E N D   O F   A N A L Y S I S  ----------
```

## 13.10 Example Problem Q4

A company is trying to determine if the installation of a new coffee machine will reduce the lines of employees waiting to buy a cup of coffee. The new machine can serve 10 cups of coffee per minute. The cycle time of the machine is fixed, so if it is run at full capacity, it will always serve exactly 10 cups per minute. If an average of five employees arrive for coffee every minute, then how many employees are typically standing in front of the coffee machine?

### 13.10.1 Problem Preparation

This is a single server model with an arbitrary service rate. Alternative 4 should be used to solve the problem. The input data are as follows:

Arrival Rate = 5 employees/minute

Service Rate = 10 employees/minute

Service Rate Standard Deviation = 0

### 13.10.2 Data Input

The following data values must be input to solve this problem after selecting model 4:

5, 10, 0, N

Figure 13.7 shows how the on-screen table looks after these data values are input.

**FIGURE 13.7**   Computer screen after input of all data for example problem Q4

|  |  |
|---|---|
| QUES - New Problem | |
| Arrival Rate | 5 |
| Service Rate | 10 |
| Number of Servers | 1 |
| Std Dev (fraction of arr) | 0 |
| Economic Analysis? | N |

### 13.10.3 Computer Output

Figure 13.8 contains the output from a run of this problem. The RESULTS show that, typically, there will be 0.75 employee standing in front of the coffee machine. (This includes both the employee who is getting coffee and the ones who are waiting in line.)

# 13.11 Example Problem Q5

The freight dock company in problem Q1 has decided to replace its loading machine with three smaller machines that cost $100 per hour to operate. Each of these new machines can service six trucks per hour. Trucks still arrive at a rate of 10 per hour and cost $50 per hour while waiting or unloading.

1. How many trucks will typically be waiting for service with this new system?
2. Typically, what will be the total hourly cost of unloading and waiting?
3. How many of the loading machines should be installed if the company wants to minimize the total hourly cost of waiting and unloading?

**FIGURE 13.8**   Output from a run of example problem Q4

```
             -=*=-   INFORMATION ENTERED   -=*=-


   ALTERNATIVE CHOSEN              :    SINGLE SERVER - ARBITRARY SERVICE

   Arrival Rate                    :         5.000
   Service Rate                    :        10.000

   Number of Servers               :         1
   Std Dev (fraction of arr)       :         0.000



                  -=*=-   RESULTS   -=*=-


   SYSTEMS IDLE (PERCENT)          :        50.000

   EXPECTED NUMBER IN SYSTEM       :         0.750

   EXPECTED NUMBER IN QUEUE        :         0.250

   EXPECTED TIME IN SYSTEM         :         0.150

   EXPECTED TIME IN QUEUE          :         0.050


         ----------   E N D   O F   A N A L Y S I S   ----------
```

### 13.11.1 Problem Preparation

This is a multiple server problem that can be solved with alternative 5. The data are as follows:

>Arrival Rate = 10 trucks/hour
>Service Rate for Each Server = 6 trucks/hour
>Number of Servers = 3
>Server Cost = $100/hour
>Customer Cost = $50/hour

### 13.11.2 Data Input

The first two questions are answered by using the ECONOMIC ANALYSIS option, but not using the OPTIMAL SERVER ANALYSIS option. The following data values must be input after selecting model 5:

>10, 6, N, 3, Y, 100, 50

Figure 13.9 shows how the on-screen table looks after these data values are input.

    The third question is answered by using the OPTIMAL SERVER ANALYSIS option. The following data values must be input to solve this question:

>10, 6, Y, 1, 5, 100, 50

Figure 13.10 shows how the on-screen table looks after these data values are input by using the EDIT CURRENT PROBLEM option to edit the original problem data values.

### 13.11.3 Computer Output

Figure 13.11 contains the output from a run with the data shown in Figure 13.9. The RESULTS show that, on the average, there will be 0.375 trucks waiting in

**FIGURE 13.9**  Computer screen after input of all data for parts 1 and 2 of example problem Q5

```
                        QUES - New Problem

    Arrival Rate             10

    Service Rate             6

    Optimal Server Analysis?  N

    Number of Servers        3


    Economic Analysis?        Y          Service Cost Rate    100
                                         Waiting Cost Rate    50
```

**FIGURE 13.10**   Computer screen after input of all data for part 3 of example problem Q5

```
                        QUES - Edit Problem

   Arrival Rate              10

   Service Rate              6

   Optimal Server Analysis?  Y
   Lower Server Limit        1        Service Cost Rate    100
   Upper Server Limit        5        Waiting Cost Rate    50



```

**FIGURE 13.11**   Output from a run of example problem Q5, parts 1 and 2

```
               -=*=-  INFORMATION ENTERED  -=*=-

   ALTERNATIVE CHOSEN              :    MULTIPLE SERVER

   Arrival Rate                   :         10.000
   Service Rate                   :          6.000

   Number of Servers              :          3

   Service Cost Rate              :        100.000
   Waiting Cost Rate              :         50.000


               -=*=-  RESULTS  -=*=-


   SERVER IDLE (PERCENT)          :         44.444

   EXPECTED NUMBER IN SYSTEM      :          2.041

   EXPECTED NUMBER IN QUEUE       :          0.375

   EXPECTED TIME IN SYSTEM        :          0.204

   EXPECTED TIME IN QUEUE         :          0.037

   COST OF SERVICE                :        300.000

   COST OF WAITING                :        102.068

   TOTAL COST                     :        402.068

      ----------  E N D  O F  A N A L Y S I S  ----------
```

line. The unloaders will cost $300 per hour, and the truck delays (waiting plus unloading) will cost $102.07 per hour. The total cost will be $402.07 per hour.

Figure 13.12 contains the output from a run with the data shown in Figure 13.10. The RESULTS from this run show that the lowest cost ($402.07) results when the three unloaders are used. One unloader does not have sufficient capacity to handle the arrivals, and two unloaders will cost $460.44.

## 13.12 Example Problem Q6

The owner of the small gas station in problem Q2 has expanded to two pumps. Customers still arrive at the rate of 20 per hour, but each pump can serve 12 customers per hour. There still is only room for three cars in the station (two being served and one waiting in line). As before, a customer who arrives when the station is full (one car in line) leaves immediately and goes to a competitor.

1. How long does a typical customer wait before being served?
2. How many customers go to a competitor in a typical hour?

**FIGURE 13.12** Output from a run of example problem Q5, part 3

```
                    -=*=-   INFORMATION ENTERED   -=*=-


     ALTERNATIVE CHOSEN              :     MULTIPLE SERVER

     Arrival Rate                    :         10.000
     Service Rate                    :          6.000

     Number of Servers               :          1     -            5

     Service Cost Rate               :        100.000
     Waiting Cost Rate               :         50.000



                     MULTIPLE SERVER PARAMETRIC ANALYSIS

                        -=*=-   RESULTS   -=*=-


        NUMBER OF          SYSTEMS          SYSTEMS           TOTAL
        SERVERS             WAIT            LENGTH            COSTS

           1         arrival rate exceeds system capacity
           2            0.522             5.209            460.438
           3            0.204             2.041            402.068
           4            0.174             1.740            486.993
           5            0.168             1.682            584.090



              ----------   E N D   O F   A N A L Y S I S   ----------
```

## 13.12.1 Problem Preparation

This problem has multiple servers with a finite waiting line. Alternative 6 should be used to solve the problem. The input data are as follows:

Arrival Rate = 20 cars/hour

Service Rate for Each Server = 12 cars/hour

Number of Servers = 2

Maximum Number of Customers in the System = 3

## 13.12.2 Data Input

The following data values must be input to solve this problem after selecting model 6:

20, 12, N, 2, 3, N

Figure 13.13 shows how the on-screen table looks after these data values are input.

## 13.12.3 Computer Output

Figure 13.14 contains the output from a run of this problem.  the RESULTS show that a typical customer waits 0.014 hour (or 0.84 minutes) for service. Since 22.2 percent of the potential customers go to competitors, and since potential customers arrive at a rate of 20 per hour, we can say that 4.44 customers would go to a competitor in a typical hour.

**FIGURE 13.13**   Computer screen after input of all data for example problem Q6

```
                         QUES - New Problem


    Arrival Rate            20

    Service Rate           12

    Optimal Server Analysis?    N

    Number of Servers       2

    Maximum in System       3

    Economic Analysis?     N
```

**FIGURE 13.14**    Output from a run of example problem Q6

```
          -=*=-  INFORMATION ENTERED  -=*=-


ALTERNATIVE CHOSEN            :    MULTIPLE SERVER - FINITE QUEUE

Arrival Rate                 :         20.000
Service Rate                 :         12.000

Number of Servers            :           2
Maximum in System            :           3



          -=*=-  RESULTS  -=*=-


BALKING RATE (PERCENT)       :         22.202

SERVER IDLE (PERCENT)        :         35.169

EXPECTED NUMBER IN SYSTEM    :          1.519

EXPECTED NUMBER IN QUEUE     :          0.222

EXPECTED TIME IN SYSTEM      :          0.098

EXPECTED TIME IN QUEUE       :          0.014



   ----------  E N D   O F   A N A L Y S I S  ----------
```

# 13.13 Example Problem Q7

The stamping plant in problem Q3 has expanded to 20 presses and now has two repairmen. Each repairman takes an average of one day to repair a press. One of the presses breaks down every one and one-third days.

Again, the plant wants to know how many presses are usually down, and how long the typical press is out of service once it breaks down.

## 13.13.1 Problem Preparation

This is a multiple server model with a finite calling population. Alternative 7 should be used to solve the problem. The input data are as follows:

Arrival Rate = 0.75 press/day

Service Rate for Each Server = 1 press/day

Number of Servers = 2

Size of Calling Population = 20 presses

### 13.13.2 Data Input

The following data values must be input to solve this problem after selecting model 7:
.75, 1, N, 2, 20, N

Figure 13.15 shows how the on-screen table looks after these data values are input.


**FIGURE 13.15**   Computer screen after input of all data for example problem Q7

```
                           QUES - New Problem

   Arrival Rate                .75

   Service Rate                1

   Optimal Server Analysis?    N

   Number of Servers           2

   Population Size             20

   Economic Analysis?          N
```

### 13.13.3 Computer Output

Figure 13.16 contains the output from a run of this problem. The RESULTS show that, typically, there will be 17.333 presses down and that a typical press will be out of service for 8.667 days.

# 13.14 Queuing Problems

For the first 27 problems, determine the following:

- Average time spent in the system
- Average time spent waiting in the queue
- Average number of customers in the system
- Average length of the queue

1. Arrival Rate = 25/hr
   Service Rate = 30/hr
   Single Server System

**FIGURE 13.16** Output from a run of example problem Q7

```
            -=*=-   INFORMATION ENTERED   -=*=-


  ALTERNATIVE CHOSEN            :   MULTIPLE SERVER - FINITE POPULATION

  Arrival Rate                  :        0.750
  Service Rate                  :        1.000

  Number of Servers             :        2
  Population Size               :        20



                -=*=-   RESULTS   -=*=-


  SERVER IDLE (PERCENT)         :        0.000

  EXPECTED NUMBER IN SYSTEM     :       17.333

  EXPECTED NUMBER IN QUEUE      :       15.333

  EXPECTED TIME IN SYSTEM       :        8.667

  EXPECTED TIME IN QUEUE        :        7.667


  ----------   E N D   O F   A N A L Y S I S   ----------
```

2. Arrival Rate = 25/hr
   Service Rate = 30/hr
   Single Server System
   Maximum Queue Length = 5

3. Arrival Rate = 25/hr
   Service Rate = 30/hr
   Single Server System
   Number of Customers = 6

4. Arrival Rate = 25/hr
   Service Rate = 30/hr
   Single Server System
   Arbitrary Service Time Distribution
   Standard Deviation of the Service Time = 1 hr

5. Arrival Rate = 25/hr
   Service Rate = 30/hr
   Single Server System
   Arbitrary Service Time Distribution
   Standard Deviation of the Service Time = 0.0011111 hr

6. Arrival Rate = 25/hr
   Service Rate = 30/hr
   Single Server System
   Arbitrary Service Time Distribution
   Standard Deviation of the Service Time = 0

7. Arrival Rate = 25/hr
   Service Rate = 30/hr
   *Two* Server System

8. Arrival Rate = 25/hr
   Service Rate = 30/hr
   *Two* Server System
   Maximum Queue Length = 5

9. Arrival Rate = 25/hr
   Service Rate = 30/hr
   Two Server System
   Number in Calling Population = 6

10. Same as problem 1, except the service rate = 75/hour

11. Same as problem 2, except the service rate = 75/hour

12. Same as problem 3, except the service rate = 75/hour

13. Same as problem 4, except the service rate = 75/hour

14. Same as problem 5, except the service rate = 75/hour

15. Same as problem 6, except the service rate = 75/hour

16. Same as problem 7, except the service rate = 75/hour

17. Same as problem 8, except the service rate = 75/hour

18. Same as problem 9, except the service rate = 75/hour

19. Same as problem 1, except the service rate = 26/hour

20. Same as problem 2, except the service rate = 26/hour

21. Same as problem 3, except the service rate = 26/hour

22. Same as problem 4, except the service rate = 26/hour

23. Same as problem 5, except the service rate = 26/hour

24. Same as problem 6, except the service rate = 26/hour

25. Same as problem 7, except the service rate = 26/hour

26. Same as problem 8, except the service rate = 26/hour

27. Same as problem 9, except the service rate = 26/hour

28. A single server system takes an average of three minutes to serve each customer. If 15 customers arrive per hour, how much time will the typical customer spend in the system?

29. Each of the servers in a three server system takes an average of four

minutes to serve each customer. How many customers will typically be in line if customers arrive for service at a rate of forty per hour?

30. The Speedo Car Wash can process an average car in five minutes. Cars arrive randomly at 10 per hour. If the car wash can only accommodate 10 cars (in addition to the car being washed), what is the average time customers will wait before they begin to wash their car? What is the probability of finding the car wash full?

31. The Speedo Car Wash is considering implementing two car wash lines, each of which can process a car in 10 minutes. Management's objective is to minimize the average time customers will wait before they begin to wash their car. Should Speedo make the change?

32. The Ajax Repair Company services 10 nuclear power plants located in the Northeast. On the average, a power plant requires service every 100 days with a mean repair time of 50 days (assume a 300-day year). Only one plant can be serviced at a time. Determine:

   a) The mean number of power plants inoperable.
   b) Mean time a power plant is inoperable.
   c) Mean time a power plant waits for service.
   d) Mean number of power plants waiting for service.

33. A department store is considering consolidating its three package wrapping stations (one for each floor) into a single station located in the basement. All three clerks will work together in the new wrapping station. Typically, customers arrive at each station at a rate of 10 per hour, and each clerk requires approximately five minutes to wrap one package. Which of these two systems will minimize the total time required to get a package wrapped?

34. If clerks are paid $4 per hour and management assigns a goodwill cost of $6 per hour for customers' waiting time, does the decision from the preceding problem change?

35. A bank is considering the following three alternative service options to handle an arrival rate of 50 per hour:

|                   | Option #1 | Option #2 | Option #3 |
|-------------------|-----------|-----------|-----------|
| Number of Servers | 5         | 7         | 10        |
| Cost per Server   | $10/Hr    | $8/Hr     | $8/Hr     |
| Service Time      | 5 Min     | 8 Min     | 8 Min     |

If the bank believes that the cost of each customer waiting for service is $5 per hour, which of the three options yields the lowest total cost?

36. High precision jigs are distributed to mechanics via a centralized tool crib. Mechanics are paid $20 per hour and arrive at the crib at an average rate of 20 per hour (Poisson arrival rate). Clerks attending the crib are paid $7 per hour and can fill a single order in 10 minutes. How many clerks should management assign to the crib in order to minimize overall costs to the company?

---

## CASE STUDY   **Talroth Construction**

Talroth Construction is a large engineering and construction firm that specializes in the design and construction of airports, refineries, and power plants on a worldwide basis. The company maintains an engineering and design staff of approximately 1000 professionals at their world headquarters in Dallas.

Talroth's engineering computer requirements are provided by a single mainframe system. This computer was the envy of the industry when it was installed five years ago, but some of the staff engineers believe that the computer is showing its age. Complaints about slow response time have become commonplace. The computer center manager agrees that system performance is worse now than last year, but claims that it is all due to a workload increase from 450 to 500 jobs per day. The result was an increase in response time from 6 minutes to 13.5 minutes per job. Management is concerned about this situation, because it costs $25 per hour while an engineer waits for a job to be processed. Each job requires one minute of computer processing time. The computer center is open nine hours per day.

The computer center manager recommends the purchase of a new computer that is made by the same company as the current computer. This new machine is twice as fast as the old current computer and will cost $1500 per day to operate. The current computer costs $1000 per day to operate. (These costs include all computer costs: machine rental, maintenance, operator salary, supplies, etc.)

The vice president in charge of facilities and services prefers to keep the current machine and has suggested hiring an extra operator. The second operator would allow the computer center to remain open for 16 hours per day. The extra operator will cost the company an additional $100 per day.

Some of the engineers have suggested that two more operators

(CONT.)

CASE STUDY  **Talroth Construction**    *(CONT.)*

should be hired (at an additional cost of $220 per day) so the computer center can be open 24 hours per day.

*NOTE*: Assume that the user workload remains constant at 500 jobs per day, and that user jobs will arrive randomly over the full time period that the computer center is open. Response time is defined as the amount of time that elapses from the moment that a job is turned in until the computer has finished processing it.

a)  Is it possible that an increase from 450 to 500 jobs per day would cause a response time increase from 6 to 13.5 minutes?

b)  Which alternative provides the fastest response time?

c)  Which is the lowest cost alternative?

d)  Which alternative results in the fewest number of users waiting for jobs to be processed?

# Appendix: Problem Solutions

## ch3 Linear Programming Problems

1a. X, Y, and P are the same as before.

1b. Slack values are the same, but constraint number 1 is now located where constraint number 3 was located in the original problem.

2a. Same as before, except that $X_1$ now stands for Y and $X_2$ stands for X.

2b. Slack values are identical and in the original order.

3. X = 2.667, Y = 1, C = 4.667. The value of C that is output may not be 4.67 due to minor differences between computers.

4. X = 1, Y = 2, P = 5.

5. X = 1, Y = 3, P = 7.

6. X = 6, Y = 0, P = 6.

7. No change.

8. X = 0, Y = 2, C = 2.

9. No change.

10. X = 2, Y = 2, C = 2.

11. C will be five units smaller.

12. Unbounded solution.

13. X = 4, Y = 0, Z = 2.333, W = 4, C = 21.333.

14a. X = 4, Y = 0, Z = 2.333, W = 4.

14b. C = 25.333.

15. $X_1 = 7$, $X_2 = 0.5$, $X_3 = 0$; Z = 22.

16. Yes.

17. $X_1 = 41.176$, $X_2 = 0$, $X_3 = 0$, $X_4 = 23.529$; X = 64.706.

18. Yes.

19. $X_1 = 5, X_2 = 10, X_3 = 0; Z = 40.$

20. 8.

21. $X_1 = 0, X_2 = 20, X_3 = 18.333, X_4 = 0; Z = 135.$

22. Any value smaller than 0.6 (such as 0.599)

23a. Unbounded.

23b. Infeasible.

23c. Multiple optimal.

23d. Infeasible.

24a. $4X + 5Y - S_1 + A_1 = 6$
$$7X - 8Y + A_2 = -9$$
$$10X + S_2 = 11$$
S = surplus
S = slack
$A_1, A_2$ = artificial

24b. $X = 1.1, Y = 2.087; P = -0.875.$

25a. $4X + 5Y - S_1 + A_1 = 6$
$$7X - 8Y + A_2 = -9$$
$$10X + S_2 = 11$$
$S_1$ = surplus
$S_2$ = slack
$A_1, A_2$ = artificial

25b. $X = 0.045, Y = 1.164; P = -2.194.$

26. $X_1 = 60, X_2 = 0, X_3 = 180; Z = 720.$

27. 12,500 pounds of cement.
187,500 pounds of concrete mix.

28. $X_1 = 120, X_2 = 300; Z = 198.$

29. EX = 2500
EY = 1666.667
NX = 0
NY = 0
REV = 2083.333

30. MAX $S = X_1 + 2X_2 + 5X_3$
$$X_1 + 2X_2 + 5X_3 \leq 100$$
$$1.5X_1 + 4X_2 + 12X_3 \leq 120$$
$$12X_3 \leq 60$$
$$X_1 \leq 50$$
$$X_2 \leq 20$$
$$X_3 \leq 10$$
$X_1 = 50, X_2 = 11.25, X_3 = 0; S = 72.5.$

31.  $H = 9.6, A = 10, S = 0; Z = 1020.$

32a.  MAX $P = 29Tc + 37Tp + 30Hc + 36Hp$
$$19Tc + 31Tp + 19Hc + 28Hp \leq 288,000.$$

32b.  $Tc + Tp = 0, Hc + Hp = 15157.894.$

32c.  $Tc = 0, Hc = 15157.894.$

33.  $40,000 stock, $60,000 new company, no borrowed money, $28,000 return.

34.  Site 1 cotton = 125 acres.
Site 2 cotton = 375 acres.
Site 1 alfalfa = 33.333 acres.
Site 3 alfalfa = 200 acres.
Site 4 alfalfa = 33.333 acres.
Site 1 walnuts = 400 acres.
Site 1 avocados = 200 acres.
Net profit = $163,333.34.

35.  $M1 = 250$ lb, $E3 = 362.5$ lb, Cost = $4150.

36a.  $P1 = 3000, P2 = 0, P5 = 0.$

36b.  $P1 = 1000, P2 = 1000, P5 = 0.$

37a.  1448.394 lb Protein Mix.
404.362 lb Powdered A.
615.128 lb Powdered C.
4032.115 lb organic Filler.

37b.  $14,887.20.

# ch4 Integer Programming Problems

1.  $X = 1, Y = 0, Z = 1, P = 11.$

2.  $X = 1, Y = 0, Z = 1, C = 15.$

3.  $X = 0, Y = 1, Z = 1, C = 12.$

4.  Denver & Los Angeles.

5a.  Smith-Chicago, Turner-Albany, Unger-Boston.

5b.  $51 million.

5c.  $54 million.

6a.  A, C, D, E.

6b.  $1.8 million.

7a.  B, D, E.

7b.  $2.27 million.

8a.  A, D, F.

8b. 200,000 votes.

9a. K, L.

9b. J.

9c. 150,000 votes.

10a. Adams-Idle, Baker-J, Cabot-K.

10b. 13,600.

10c. $192.

11a. Adams-Idle, Baker-J, Cabot-K.

11b. 12,240.

11c. 1360.

11d. $190.64.

12a. Computer, Seismic, Life Support.

12b. $115,000.

# ch5 Transportation Problems

1.

| 0 | 15 | 30 |
|---|----|----|
| 10 | 5 | 0 |

Minimum cost = 175

2.

| 0 | 5 | 0 |
|---|---|---|
| 0 | 8 | 0 |
| 10 | 7 | 21 |
| 0 | 0 | 9 |

Minimum cost = 332

3.

| 0 | 13 | 5 |
|----|----|---|
| 21 | 2 | 0 |
| 4 | 0 | 0 |
| 10 | 0 | 0 |

Minimum cost = 224

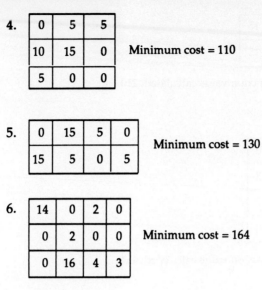

**4.**

| 0 | 5 | 5 |
|---|---|---|
| 10 | 15 | 0 |
| 5 | 0 | 0 |

Minimum cost = 110

**5.**

| 0 | 15 | 5 | 0 |
|---|----|---|---|
| 15 | 5 | 0 | 5 |

Minimum cost = 130

**6.**

| 14 | 0 | 2 | 0 |
|----|---|---|---|
| 0 | 2 | 0 | 0 |
| 0 | 16 | 4 | 3 |

Minimum cost = 164

**7.**

| 0 | 0 | 6 |
|---|---|---|
| 1 | 9 | 0 |
| 2 | 0 | 6 |
| 2 | 0 | 0 |

Minimum cost = 59

**8.**

| 0 | 0 | 4 |
|---|---|---|
| 5 | 5 | 0 |
| 0 | 3 | 3 |

Minimum cost = 84

**9.**

| 0 | 800 | 200 | 0 |
|---|-----|-----|---|
| 0 | 0 | 1500 | 0 |
| 0 | 0 | 0 | 1200 |
| 1400 | 300 | 0 | 300 |

Minimum cost = 16,746

10.

| 10 | 20 | 15 |
|----|----|----|
| 0  | 0  | 15 |

Objective function value calculated: 210

11.

| 5 | 0  | 0  |
|---|----|----|
| 5 | 0  | 3  |
| 0 | 11 | 27 |
| 0 | 9  | 0  |

Objective function value calculated: 454

12.

| 18 | 0  | 0 |
|----|----|---|
| 17 | 1  | 5 |
| 0  | 4  | 0 |
| 0  | 10 | 0 |

Objective function value calculated: 373

13.

| 10 | 0  | 0 |
|----|----|---|
| 5  | 15 | 5 |
| 0  | 5  | 0 |

Objective function value calculated: 155

14.

| 15 | 0  | 0 | 5 |
|----|----|---|---|
| 0  | 20 | 5 | 0 |

Objective function value calculated: 170

15.

| 0 | 13 | 0 | 3 |
|---|----|---|---|
| 0 | 0 | 2 | 0 |
| 14 | 5 | 4 | 0 |

Objective function value calculated: 234

16.

| 5 | 1 | 0 |
|---|---|----|
| 0 | 0 | 10 |
| 0 | 8 | 0 |
| 0 | 0 | 2 |

Objective function value calculated: 122

17.

| 0 | 0 | 4 |
|---|---|---|
| 2 | 8 | 0 |
| 3 | 0 | 3 |

Objective function value calculated: 105

18.

| 0 | 0 | 0 | 1000 |
|------|------|------|------|
| 0 | 1000 | 0 | 500 |
| 1200 | 0 | 0 | 0 |
| 200 | 100 | 1700 | 0 |

Objective function value calculated: 22,551

19.

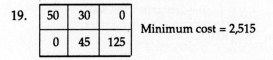

| 50 | 30 | 0 |
|----|----|-----|
| 0 | 45 | 125 |

Minimum cost = 2,515

20.

| | 1 | 2 | 3 | 4 | X | |
|---|---|---|---|---|---|---|
| 1 | 0 | 2.20 | 4.40 | 6.60 | 0 | 1000 |
| 2 | 20 | 0 | 2.20 | 4.40 | 0 | 1000 |
| 3 | 40 | 20 | 0 | 2.20 | 0 | 1000 |
| 4 | 60 | 40 | 20 | 0 | 0 | 1000 |
| | 1500 | 0 | 1700 | 0 | 800 | |

Solution

| | | | | |
|---|---|---|---|---|
| 1000 | 0 | 0 | 0 | 0 |
| 500 | 0 | 500 | 0 | 0 |
| 0 | 0 | 1000 | 0 | 0 |
| 0 | 0 | 200 | 0 | 800 |

Minimum cost = $15,100

21.

| | R1 | B1 | R2 | B2 | R3 | B3 | R4 | B4 | X | |
|---|---|---|---|---|---|---|---|---|---|---|
| 1 | 0 | 0 | 2.20 | 2.20 | 4.40 | 4.40 | 6.60 | 6.60 | 0 | 1000 |
| 2 | 20 | 20 | 0 | 0 | 2.20 | 2.20 | 4.40 | 4.40 | 0 | 1000 |
| 3 | 40 | 40 | 20 | 20 | 0 | 0 | 2.20 | 2.20 | 0 | 1000 |
| 4 | 60 | 60 | 40 | 40 | 20 | 20 | 0 | 0 | 0 | 1000 |
| | 1000 | 500 | 0 | 0 | 100 | 1600 | 0 | 0 | 800 | |

| | | | | | | | | |
|---|---|---|---|---|---|---|---|---|
| 1000 | 0 | 0 | 0 | 0 | 0 | 0 | 0 | 0 |
| 0 | 500 | 0 | 0 | 0 | 500 | 0 | 0 | 0 |
| 0 | 0 | 0 | 0 | 100 | 900 | 0 | 0 | 0 |
| 0 | 0 | 0 | 0 | 0 | 200 | 0 | 0 | 800 |

Minimum cost = $15,100

22.

| | R1 | B1 | R2 | B2 | R3 | B3 | R4 | B4 | X | |
|---|---|---|---|---|---|---|---|---|---|---|
| 1 | 0 | 0 | 2.20 | 2.20 | 4.40 | 4.40 | 6.60 | 6.60 | 0 | 1000 |
| 2 | 20 | 1000 | 0 | 0 | 2.20 | 2.20 | 4.40 | 4.40 | 0 | 1000 |
| 3 | 40 | 1000 | 20 | 1000 | 0 | 0 | 2.20 | 2.20 | 0 | 1000 |
| 4 | 60 | 1000 | 40 | 1000 | 20 | 1000 | 0 | 0 | 0 | 1000 |
| | 1000 | 500 | 0 | 0 | 100 | 1600 | 0 | 0 | 800 | |

| | | | | | | | | |
|---|---|---|---|---|---|---|---|---|
| 500 | 500 | 0 | 0 | 0 | 0 | 0 | 0 | 0 |
| 400 | 0 | 0 | 0 | 0 | 600 | 0 | 0 | 0 |
| 0 | 0 | 0 | 0 | 0 | 1000 | 0 | 0 | 0 |
| 100 | 0 | 0 | 0 | 100 | 0 | 0 | 0 | 800 |

Minimum cost = $17,320

23.

| | R1 | B1 | R2 | B2 | R3 | B3 | R4 | B4 | X | |
|---|---|---|---|---|---|---|---|---|---|---|
| 1 | 0 | 0 | 220 | 220 | 440 | 440 | 660 | 660 | 0 | 10 |
| 2 | 2000 | 2000 | 0 | 0 | 220 | 220 | 440 | 440 | 0 | 10 |
| 3 | 4000 | 4000 | 2000 | 2000 | 0 | 0 | 220 | 220 | 0 | 10 |
| 4 | 6000 | 6000 | 4000 | 4000 | 2000 | 2000 | 0 | 0 | 0 | 10 |
| | 10 | 5 | 0 | 0 | 1 | 16 | 0 | 0 | 8 | |

| | | | | | | | | |
|---|---|---|---|---|---|---|---|---|
| 10 | 0 | 0 | 0 | 0 | 0 | 0 | 0 | 0 |
| 0 | 5 | 0 | 0 | 0 | 5 | 0 | 0 | 0 |
| 0 | 0 | 0 | 0 | 1 | 9 | 0 | 0 | 0 |
| 0 | 0 | 0 | 0 | 0 | 2 | 0 | 0 | 8 |

Minimum cost = $15,100

24.

| | S | D | LA | C | |
|---|---|---|---|---|---|
| LA | 6 | 6 | 2 | 9 | 830 |
| C | 11 | 7 | 9 | 1 | 1050 |
| | 500 | 600 | 560 | 220 | |

| | | | | |
|---|---|---|---|---|
| 270 | 0 | 560 | 0 | Minimum cost = $9,690 |
| 230 | 600 | 0 | 220 | |

25.

| | S | D | LA | C | X | |
|---|---|---|---|---|---|---|
| LA | 6 | 6 | 2 | 9 | 0 | 830 |
| C | 11 | 7 | 9 | 1 | 0 | 1050 |
| | 500 | 600 | 560 | 120 | 100 | |

| | | | | | |
|---|---|---|---|---|---|
| 270 | 0 | 560 | 0 | 0 | Minimum cost = $9,590 |
| 230 | 600 | 0 | 120 | 100 | |

26.

| | S | D | LA | C | X | |
|---|---|---|---|---|---|---|
| LA | 6 | 6 | 2 | 9 | 3 | 830 |
| C | 11 | 7 | 9 | 1 | 8 | 1050 |
| | 500 | 600 | 560 | 120 | 100 | |

| | | | | | |
|---|---|---|---|---|---|
| 270 | 0 | 560 | 0 | 0 | Minimum cost = $10,390 |
| 230 | 600 | 0 | 120 | 100 | |

**27.**

|      | S  | D | LA | C |      |
|------|----|---|----|---|------|
| LA   | 6  | 6 | 2  | 9 | 830  |
| C    | 11 | 7 | 9  | 1 | 1050 |
| X    | 0  | 0 | 0  | 0 | 100  |

500   600   560   320

| 270 | 0   | 560 | 0   |
|-----|-----|-----|-----|
| 130 | 600 | 0   | 320 |
| 100 | 0   | 0   | 0   |

Minimum cost = $8,690

**28.**

|      | S  | D  | LA | C |      |
|------|----|----|----|---|------|
| LA   | 6  | 6  | 2  | 9 | 830  |
| C    | 11 | 7  | 9  | 1 | 1050 |
| X    | 4  | 10 | 4  | 4 | 100  |

500   600   560   320

| 270 | 0   | 560 | 0   |
|-----|-----|-----|-----|
| 130 | 600 | 0   | 320 |
| 100 | 0   | 0   | 0   |

Minimum cost = $9,090

**29.**

|                    |      | KC  | C   | NO  | X |    |
|--------------------|------|-----|-----|-----|---|----|
| Own Computer       |      | 310 | 350 | 370 | 0 | 22 |
|                    | KC   | 500 | x   | x   | 0 | 15 |
| Service Bureau     | C    | x   | 450 | x   | 0 | 12 |
|                    | NO   | x   | x   | 550 | 0 | 8  |

15   12   8   22

Own Computer—KC = 15
Own Computer—NO = 7
Service Bureau—C = 12
Service Bureau—NO = 1
Minimum cost = $13,190

30.

|  | 2.7 T | 2.6 HK | 3.2 M |  |
|---|---|---|---|---|
| 0.10 J | 0.01 | 0.015 | 0.03 | 20,000 |
| 0.14 US | 0.025 | 0.035 | 0.005 | 40,000 |
|  | 70,000 | 40,000 | 50,000 |  |

|  | T | HK | M |  |
|---|---|---|---|---|
| J | 2.81 | 2.715 | 3.33 | 20,000 |
| US | 2.865 | 2.775 | 3.345 | 40,000 |
| X | 0 | 0 | 0 | 100,000 |
|  | 70,000 | 40,000 | 50,000 |  |

Minimum cost = $167,100
J—HK = 20,000, US—T = 20,000, US—HK = 20,000

31.

|  | E | C | W |  |
|---|---|---|---|---|
| I | 5.60 | 6.80 | 9.10 | 2000 |
| B | 6.90 | 7.65 | 9.80 | 3000 |
| X | 0 | 0 | 0 | 8500 |
|  | 7500 | 2000 | 4000 |  |

Maximum Profit = $45,450
I—W = 2000, B—C = 1000, B—W = 2000

32.

|   | $E_1$ | $C_1$ | $W_1$ | $E_2$ | $C_2$ | $W_2$ |      |
|---|-------|-------|-------|-------|-------|-------|------|
| I | 5.60  | 6.80  | 9.10  | 5.60  | 6.80  | 9.10  | 2000 |
| B | 6.90  | 7.65  | 9.80  | 6.90  | 7.65  | 9.80  | 3000 |
| X | −100  | −100  | −100  | 0     | 0     | 0     | 8500 |
|   | 1000  | 1000  | 1000  | 6500  | 1000  | 3000  |      |

Maximum Profit = $42,550
$I—W_1 = 1000$
$I—W_2 = 1000$
$B—E_1 = 1000$
$B—C_1 = 1000$
$B—W_2 = 1000$

# ch6 Assignment Problems

1. A—F, B—D, C—E, minimum = 14.
2. A—M, B—K, C—L, D—N, minimum = 19.1.
3. A—X, B—Z, C—Y, maximum = 38.
4. X1—Y4, X2—Y1, X3—Y3, X4—Y2, maximum = 46.
5. A—G, B—E, C—F, D—unassigned, maximum = 17.
6. A—E, B—C, D and F unassigned, minimum = 7.
7. W1—X1, W2—X2, W3—X3, minimum = 28.
8. A—D, B—F, C—E, maximum = 21.
9. A1—B2, A2—B3, A3—B1, B4 unassigned, maximum = 42.
10. S1—D1, S2—D2, S5—D3, S3 and S4 unassigned, minimum = 35.
11. W1—M3, W2—M1, W3—M2, cost = 15.
12. E1—M2, E2—M3, E3—M1, E4 idle, 12 defective parts.
13. E1—M2, E2 idle, E3—M3, E4—M1, 13 defective parts.
14. E1—M2, E2—M3, E3—M1, E4 idle, 12 defective parts.
15. E1—M2, E2 idle, E3—M1, E4 idle, 8 defective parts.
16. SR1—T3, SR2—T4, SR3—T2, SR4—T1, SR5—T5, 860 sales.
17. Ajax—Altoona, Consolidated—Sespi, Beta—Dayton, $9,100,000.
18. $600,000.
19. $500,000.
20. New York—Los Angeles; Bombay—Paris; Singapore—Hong Kong.

21. S1—L4, S2—L3, S3—L2, S4 idle, S5—L1, 168 seconds.

22a. Alan—valve floaters.
Bob—finial harps.
Carl—index pins.
Don—knurls.

22b. 9.486 hours.

23a. Same as problem 22.

23b. $62.74.

24a. Smith—Boston, Turner—Albany, Unger—Chicago.

24b. $54,000,000.

25a. Smith—Chicago, Turner—Albany, Unger—Boston.

25b. $51,000,000.

26a. Adams—Idle, Baker—M2, Cabot—M1.

26b. 1700.

26c. $1304.

# ch7 Project Scheduling Problems

1. Critical path = B,F.
Time = 14.

2a. Time = 16.

2b. Yes.

3. Critical path = B, C, D, E, G.
Time = 29.

4a. No change, time is still 29.

4b. Yes.

5.

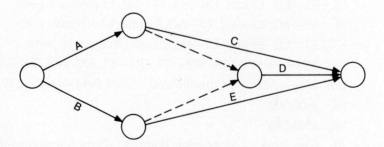

6. Critical path = B, D.
   Time = 52.

   Tenth day cost total = $1,958.33.

7a. No change, time is still 52.

7b. Yes.

8.

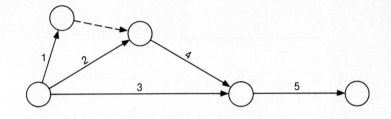

9. Critical path = 1, 4, 5.
   Time = 19 hours.
   Total cost = $990

10a. Time is still 19, but critical path is 1, 3, 4, 5.

10b. Yes, time is still 19, and critical path is 1, 3, 4, 5.

11a. 36.

11b. B = 2, E = 2, all others = 0.

11c. A, C, D, F.

11d. _____

| Job | Immediate Predecessors | Time |
|-----|------------------------|------|
| A | – | 10 |
| B | A | 15 |
| C | A | 8 |
| D | C | 12 |
| E | B | 3 |
| F | D,E | 6 |

12a. 32.

12b. B = 3, D = 3, E = 3, all others = 0.

12c. A, C, F, G.

12d. ────────────

| Job | Immediate Predecessors | Time |
|-----|-----------------------|------|
| A | – | 6 |
| B | – | 10 |
| C | A | 12 |
| D | B | 5 |
| E | B | 11 |
| F | C,D | 6 |
| G | E,F | 8 |

13a. 38.

13b. A—2, C—12, D—13, E—2, G—12.

13c. B—F—H—I.

13d. ────────────

| Job | IP | Time |
|-----|-----|------|
| A | – | 7 |
| B | – | 6 |
| C | – | 12 |
| D | B | 5 |
| E | A | 12 |
| F | B | 15 |
| G | C,D | 10 |
| H | E,F | 13 |
| I | G,H | 4 |

14a. 24 days.

14b. 3 days.

14c. None.

15a. 25 weeks.

15b. 2 weeks, because there is 1 week slack, and 8 weeks (the delayed time) are 3 weeks longer than 5 weeks (the usual time).

16a. Time = 19.333
Critical path = A—C—E.

16b. Variance = 4.556.

17a. 19.667

17b. 2.944

17c. 12.667

18. 27.333 days
19. 36.667 days

# ch8 Network Problems

## Minimum Spanning Tree Problems

1. AB, BC, BD, DE distance = 10.
2. 1—3, 3—4, 4—5, 1—2, 5—6 distance = 16.
3. AG, BG, BC, GH, CE, EF, DH distance = 94.
4. AD, DF, FG, DC, CE, EH, BH distance = 35.
5. AC, BC, BD, AF, DI, EI, FG, GH distance = 76.
6. AB, BD, AC distance = 9 miles.
7. AB, BE, BD, AC distance = 11 miles.
8a. Copperville—Adams Junction.
    Adams Junction—Gold City.
    Durango—Copperville.
8b. $470,000.
9. 2.8 million dollars.
10. AD, AB, BE, BC, 16 million dollars.

## Maximum Flow Problems

11. 4.
12. 10.
13. 13.
14. 13 gal min.
15. 12 ft$^3$/min.
16. 15 gal/min.
17. 6.
18. 2100.
19. 19,000 vehicles/hour.
20. 19,000 vehicles/hour.

## Shortest Route Problems

21. ABE, distance = 7.
22. 1—3—4—5—6, distance = 11.

23.  2—1—3, distance = 7.

24.  ACE, distance = 13.

25.  DAF, distance = 13.

26.  ABD, distance = 5 miles.

27.  ABE, distance = 4 miles.

28.  ACD, distance = 4 miles.

29.  FORMULATION (all costs are in thousands of dollars):

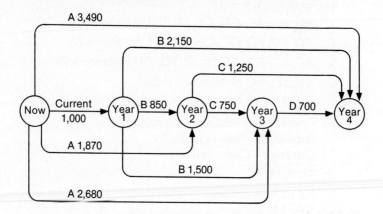

ANSWER:

Keep current computer for one year.
Get computer B for the next year.
Get computer C for the last two years.
Total cost = $3,100,000.

30.  FORMULATION:

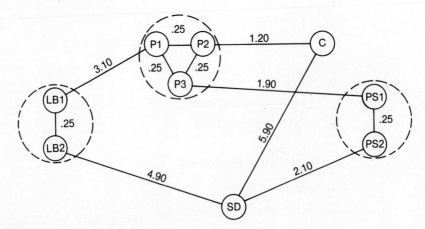

ANSWER:
Colton—Pomona—Palm Springs—San Diego.
Total Cost = $5.70.

# ch9 Decision Analysis Problems

1a.  A4.

1b.  300 (Profit).

1c.  A2.

1d.  –50 (Loss).

1e.  A3.

1f.  33.33 (Profit).

1g.  A1.

1h.  250 (Regret).

1i.  A3.

1j.  20 (Profit).

2a.  A1.

2b.  0 (Cost).

2c.  A1.

2d.  200 (Cost).

2e.  A1.

2f.  87.5 (Cost).

2g.  A1.

2h.  100 (Regret).

2i.  A1.

2j.  60 (Cost).

3a.  A1.

3b.  1000 (Profit).

3c.  A1.

3d.  0 (Profit).

3e.  A1.

3f.  400 (Profit).

3g.  A1.

3h.  800 (Regret).

3i. A1.

3j. 200 (Profit).

4a. Large order.

4b. $10,000.

4c. Medium order.

4d. $6,000.

4e. Large order.

4f. $7,666.67

4g. Large order.

4h. $2,000 Regret.

4i. Large order.

4j. $7,500.

5a. Patch.

5b. $100,000 Cost.

5c. Reroof.

5d. $250,000 Cost.

5e. Spray.

5f. $250,000 Cost. (Reroofing costs the same, but this program does not find multiple optimal solutions.)

5g. Spray.

5h. $100,000 Regret.

5i. Patch.

5j. $140,000 Cost. (Computer roundoff errors cause the 0.02 on the output.)

6a. $A_3$.

6b. Expected payoff = 70.

6c. EVPI = 120.

7a. Supply 200 or 300 (EV = 12)

7b. $24.

8. A1 (EV = 70)

9a. 3.

9b. 720.

9c. 410.

10. 250.

11a.

| 1000 | 0 | –1000 |
|---|---|---|
| –1500 | 2000 | 1000 |
| –4000 | –500 | 3000 |

11b. 300 units
EV = 800.

12a. Introduce.
EV = 290,000.

12b. No.

12c. $21,000.

13. Buy Sav-Less.
EV = $15M.

14. $18.5M.

15. The maximum value of the forecast is $22.5M.

# ch10 Decision Tree Problems

1. $P(S_1/I_1) = .8421$, $P(S_2/I_2) = .8710$

2. $P(S_1/I_1) = .35$, $P(S_2/I_1) = .44$, $P(S_3/I_1) = .07$, $P(S_4/I_1) = .13$.
   $P(S_1/I_2) = .19$, $P(S_2/I_2) = .62$, $P(S_3/I_2) = .16$, $P(S_4/I_2) = .03$.

   *Note*: these answers are all rounded to the nearest hundredth

3a. $P(R/r) = .6585$

3b. $P(S/s) = .9492$

4a. .84

4b. .5714

5.

| 0.6957 | 0.2609 | 0.0435 | 0 |
|---|---|---|---|
| 0.0741 | 0.6667 | 0.1111 | 0.1481 |
| 0 | 0.3750 | 0.6250 | 0 |
| 0.0476 | 0.0714 | 0.0238 | 0.8571 |

6. $P(A|a) = .7742$, $P(B|b) = .913$.

7.

| 0.3529 | 0 | 0.0588 | 0.4706 | 0.1176 |
|--------|--------|--------|--------|--------|
| 0 | 0.7692 | 0.0769 | 0 | 0.1538 |
| 0 | 0.3158 | 0.3684 | 0.2105 | 0.1053 |
| 0.0556 | 0.1111 | 0 | 0.7778 | 0.0556 |
| 0.1333 | 0 | 0.0667 | 0 | 0.8000 |

8. $P(LT \mid w) = .75$.

9.        State

|   | O | D |
|---|------|------|
| O | .9697 | .0303 |
| D | .4706 | .5294 |

10a. $P(P \mid p) = .7941$

10b. $P(A \mid C) = .2286$

11.   Build small plant: if demand is strong—add on.

12.   $A_1$ (EV = 640).

13.   EV = 1620.

14.   $A_2$ (EV = 75).

15a. 3 million.

15b. Use the well-tested process.

15c. 1.2 million.

16a. Select Alternative 1.

16b. EV = 900.

17a. Introduce.
EV = 290,000

17b. No.

17c. $21,000.

18.   Buy Sav-Less.
EV = $15M.

19a. Yes.

19b. $18.5M.

20.   Willing to pay up to $22.5M.

# ch11 **Markov Problems**

1. .294, .382, .324.
2a. P1 = .27, P2 = .51, P3 = .22.
2b. P1 = .402, P2 = .324, P3 = .275.
2c. 5.714 periods.
2d. 3.091 periods.
3a. P1 = .13, P2 = .253, P3 = .395, P4 = .222.
3b. P1 = .125, P2 = .167, P3 = .573, P4 = .135.
3c. 7.455 periods.
3d. 6 periods.
4a. 1.25 times.
4b. 87.5% good parts.
5a. T(S3) = 2.963, T(S1) = 1.8519
5b. P(S1 → S2) = .741, P(S3 → S2) = .185.
6a. .3, .667, .033 .
6b. .433, .512, .056.
7a. .291, .519, .19.
7b. 3.435, 1.927, 5.267
8a. 0.6.
8b. .312.
8c. .667 (operational), .333 (down).
9. 0.
10a. 52.5% foreign, 47.5% US (two years).
      59.1% foreign, 40.9% US (five years).
10b. 60% foreign, 40% US.
11a. .186, .259, .291, .264.
11b. 5.388, 3.856, 3.433, 3.791.
12. S2 = 4.6341, S3 = 5.7724, S4 = 6.2602.
13a. If a trustee = 5.5556 periods. If in solitary confinement = 8.8889 periods.
13b. 100%.
14a. 2.9167 months from the time that drilling begins.
14b. .708.

# ch12 Inventory Problems

(All money values are rounded to the nearest cent.)

1a. $Q^* = 34.641$.

1b. $173.20.

2a. $Q^* = 219.089$.

2b. Total cost = $1,095.44.

3a. $Q^* = 109.545$.

3b. $1,314.53.

4a. $Q^* = 44.272$.

4b. $442.72.

5a. $Q^* = 223.607$.

5b. $321.99.

6a. $Q^* = 816.497$.

6b. $1,837.12

7a. $Q^* = 50$.

7b. 2,880.

8a. $Q^* = 64.807$.

8b. $92.58.

9a. $Q^* = 38.079$.

9b. $157.57.

10a. $Q^* = 536.657$.

10b. Total cost = $447.21.

11. 20.

12. 144.

13. $Q^* = 577.35$.

14a. $Q^* = 447.214$.

14b. $5,366.56.

15a. $Q^* = 632.456$

15b. 316.228.

15c. $3,794.73 per year.

16a. $Q^* = 774.597$.

16b. 258.199.

16c. $3,098.39.

17. 23.

18. $1961 ($1800 production cost plus $161.00 inventory cost).

19. 38.188.

20a. $Q^* = 1291$.

20b. 1000.

20c. $1,936.49.

21. Optimal order quantity = 7071.244, reorder level = 20,079.998, total cost = $1,836.48 per year.

22. Optimal order quantity = 346.411, reorder level = 1935.882, total cost = $10,107.50 per year.

23a. Reorder quantity = 20.

23b. Order point = 52.175.

23c. Cost = $77,219.67.

24a. Order point = 60.429.

24b. Cost = $104,120.09.

24c. These costs are higher than those in problem 23.

# ch13 **Queuing Problems**

1. $W = 0.2$ hr., $Wq = 0.167$ hr., $L = 5$, $Lq = 4.167$.

2. $W = 0.099$ hr., $Wq = 0.066$ hr., $L = 2.29$, $Lq = 1.521$.

3. $W = 0.16$ hr., $Wq = 0.127$ hr., $L = 4.801$, $Lq = 3.803$.

4. $W = 75.117$ hr., $Wq = 75.083$ hr., $L = 1877.917$, $Lq = 1877.083$.

5. $W = 0.117$ hr., $Wq = 0.083$ hr., $L = 2.919$, $Lq = 2.086$.

6. $W = 0.117$ hr., $Wq = 0.083$ hr., $L = 2.917$, $Lq = 2.083$.

7. $W = 0.04$ hr., $Wq = 0.007$ hr., $L = 1.008$, $Lq = 0.175$.

8. $W = 0.04$ hr., $Wq = 0.007$ hr., $L = 0.999$, $Lq = 0.167$.

9. $W = 0.065$ hr., $Wq = 0.031$ hr., $L = 3.704$, $Lq = 1.79$.

10. $W = 0.02$ hr., $Wq = 0.007$ hr., $L = 0.5$, $Lq = 0.167$.

11. $W = 0.020$ hr., $Wq = 0.007$ hr., $L = 0.497$, $Lq = 0.164$.

12. $W = 0.044$ hr., $Wq = 0.031$ hr., $L = 3.156$, $Lq = 2.209$.

13. $W = 18.767$ hr., $Wq = 18.753$ hr., $L = 469.167$, $Lq = 468.833$.

14. $W = 0.017$ hr., $Wq = 0.003$ hr., $L = 0.417$, $Lq = 0.084$.

15. $W = 0.017$ hr., $Wq = 0.003$ hr., $L = 0.417$, $Lq = 0.083$.

16. $W = 0.014$ hr., $Wq = 0.000$ hr., $L = 0.343$, $Lq = 0.010$.

17. $W = 0.014$ hr., $Wq = 0.000$ hr., $L = 0.343$, $Lq = 0.010$.

18.  W = 0.018 hr., Wq = 0.004 hr., L = 1.832, Lq = 0.443.

19.  W = 1 hr., Wq = 0.962 hr., L = 25, Lq = 24.038.

20.  W = 0.13 hr., Wq = 0.092 hr., L = 2.843, Lq = 2.004.

21.  W = 0.191 hr., Wq = 0.152 hr., L = 4.961, Lq = 3.961.

22.  W = 325.519 hr., Wq = 325.481 hr., L = 8,137.975, Lq = 8,137.014.

23.  W = 0.52 hr., Wq = 0.481 hr., L = 12.991, Lq = 12.029.

24.  W = 0.519 hr., Wq = 0.481 hr., L = 12.981, Lq = 12.019.

25.  W = 0.05 hr., Wq = 0.012 hr., L = 1.251, Lq = 0.289.

26.  W = 0.049 hr., Wq = 0.011 hr., L = 1.221, Lq = 0.263.

27.  W = 0.079 hr., Wq = 0.04 hr., L = 3.977, Lq = 2.033.

28.  W = 0.2 hr.

29.  Lq = 4.999.

30a. Wq = 0.274 hr.

30b. 0.02526.

31.  Yes, Wq is now 0.246 hr.

32a. L = 8.

32b. W = 1.333 yr.

32c. Wq = 1.167 yr.

32d. Lq = 7.

33.  The consolidated system (W = 0.192 hr. vs. 0.5 hr. in the current system).

34.  No, current system costs $108 (3 stations at a cost of $34 each) and the consolidated station costs $46.46.

35.  Option 1 ($84.72/hr.).

36.  6 clerks ($112.37/hr.).

# *Index*